FEAST OF SPAIN

edited by Luis Bettonica

300 recipes illustrated in colour

A & W Publishers, Inc.
New York

The publisher thanks the following restaurants for their help in compiling the text and providing the photographic illustrations: Agut d'Avignon (Barcelona), Akelaré (San Sebastián), Ama Lur (Barcelona), Ampurdán (Figueres-Gerona), Ancora (Palma de Mallorca), Arzak (San Sebastián), Caballo Rojo (Córdoba), Can Borrell (Meranges-Gerona), Can Gatell (Cambrils-Tarragona), Can Toni (San Feliú de Guixols-Gerona), Casa Fermín (Oviedo), Casa Gatell (Cambrils-Tarragona), Casa Ortega (Albacete), Casas Colgadas (Cuenca), Duna II (La Coruña), El Bodegón (Madrid), Eldorado Petit (San Feliú de Guixols-Gerona), El Faro (Cadiz), Eugenia (Cambrils-Tarragona), Farín (Barcelona), Formentor (Palma de Mallorca), Gaitán (Jerez-Cadiz), Gorría (Barcelona), Hispania (Arenys de Mar-Barcelona), Hostal Galbis (Alcudia de Carlet-Valencia), Hostal La Gavina (S'Agaró-Gerona), Hostal San Jordi (Barcelona), La Fragua (Valladolid), La Merced (Logroño), La Rinconada de Lorenzo (Saragossa), O'Pazo (Madrid), Orotava (Barcelona), Pasteleria Baixas (Barcelona), Patxiku-Kintana (San Sebastián), Rincón de Pepe (Murcia), Torre del Mar (Ibiza), Virrey Palafox (Burgo de Osma-Soria).

The photograph on the jacket was taken in the La Tranca restaurant in Milan.

Photographs by Antonio Murillo except for the following:
p. 17 r, p. 34 r, p. 45 l, p. 64 r, pp. 68–75 inc, p. 80 r, p. 110 r, p. 150 l, p. 163 l (Enrique Puigdengolas) and p. 173, p. 174 l, p. 176, p. 179 l, p. 183, p. 184 r (Tullio Gatti).
The jacket photographs are by Jürgen Becker.

First published in the United States of America in 1982 by
A & W Publishers, Inc.
95 Madison Avenue
New York, New York 10016
By arrangement with Arnoldo Mondadori Editore S.p.A., Milan

Translated from the Italian by Olive Ordish

Library of Congress Catalog Card Number: 82–72823
ISBN: 0-89479-128-1

Printed and bound in Italy by
Officine Grafiche di Arnoldo Mondadori Editore, Verona

CONTENTS

FOREWORD

First of all we must stress that, strictly speaking, there is no such thing as "Spanish" cooking in the true sense of the word. The term makes sense only when it is applied to the whole, made up of all the various regional cookeries of the land, each one different and independent of the others, and each influenced by the history, culture and characteristic temperament—sometimes in strong contrast—of each of the peoples inhabiting Spain.

This gastronomic diversity derives from the geographical complexity of the Iberian Peninsula, the variety of its climates, and the different economic conditions, past and present, of the separate regions. Without doubt, all things considered, Spanish cookery is particularly varied and "anarchic," a most heterogeneous assembly of dishes.

However, some characteristics are common to the kitchen repertory of all or at least a number of the provinces, while certain recipes have crossed their original geographical boundaries to be adopted in other parts of the country. It is the Basques, most of all, who have "exported" their cookery. Their "Hake à la Basque," their dishes based on elvers (baby eels), and certain recipes from the so-called "new Basque cuisine" have become famous all over Spain. Conversely, gazpacho, paella and potato tortillas are popular in the Basque country.

One single dish stands out against the amazingly diversified panorama of Spanish regional cookery by being truly "national," namely *cocido*, a sort of meat and vegetable stew, a tasty and substantial dish with richly assorted ingredients, to be found on practically every Spanish table, with only slight differences between one region and the next.

Thus, in order to illustrate the Spanish way of eating, a wide knowledge of their regional cookery becomes absolutely essential, and that is the criterion we have adopted in planning this book. Since limited space makes it impossible to devote a separate chapter to each region, we have decided to group under the same heading recipes from two or three regions which, although differentiated on the gastronomical plane, are bound together by links of history, geography and custom. It is a mere formal subdivision, not intended to mark any order of merit or preference between such very individual cooking traditions, each of which is interesting in its own right.

There are two basic cooking fats used in the Spanish kitchen: olive oil and lard. Cooking with butter is infrequent. The produce of the sea is present in abundance, making it possible to create an infinite number of dishes based on fish and molluscs, and earning Spain a place of honour in the sphere of seafood cookery. In the eyes of foreigners, however, that renown has to some extent overshadowed her claims to excellence in other types of cookery. These include a great variety of dishes composed of rice, vegetables, pork, game and a wide range of hors-d'oeuvres and desserts.

We hope this book will prove an invaluable guide to the discriminating reader embarking on the quest for genuine Spanish food.

Luis Bettonica

BASQUE PROVINCES

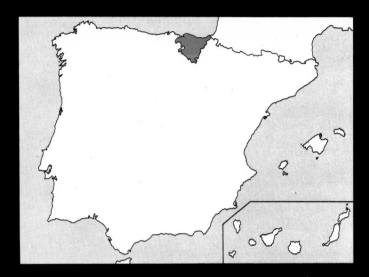

To say that the Basque Provinces taught the culinary arts to the rest of Spain is no over-enthusiastic claim, but a statement of fact based on undeniable evidence. Basque cookery has been, and continues to be, the most widely diffused in the peninsula. Basque restaurants are found almost throughout the country. This cuisine's high renown comes, above all, from its variety of exquisite fish dishes, characterized by four basic sauces: a white sauce for "Pil-pil," a green sauce for "Hake à la Basque," a red sauce called "Vizcaina," and a special black sauce for stewed cuttlefish. These sauces accompany the many fishes of Cantabria and are the gastronomical pride of that northern region. Basque seafood cookery includes a vast number of recipes, from dried salt cod to hake, from cuttlefish to elvers, from sea bream to sardines, to say nothing of delicious crustaceans and shellfish. Other Basque specialities are meat dishes such as their tasty veal cutlets and beef steaks. Some of their vegetable dishes too are of the highest quality, especially "Alubias rojas," whose main ingredient is a red kidney bean. From these basic materials the shining genius of Basque cooks has created a masterly culinary art.

Alubias rojas de Tolosa
Kidney beans with sausages

Sopa de malvices y trufas
Thrush and truffle soup

For 4 persons

Time: *preparation 15 min. ● cooking 60 min.*
Ingredients: *2 cups/1 lb/500 g fresh red kidney beans ● salt ●*
¼ cup/4 fl. oz/1 dl olive oil ● 1 small onion ● 4 oz/100 g Chorizo sausage*
all in one piece ● 4 oz/100 g blood sausage (or black pudding)** all in one
piece ● 2 green peppers, seeded and chopped ● 4 cloves garlic, crushed ●
4 oz/100 g fat (streaky) bacon.

For 6 persons

Time: *preparation 30 min. ● cooking 45 min.*
Ingredients: *1 onion, chopped ● ¼ cup/4 fl. oz/1 dl olive oil ●*
4 cloves garlic ● 6 thrushes (including the liver)* ● ¼ cup/4 fl. oz/1 dl dry
white wine ● 4½ cups/1¾ pints/1 liter good stock ● 2 truffles, sliced ●
liquid from the can of truffles ● 4 tablespoons/2 oz/½ dl goose fat ● salt ●
pepper ● chervil ● Can be served with: croutons of fried bread.

● Put the beans in a saucepan, cover with cold water, add salt, a little oil and half the onion. ● Cook over a low heat for 1 hour. ● Separately, cook the sausages (pricked beforehand so that they do not burst) together with the bacon. ● Cut the sausages into thick chunks and set them aside. ● Fry the green peppers, garlic and the rest of the onion, chopped. ● Add the sausages and all the other ingredients to the cooked beans. ● Mix very thoroughly, salt to taste and serve.

* Chorizo is a special, very piquant, small salami sausage that is used in many Spanish dishes. If unavailable, the same quantity of Neapolitan salami— which has a similar flavour—or other salami can be used.
** Blood sausages, or black puddings, are sausages made from the blood of a freshly killed pig, with groats, fat and oatmeal. If unavailable, use best quality pork sausages.

● Sweat the chopped onion in oil. ● Add the garlic cloves. ● When brown, remove from pan and put to one side. ● Clean the birds and sprinkle with salt and pepper. ● Add them to the pan, not forgetting the livers. ● When everything is well browned add the white wine, bring to a rapid boil and let it evaporate. ● Now pour in the stock. ● As soon as the birds are tender remove them from the pan, bone them and put the meat on one side. ● Return the bones to the pan and simmer for 15 minutes. ● When the stock has thickened slightly, strain it. ● Warm up the meat and the sliced truffles in a little of the stock. ● Divide the meat and truffles equally into six soup plates. ● Return the slightly thickened broth to the pan, and add the liquid from the truffle can. ● Bring back to the boil and add 2 of the lightly browned cloves of garlic, mashed with a fork, and the goose fat. ● Mix well. ● Taste for seasoning. ● Pour the soup into the plates. ● Sprinkle with finely chopped chervil and serve with fried croutons.

* Or use 1 guinea hen (guinea fowl).

Crêpes de hongos
Mushroom pancakes

Pimientos rellenos de bacalao
Peppers stuffed with dried salt cod

For 4 persons

Time: *preparation 15 min. ● cooking 1 hour.*
Ingredients: For the pancakes: *1 cup/4 oz/100 g flour ● salt ● 2 eggs ● 3 tablespoons/1½ oz/40 g butter, melted ● 1¼ cups/½ pint/3 dl lukewarm milk.* For the filling: *2 lb/1 kg mushrooms ● salt ● pepper ● ¾ cup/6 fl. oz/2 dl olive oil ● 6 cloves garlic, chopped ● 1¾ cups/¾ pint/4 dl light (single) cream ● 1 small glass brandy.*

For 4 persons

Time: *preparation 40 min. + 24 hours for soaking of dried salt cod ● cooking 1 hour.*
Ingredients: *1 large onion, sliced ● 1 carrot, finely sliced ● olive oil ● 1 tablespoon tomato sauce (see p. 187) ● 1 tablespoon paprika ● chopped parsley ● flour ● ½ glass white wine ● stock ● salt ● pepper ● 1 onion, chopped ● 2 cloves garlic, chopped ● 1 lb/400 g dried salt cod ● 1 cup/4 oz/100 g breadcrumbs soaked in milk ● 2 egg yolks ● 8 sweet red peppers ● 1 whole egg.*

● Sift flour and salt into a large bowl. ● Add the eggs and stir well. ● Add the melted butter and slowly beat in the lukewarm milk to form a smooth cream. ● Pass through a fine sieve into another bowl. ● Let the batter rest for at least an hour. ● Then pour about 2 tablespoonfuls into a small, very hot, frying pan greased with butter. ● Move the pan around so that the mixture spreads evenly. ● When the crêpe is lightly browned on the underside turn it over to brown other side. ● Make 8 pancakes in all and keep them warm. ● Clean the mushrooms, removing and slicing the stalks. ● Place them in an ovenproof dish, season with salt and pepper, and add the oil and chopped garlic. ● Put them in a moderate oven (350°F/mark 4/175°C) for about 20 minutes. ● After leaving them to get cold, chop them finely. ● Fill the crêpes with this mixture, reserving a little of it, then roll them up and arrange them side by side in an ovenproof dish. ● Mix the cream with the brandy and the remaining mushroom filling. ● Pour the resulting sauce over the pancakes and put the dish in a hot oven (425°F/mark 7/220°C) for 10–15 minutes. ● Place 2 pancakes with sauce on each person's plate.

● Soak the dried salt cod for 24 hours, changing the water several times. ● Rinse thoroughly and dry. ● Prepare the sauce as follows. ● In a frying pan sweat a sliced onion and carrot in olive oil. ● Add tomato sauce, paprika, chopped parsley and 2 tablespoons flour. ● When well mixed add the white wine, a little cold water or stock, salt and pepper. ● Bring to the boil, then lower the heat and simmer. ● Meanwhile, heat 4 tablespoons olive oil in another frying pan. ● Add the other onion, chopped and mixed with chopped garlic. ● Leave them to sweat a little before adding the cod (bones and skin removed) cut into small pieces. ● Fry thoroughly, stirring, then add the milk-steeped breadcrumbs. ● Season with salt and pepper and allow to cook gently, stirring from time to time. ● Add the egg yolks and 1 tablespoon chopped parsley. ● Take from heat and leave to get cold. ● Remove skin and seeds from the red peppers.* ● Fill them with the cod mixture. ● Dip them in beaten egg and then in flour and fry in hot oil until brown. ● Strain the sauce into a flameproof serving dish and add the fried stuffed peppers. ● Leave to cook until tender.

*To peel peppers, put under the broiler (grill) until the skins are charred, plunge into cold water, and rub skin off.

Porrusalda
Dried salt cod with leeks and potatoes

Pastel de verduras
Vegetable timbale

For 4 persons

Time: *preparation 15 min. + 24 hours for soaking cod ● cooking 50 min.*
Ingredients: *½ lb/200 g dried salt cod ● 2 cloves garlic ●*
1 cup/8 fl. oz/2 dl olive oil ● 1 lb/400 g leeks, thickly sliced ● ¾ lb/300 g
potatoes, finely sliced ● 3 or 4 carrots, chopped ● 1 bay leaf ● salt ● pepper ●
1 cup/8 fl. oz/2.5 dl fish stock.

For 4 persons

Time: *preparation 20 min. ● cooking 2 hours.*
Ingredients: *3 carrots ● 2 leeks ● handful spinach ● 2 smallish turnips ●*
2 radishes ● 1 cup/4 oz/100 g green (French or runner) beans ● 3 eggs ●
3 tablespoons tomato sauce (see p. 187) ● salt ● dried breadcrumbs. For
the sauce: 2 onions, chopped ● olive oil ● ½ lb/250 g mushrooms,
chopped ● 1 cup/8 fl. oz/2.5 dl of the water the leeks were cooked in ●
3 tablespoons light (single) cream.

● Soak the dried salt cod for 24 hours, changing the water several times. ● Rinse thoroughly and pat dry. ● Cook the cod in 2 cups/¾ pint/5 dl water for 7 minutes. ● Gently fry the garlic in oil in a frying pan. ● When browned take it out and set it aside. ● Put in the sliced leeks, the sliced potatoes, the chopped carrot and the bay leaf. ● Sweat them all well without allowing them to brown. ● Add the finely chopped cod without bones or skin, a pinch of pepper, the water in which the cod was boiled and 1 cup/8 fl. oz/2.5 dl hot water or fish stock. ● Simmer for 30 minutes till the potatoes are just beginning to disintegrate. ● During the cooking add the garlic, which has been finely chopped and heated up in some of the stock. ● Season to taste. ● Remove the bay leaf before serving.

● Clean the vegetables. ● Scrape and finely slice the carrots, finely chop the other vegetables and cook them each separately, steaming them if possible. ● Grease a 1 quart (1 lb) loaf pan (loaf tin) or mould with butter and sprinkle with breadcrumbs. ● Arrange the vegetables in separate layers, and when a layer of each vegetable has been used pour in a little of the mixture made by beating the eggs with tomato sauce and a little salt. ● Continue in this way, alternating vegetables and egg mixture and finishing with a layer of spinach. ● Place the mould in a bain-marie in the oven and cook at 400°F/mark 6/200°C for 1½ hours. ● If the timbale appears to be getting too brown, cover the top with aluminum foil. ● Now prepare the sauce. ● Sweat the chopped onions in oil and add the mushrooms. ● When these are thoroughly softened together pour in 1 cup/8 fl. oz/2.5 dl of the water in which the leeks were cooked. ● Simmer for an hour, adding the cream little by little during the last 10 minutes. ● Strain the sauce. ● Take the mould out of the oven. ● Turn it out and set it on a serving dish. ● Cut it into slices and serve with the sauce.

Sopa de pescado y mariscos
Fish and seafood soup

Huevos con trufas y tuétano
Eggs with truffles and bone marrow

For 6 persons

Time: *preparation 30 min.* ● *cooking 1½ hours.*
Ingredients: *1 cup/8 fl. oz/2 dl olive oil ● 1 onion, chopped ● 1 carrot, chopped ● 1 leek, chopped ● 1 bay leaf ● sprig of thyme ● a few leaves of tarragon ● 2 crawfish (crayfish) ● 2 jumbo shrimp (prawns) ● 1 small wine glass brandy ● 1 small glass white wine ● 2 ripe tomatoes, peeled ● 2 tablespoons tomato sauce (see p. 187) ● the head of a cod (or other fish) ● 1 tablespoon rice ● salt ● clams and mussels (optional) ● 2 small shrimp per person, uncooked.*

For 4 persons

Time: *preparation 6 hours to soften the marrow ● cooking 40 min.*
Ingredients: *1 cup/½ lb/250 g butter ● 2 egg yolks ● juice of ½ lemon ● salt and pepper ● 4 tablespoons liquid from the truffle can (or port or madeira) ● 8 eggs ● 4 tablespoons wine vinegar ● 8 slices fried bread ● 4 truffle slices ● 4 round slices of bone marrow.*

● Put the oil in a cast iron casserole, add a chopped mixture of onion, carrot and leeks plus herbs, and sweat over a low heat. ● Add the crawfish (crayfish) and jumbo shrimp (prawns), pounded in a mortar, and fry gently, stirring. ● Add brandy, heat and set alight, then pour in the white wine. ● Slice the tomatoes and put them in the pot together with the tomato sauce. ● In a separate saucepan boil the fish head with the carrot scrapings and the green part of the leeks, for about 10 minutes. ● Add the small shrimp and cook a further 3 minutes. ● Strain the resulting broth into the casserole. ● Shell the shrimp, bone the fish head and set them aside. ● When the soup begins to boil throw in the rice. ● Leave to simmer for 45 minutes. ● Strain, adjust seasoning. ● As a garnish for the soup, use the small shrimp, a few clams or mussels, and morsels of fish.

● Melt the butter in a pan and leave it in a warm place ● Mix the egg yolks, lemon juice and salt and pour into a casserole dish. ● Stand it in hot but not boiling water and little by little add the melted butter. ● Without ever letting the water boil, stir the sauce until it thickens to the consistency of mayonnaise. ● It is very important that the temperature of the eggs should be the same as that of the butter. ● Add the truffle liquid or wine (in which the truffles should have been heated up). ● Poach the eggs for 3 minutes in boiling water with salt and vinegar. ● Take them out, drain, and place 2 eggs on fried bread slices on each plate. ● Cover the eggs with the sauce, and garnish each one with a slice of truffle and a round of marrow (soaked for 6 hours and cooked in advance). ● Heat up and serve.

Arroz con almejas
Rice with clams

Huevos Igueldo
Eggs Monte Igueldo

For 4 persons

Time: *preparation 15 min. ● cooking 30 min.*
Ingredients: *¾ cup/6 fl. oz/2 dl olive oil ● 1 green pepper, chopped ● 2 cloves garlic, chopped ● 2 cups/1 lb/500 g rice ● 1 pint/1 lb/500 g clams or mussels ● chopped parsley ● 7 cups/2½ pints/1.5 liters good stock ● salt.*

For 1 person

Time: *preparation 10 min. ● cooking 30 min.*
Ingredients: *2 eggs ● wine vinegar ● 1 tablespoon/½ oz/15 g butter ● a few drops of olive oil ● 1 shallot, chopped ● 4 mushrooms, sliced ● ½ truffle, finely sliced ● a little brandy ● 1 cup/8 fl. oz/2 dl light (single) cream ● 2 tablespoons Sauce Hollandaise (see p. 187) ● 2 pieces flaky or puff pastry, rolled out to 4 in./10 cm squares and baked beforehand.*

● Pour the oil into a fireproof dish and add the chopped green pepper. ● When it begins to soften add the chopped garlic. ● When these have sweated sufficiently throw in the rice and clams. ● When all has browned a little sprinkle with chopped parsley and cover with stock. ● Cook over a lively heat for 20 minutes. ● When the rice is nearly cooked turn off the heat, cover tightly and leave for 5 minutes. ● Taste and add salt if necessary.

● Poach the eggs one at a time in water and a little vinegar for 3 minutes. ● Drain carefully, then leave in hot salted water without vinegar. ● To make the sauce, put the butter, oil and chopped shallot in a small frying pan and fry gently. ● Add the sliced mushrooms and truffle. ● Add brandy, set alight and stir in the cream. ● At the last moment add 2 tablespoons Sauce Hollandaise. ● Arrange the hot and well drained eggs on the slices of baked puff pastry and cover with sauce.

Besugo a la donostiarra
Red sea bream à la San Sebastián

"Zurrukutuna"
Dried salt cod and green pepper soup

For 4 persons

Time: *preparation 80 min. ● cooking 35 min.*
Ingredients: *1 red sea bream* (about 2 lb/1 kg) ● salt ● juice of 2 lemons ● 1 cup/8 fl. oz/2 dl olive oil ● 6 cloves garlic, finely chopped ● chili pepper.*

For 5 or 6 persons

Time: *preparation 30 min. + 12 hours for softening the peppers and 24 hours for soaking the fish ● cooking 2 hours.*
Ingredients: *6 large green peppers ● 1 cup/½ pint/2.5 dl olive oil ● 3 cloves garlic, chopped ● 1 chili pepper ● ½ lb/250 g dried salt cod ● 4 slices stale bread, cut up ● vegetable stock ● 5–6 poached eggs (optional).*

● Open the bream and remove the backbone. ● Wash the fish and dry with a cloth. ● Sprinkle it with salt, the juice of 1 lemon and a few drops of olive oil. ● Leave it to marinate for an hour in a cool place. ● Place the fish gently on a charcoal grill or on the top shelf of a hot oven (425°F/mark 7/220°C). ● Baste it with olive oil now and again and turn it often so that the skin becomes crisp on both sides. ● Lay the cooked bream on a serving dish and sprinkle it with the oil, in which the garlic and chili have been fried. ● Salt lightly and add a few spoonfuls of lemon juice. ● Serve very hot.

* Or use scup/porgy.

● Soak the dried salt cod for 24 hours, changing the water several times. ● Rinse thoroughly, dry and chop. ● Soak peppers in water for 12 hours, drain, remove seeds, and purée in blender. ● Heat the oil in a flameproof pot with the chopped garlic and chili. ● Add the chopped cod and bread pieces, and fry gently, stirring. ● Cover with vegetable stock and add the puréed peppers. ● Simmer over a low heat for 1½ hours. ● While the broth is cooking, mash the bread with a wooden spoon. ● When ready the soup should be very thick. ● Bring it to table with a poached egg in each serving.

Bacalao a la vizcaina
Bay of Biscay cod

Bacalao al pil-pil
Dried salt cod à la pil-pil

For 4 persons

Time: *preparation 30 min. + 24 hours for soaking of cod ● cooking 2½ hours.*
Ingredients: *1 cup/8 fl. oz/2.5 dl olive oil ● ½ cup/4 oz/110 g lard ● ¾ cup/6 oz/170 g bacon (streaky bacon), chopped ● 6 onions, chopped ● 3 cloves garlic, chopped ● 3 sprigs parsley, chopped ● pepper ● 6 large green peppers ● ¾ cup/2½ oz/75 g breadcrumbs ● 1 hard-boiled egg yolk ● 1¼ lb/600 g dried salt cod ● sugar.*

For 4–6 persons

Time: *preparation 15 min. + 24 hours for soaking the dried salt cod ● cooking 35 min.*
Ingredients: *2 lb/1 kg best quality dried salt cod ● 2¼ cups/1 pint/6 dl olive oil ● 4 cloves garlic ● 1 glass cold water.*

● Soak the cod for 24 hours, changing the water several times. ● Rinse thoroughly and pat dry. ● Put the oil, lard and chopped bacon into a frying pan. ● When they begin to cook add the chopped onion, garlic, parsley and pepper. ● Simmer until the onions are soft. ● After an hour add as much boiling water as necessary to keep mixture from sticking and cook for a further hour. ● Soak the green peppers in warm water; remove the seeds, plunge into boiling water to remove skins and put the flesh into the pot. ● Pound the pepper skins into the breadcrumbs and add a little of the water in which the dried cod was soaked. ● Mix thoroughly and add to the cooking mixture. ● Dilute the crumbled hard-boiled egg yolk with a little water and mix this into the pot. ● Let the mixture cook a little longer, then press it through a sieve. ● Descale the cod, put it into a saucepan and cover it with cold water. ● Bring to the boil, then remove from heat. ● Drain and bone carefully. ● Cut into 4. ● Put 2 tablespoons/1 oz/30 g lard in a flameproof serving dish with a little of the hot sauce, and lay the fish pieces on top. ● Cover with the remaining sauce. ● Finish cooking, gradually adding some more lard. ● Adjust seasoning and add the sugar. ● Stir before serving so that the sauce is evenly distributed.

● Cut the dried cod in pieces, without removing the skin, and leave it to soak in cold water for 24 hours, changing the water several times. ● Rinse thoroughly. ● Put the fish in a saucepan and cover with cold water. ● Bring to the boil. ● As soon as white scum appears on the surface take the pan from the heat, drain the fish pieces and remove the bones very carefully. ● Heat 1¼ cups/½ pint/3 dl olive oil in flameproof serving dish and lightly brown the garlic cloves. ● Remove and set aside. ● Now put the fish into the oil with a glass of cold water and cook over a low heat, turning the pan and stirring from time to time so that the sauce becomes really thick. ● Add 2 of the garlic cloves, crushed and mingled with a little water, and finally add the rest of the pre-heated oil gradually. ● Cook on for about 20 minutes (the sauce should resemble a mayonnaise). ● Garnish with remaining 2 cloves of garlic, sliced.

Filetes de lenguado al Txakoli
Fillets of sole Txakoli

"Marmitako"
Casserole of mackerel

For 4 persons

Time: *preparation 20 min. ● cooking 30 min.*
Ingredients: *1 tablespoon/$\frac{1}{2}$ oz/15 g butter ● 1 shallot ● 8 fillets of sole (i.e., 1 complete sole per person) ● salt ● white pepper ● $\frac{1}{2}$ cup/4 fl. oz/1 dl Txakoli (or other dry white wine) ● 8 button mushrooms ● 16 cooked jumbo shrimp (prawns) ● 8 mussels, steamed open ● 1 cup/8 fl. oz/2.5 dl thin white sauce (see p. 187) or light (single) cream ● 4 tablespoons Sauce Hollandaise (see p. 187).*

For 6 persons

Time: *preparation 40 min. + 12 hours for soaking the sweet peppers ● cooking 40 min.*
Ingredients: *3 lb/1$\frac{1}{2}$ kg mackerel ● 1 onion, sliced ● 1 green pepper, finely chopped ● 1 cup/8 fl. oz/2 dl olive oil ● 2 lb/1 kg potatoes, peeled and quartered ● salt ● 6 sweet red peppers.*

● Grease a casserole dish with butter. ● Scatter the chopped shallot and lay the fillets of sole on top. ● Season with salt and white pepper. ● Moisten with white wine and add the mushrooms, shrimp (prawns) and mussels, removed from their shells. ● Bake in a pre-heated oven (350°C/mark 4/ 175°C) for about 7 minutes. ● Remove the fillets and arrange them on a flameproof serving dish. ● Heat up the liquid remaining in the casserole and strain it. ● Mix with the white sauce or cream and heat. ● Remove from heat, add the Sauce Hollandaise and mix well. ● Adjust seasoning. ● Pour sauce over the fillets and brown in the oven or under the broiler (grill). ● Garnish with the mushrooms, shrimp (prawns) and mussels from the strained liquid.

● Clean and fry the mackerel. ● When cooked remove skin and bones and chop into pieces. ● In a flameproof casserole dish sweat the sliced onion and chopped green pepper in oil. ● When they are soft but not brown add the potatoes cut into quarters. ● Cover with water, bring to a boil and continue cooking. ● When the potatoes are done add the mackerel. ● Add salt. ● Cook for another 5–10 minutes, being careful not to let the mackerel disintegrate. ● Finally, add the sweet peppers, which have been soaked for 12 hours and put through a blender or sieve. ● Serve hot.

Anchoas al estilo del muelle donostiarra
Anchovies à la San Sebastián

Angulas
Fried elvers

For 6 persons

Time: *preparation 20 min. ● cooking 35 min.*
Ingredients: *2 cups/¾ pint/5 dl olive oil ● 2 onions, finely chopped ●
¾ lb/350 g green peppers, seeded and finely chopped ● 3 cloves garlic,
finely chopped ● 1 tablespoon paprika ● 6 dozen anchovies ●
1 cup/8 fl. oz/2.5 dl dry white wine ● 1 cup/8 fl. oz/2.5 dl vinegar ●
½ cup/4 fl. oz/1 dl fish stock ● 4 sprigs parsley, chopped.*

For 1 person

Time: *preparation and cooking 10 min.*
Ingredients: *1 clove garlic per person ● chili pepper ● olive oil ●
¾ cup/6 oz/150 g elvers (baby eels) per person.*

● In a large pan put oil with the finely chopped onions, green peppers and garlic. ● Fry over a low heat, stirring. ● Add the paprika. ● Stir in the anchovies and allow to cook for 5 minutes on both sides. ● Little by little pour in the white wine, vinegar and fish stock. ● Simmer for another 10 minutes. ● Serve very hot in an earthenware dish and sprinkle with chopped parsley.

● Sweat the garlic cloves and chili pepper in oil in a frying pan. ● When the garlic begins to brown take it out. ● Set aside. ● Throw the elvers into the oil, which should not be too hot. ● Cook them for about a minute or until they are done, but take care not to overcook. ● Serve immediately.

Centollo o "Txangurro"
Crab au gratin

"Txipirones" en su tinta
Cuttlefish stew

For 4 persons

Time: *preparation 20 min. • cooking 40 min.*
Ingredients: *4 small crabs • 2 leeks • parsley • 2 onions •
½ cup/¼ pint/1 dl olive oil • ¼ cup/2 oz/50 g butter • 2 carrots •
1 clove garlic • 1 tablespoon tomato sauce (see p. 187) • liqueur glass of
brandy • ½ glass dry white wine • fish or vegetable stock • dried
breadcrumbs • salt.*

For 4 persons

Time: *preparation 30 min. • cooking 50 min.*
Ingredients: *32 little cuttlefish* • 2 onions, finely chopped • 2 green
peppers • 4 cloves garlic • ½ cup/¼ pint/1 dl olive oil • salt • 2 tomatoes,
peeled and chopped • breadcrust. • 2 cups/1 pint/5 dl vegetable stock •
As a garnish: 4 slices fried bread.*

• Cook the crabs in sea (or salted) water with the green part of
the leeks, a little parsley and a slice of onion for about 10
minutes. • Let them get cold, extract the meat from the shells
and claws, and put the shells with the liquid contained in them
on one side. • Fry gently in oil and butter the onions, leeks,
carrots and garlic, all finely chopped. • When all are well
browned add the tomato sauce and crabmeat. • Pour the
brandy over and set alight. • Add the juice from the shells and
the white wine. • Cook for about 10 minutes. • Moisten with a
little fish or vegetable stock and season with salt. • Divide the
mixture into the four crab shells, dot with butter and sprinkle
the top with breadcrumbs. • Brown in a very hot oven or under
the broiler (grill) and serve at once.

• Clean the cuttlefish, keeping the ink sacs on one side. •
Remove the eyes. • Wash the cuttlefish in running water. •
Sweat 1½ onions finely chopped, 1 finely chopped green
pepper and 2 cloves finely chopped garlic in a frying pan with
half the olive oil. • Add the cuttlefish tentacles cut into small
pieces. • Mix well and fry, stirring, over a lively heat; add salt. •
Fill the cuttlefish bodies with the fried mixture, fixing each one
with cocktail sticks or toothpicks. • Fry in the oil with the third
clove of garlic. • Now make the sauce. • In a saucepan with
the remaining olive oil put the remaining half onion, the
remaining green pepper, sliced, the peeled and chopped
tomatoes, the fourth clove of garlic, crushed, and a small crust
of bread. • Simmer very gently while adding the stock. • Stir
well. • Empty the cuttlefish ink into a small amount of stock
and add to the sauce. • Strain the sauce, then add the
cuttlefish rolls (after removing the cocktail sticks) and adjust
seasoning. • Continue to cook gently. • When the sauce has
thickened, serve the cuttlefish stew with a triangular piece of
fried bread on each individual plate.

* Squid, octopus or calamari may be used.

Caracoles sin trabajo
Snails in pastry

"Kokotxas" a la donostiarra
"Kokotxas" à la San Sebastián

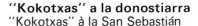

For 4 persons

Time: *preparation 30 min. + time for preparing the snails ● cooking 1 hour.*
Ingredients: *80 snails ● wine vinegar ● salt ● 1 tablespoon/½ oz/15 g butter ● olive oil ● 1 shallot, chopped ● 2 cloves garlic, crushed ● liqueur glass of brandy ● small glass of sherry ● handful of watercress, finely chopped ● 4 tablespoons tomato sauce (see p. 187) ● 2 tablespoons meat sauce or Spanish Sauce (see p. 187) ● 4 thin rounds of flaky pastry, uncooked ● 1 egg.*

For 4 persons

Time: *preparation 15 min. ● cooking 15 min.*
Ingredients: *2 lb/1 kg "kokotxas" (hake)* ● salt ● 1 clove garlic, crushed ● 1 cup 8 fl. oz/2.5 dl olive oil ● 1 tablespoon parsley, chopped.*

● Clean and wash the snails, then put them in a saucepan with cold water to cover, 2 tablespoons wine vinegar and salt. ● Cook for 1 hour. ● Drain and put snails back in cold water for 1¼ hours. ● Remove from shells and discard intestinal sacs. ● Reserve 4 of the shells. ● Put butter and a little oil into a saucepan. ● Lightly brown a chopped shallot and the garlic in it, then add the snails. ● Add brandy and set alight, then add sherry. ● Stir in a handful of finely chopped watercress, the tomato sauce and the meat sauce or Spanish Sauce. ● Continue cooking for 10 minutes more. ● Take 4 thin rounds of flaky pastry, brush them with beaten egg and place a snail shell on each one. ● Slide them into a hot oven (450°F/mark 8/230°C) to bake. ● When they are golden brown take them out and split each one in half horizontally. ● Arrange the snails with their sauce on the bottom half. ● Place the other half on top like a lid, garnish with the snail shell and serve.

● Bone the kokotxas and sprinkle with salt. ● In a frying pan sweat the garlic in oil, then add the kokotxas and parsley. ● When the oil begins to brown take the pan from the heat and allow the fish to finish cooking in the gradually cooling oil. ● Stir from time to time to form a smooth sauce, which will be thickened by the gelatin that is contained in the kokotxas themselves. ● Before serving reheat in a moderate oven (325°F/mark 3/165°C). ● The kokotxas are served with the darker side downwards.

*"Kokotxas" actually refers to the front part of the hake, around the gill area. The whole fish may be used.

Lubina a la pimienta verde
Sea bass with green peppercorns

For 1 person

Time: *preparation 5 min.* ● *cooking 15 min.*
Ingredients: *1 shallot, chopped* ● *½ cup/¼ pint/1 dl olive oil* ●
1 tablespoon/½ oz/15 g butter ● *½ lb/200 g fillets of sea bass* ● *½ liqueur
glass of Calvados* ● *3 tablespoons green peppercorns* ● *1 cup/8 fl. oz/2 dl
light (single) cream* ● *salt* ● *pepper.*

● Sweat the shallot in oil and butter. ● Add the salted,
peppered fillets of sea bass. ● Brown on both sides. ● Heat the
Calvados, pour it over the fish and set alight. ● Add
peppercorns and cream. ● Adjust seasoning. ● Bake in a very
hot oven (450°F/mark 8/230°C) for about 5 minutes, taking
care not to let the sauce boil. ● Arrange the fillets on a heated
serving plate and cover with sauce. ● Can be garnished with
pieces of pastry cut into fish shapes and baked until brown.

Merluza capricho
Hake caprice

For 6 persons

Time: *Preparation 15 min.* ● *cooking 30 min.*
Ingredients: *3 lb/1½ kg hake* ● *salt* ● *4½ cups/1¾ pints/1 liter olive oil* ●
3 onions, finely chopped ● *5 cloves of garlic, chopped* ● *2 pints/2 lb/1 kg
clams* ● *1¼ lb/600 g kokotxas (see p. 19)* ● *4½ cups/1¾ pints/1 liter fish
stock* ● *8 sprigs parsley, chopped.*

● Cut the hake in small pieces and sprinkle sparsely with salt. ●
In a pan containing a third of the oil, half the chopped onion
and a third of the chopped garlic place the clams. ● Cover, and
heat until clams have opened. ● Remove from heat and set
aside. ● In a second pan cook the hake pieces together with
the rest of the onion and half the remaining garlic in a third of
the oil for about 10 minutes. ● Finally, cook the kokotxas and
the rest of the garlic in the remaining oil in a third pan for about
7 minutes. ● When the fish has browned baste it with the
stock. ● In a large earthenware casserole put the hake pieces,
then the kokotxas and finally the clams. ● Pour the cooking
juices from the three pans into a single saucepan and let
thicken over a low heat until you have a smooth sauce. ●
Adjust seasoning, then pour the sauce over the fish, and
sprinkle over the chopped parsley. ● Cook in a moderate oven
(350°F/mark 4/175°C) for about 30 minutes.

San Pedro con salsa de ortigas
John Dory with nettle sauce

Lubina con salsa de espinacas y quisquillas
Sea bass with spinach and shrimp (prawn) sauce

For 4 persons

Time: *preparation 20 min. ● cooking 30 min.*
Ingredients: *bunch of young stinging nettles ● salt ● 1 John Dory fish**
weighing about 3 lb/1.5 kg ● 1 shallot ● 1 cup/8 fl. oz/2.5 dl white wine ●
¼ cup/2 oz/50 g butter, melted ● 1 cup/8 fl. oz/2.5 dl light (single) cream ●
½ cup/4 fl. oz/1 dl Sauce Hollandaise (see p. 187).

For 4 persons

Time: *preparation 15 min. ● cooking 20 min.*
Ingredients: *1 sea bass weighing about 2 lb/1 kg ● salt ●*
1 cup/8 fl. oz/2 dl vegetable stock or water ● 1 lb/500 g spinach ● 4 large
shrimp (prawns) ● 4 tablespoons/2 oz/50 g butter ● 1¼ cups/½ pint/3 dl
light (single) cream.

● Handle the nettles with gloved hands and plunge them into boiling salted water. ● Boil for 3 minutes, then drain. ● Clean and bone the fish and divide it into 4 portions. ● Put into a shallow pan with the chopped shallot, pour the white wine and melted butter over them and bake in a moderate oven (350°F/mark 4/175°C) for about 12–15 minutes. ● Salt and arrange the cooked nettles on each fish serving. ● Add the cream and leave it to thicken. ● After adjusting the seasoning, strain the resulting sauce. ● Mix in the Sauce Hollandaise and pour all over the fish. ● A little of the strained cooked nettles may be used for a garnish.

* Turbot or sole may be used.

● Divide the bass into 4 portions of about ½ lb/250 g each and sprinkle with salt. ● Put the stock or water into a steamer and arrange the fish portions, the spinach and the shrimp (prawns) on a trivet or perforated insert above the water level. ● Cover the pan and steam for about 10 minutes. ● Be careful not to overcook. ● Take out the shrimp (prawns) and set aside. ● Remove the spinach, sieve it into a purée, and add butter and cream. ● Put a few tablespoons of the spinach sauce onto each plate, add the fish portions, garnish with shrimp (prawns) and serve.

Merluza al vapor con algas
Steamed hake with seaweed

Solomillo al estragón con tuétano
Fillet steak with tarragon

For 4 persons

Time: *preparation 15 min.* ● *cooking 30 min.*
Ingredients: *salt* ● *olive oil* ● *pepper* ● *handful of seaweed** ● *1 hake (about 2 lb/1 kg* ● *1 onion* ● *2 carrots* ● *1 leek* ● *1 stick celery* ● *1 shallot, chopped* ● *½ cup/4 fl. oz/1 dl white wine* ● *½ cup/4 fl. oz/1 dl white wine vinegar* ● *2 tablespoons light (single) cream* ● *½ cup/4 oz/100 g butter, melted* ● *lemon juice.*

For 4 persons

Time: *preparation 10 min.* ● *cooking 10–25 min + 30 min. for the bone marrow.*
Ingredients: *4 broiling (fillet) steaks 5–6 oz/150 g each* ● *salt* ● *pepper* ● *½ cup/4 oz/100 g butter* ● *1 tablespoon chopped shallot* ● *½ glass dry white wine* ● *1¾ cups/¾ pint/4 dl light (single) cream* ● *handful of chopped tarragon* ● *4 rounds of pre-cooked marrow* ● *As a garnish: small new carrots and turnips.*

● Using a steam cooker (steamer saucepan), turn its perforated insert upside down so that the fish you are going to steam on it will not come into contact with the water. ● Pour into the pan salted water, a few drops of olive oil, a pinch of pepper and some seaweed. ● Bring to the boil, meanwhile cutting the hake into 4 portions. ● Cut the vegetables into thin strips and arrange on top of the fish in the steamer. ● Cover the pan and steam the contents for 7 minutes. ● During that time prepare the sauce. ● Put into a small saucepan the chopped shallot, white wine and wine vinegar, and bring to the boil. ● Let the liquid evaporate almost entirely, then pour in 1 tablespoon of the cream. ● Let it just simmer, stirring with a wooden spoon while you add, a little at a time, the melted butter and a few drops of lemon juice. ● Adjust seasoning. ● Arrange the hake portions on separate serving plates and cover with the sauce.

● Season the steaks with salt and pepper. ● Put butter in a frying pan, add the chopped shallot and then the fillets. ● When they are browned outside but still red inside take them out of the pan and keep them hot between two soup plates. ● Add the wine, cream and chopped tarragon to the cooking juices, and let thicken over a high heat. ● Finally, add the juices from the steaks, which will have accumulated on the bottom plate. ● Arrange the steaks on separate plates and keep warm in the oven. ● Just before serving pour over the sauce, very hot and mixed with the butter. ● On top of each fillet place a round of pre-cooked bone marrow. ● A pleasant suggestion is to serve the steaks on a bed of baby carrots and turnips which have been cooked separately.

* Dried seaweed can be bought in some delicatessens or specialty shops, such as oriental foodshops. Use a couple of "sheets" or layers.

Mollejas de ternera al oporto
Veal sweetbreads with port

Codornices con foie gras y uva
Quail with foie gras and grapes

For 4 persons

Time: *preparation 20 min.* ● *cooking 1¾ hours.*
Ingredients: *2 lb/900 g veal sweetbreads* ● *½ cup/4 fl. g/1 dl olive oil* ●
salt ● *1 onion, chopped* ● *1 carrot, chopped* ● *1 leek, chopped* ● *1 bouquet
garni* ● *1 tablespoon brandy* ● *1 tablespoon red wine* ● *½ cup/4 fl. oz/1 dl
port* ● *2 ripe tomatoes* ● *½ cup/4 fl. oz/1 dl meat sauce or Spanish Sauce
(see p. 187)* ● *½ cup/4 fl. oz/1 dl light (single) cream.*

For 4 persons

Time: *preparation 40 min.* ● *cooking 1½ hours.*
Ingredients: *1 onion* ● *1 carrot* ● *2 leeks* ● *½ cup/¼ pint/1 dl olive oil* ●
12 quail ● *1 liqueur glass brandy* ● *2 cups/¾ pint/5 dl vegetable stock* ●
salt ● *2 cups/1 lb/500 g pâté de foie gras* ● *2 cups/¾ pint/5 dl port* ●
1 cup/4 oz/100 g currants ● *4 tablespoons/2 oz/50 g butter* ● *pepper. As an
accompaniment: baked (jacket) potatoes* ● *Concorde (black) grapes.*

● Clean the sweetbreads and blanch them in boiling water for
5 minutes. ● Let them cool, then remove the fat and skin. ●
Heat oil in a pan and add the salted sweetbreads. ● Brown on
both sides, then take out of the oil and drain well. ● In the same
pan fry the onion, carrot, leek and bouquet garni, stirring all
the while. ● Put back the sweetbreads, cover and cook over a
low heat for about 10 minutes. ● Sprinkle with brandy and set
alight. ● Add the red wine and port, cover and simmer for 10
minutes to gather flavour. ● Add the sliced tomatoes, meat
sauce or Spanish Sauce. ● Continue cooking for 1 hour. ●
Remove the sweetbreads, cut them into slices and arrange on
separate plates. ● Strain the sauce and add the cream. ● Bring
the sauce back to the boil and pour it over the sweetbreads. ●
Garnish as you please.

● Finely slice the onion, carrot and leeks. ● Lightly brown them
in oil. ● Add 4 of the quails, plucked, cleaned and jointed. ●
When they are golden brown moisten them with some brandy
and add the vegetable stock. ● Cook for 20 minutes. ● Take out
the birds, bone them, return the meat to the pan and cover with
the cooking juices. ● Break it all up and sieve or put it through
a meat grinder (mincer). ● Pluck and clean the remaining 8
quails. ● Pour the rest of the brandy over them and set alight. ●
Sprinkle the quails with salt and stuff with half the pâté de foie
gras. ● Place in a casserole dish and bake in a moderately hot
oven (375°F/mark 5/190°C) for 10 minutes. ● Remove from
casserole and keep them warm. ● Skim the cooking juices and
dilute with port. ● Add the currants and the sauce obtained
from the first 4 quails. ● Bring to a boil and reduce over high
heat for 5 minutes, adding the rest of the pâté cut into 8 thin
slices. ● Halve the 8 quails and arrange 4 pieces on each plate.
● Heat the sauce, stirring in the butter and a little salt, and pour
over the birds. ● Garnish each quail portion with a slice of
heated pâté. ● Serve with baked (jacket) potatoes which have
been halved, hollowed out and filled with peeled, seeded
grapes whisked through the hot gravy.

Becada asada a la guipuzcoana
Roast woodcock à la Basque

Pichón con salsa de hongos
Pigeon with mushroom sauce

For 4 persons

Time: *preparation 40 min.* ● *cooking 20 min.*
Ingredients: *4 woodcock* ● *salt* ● *4 slices salt pork or fat bacon* ● *4 tablespoons olive oil* ● *½ liqueur glass brandy* ● *pepper.* As an accompaniment: *4 square-cut slices of bread.*

For 4 persons

Time: *preparation 30 min.* ● *cooking 1¼ hours.*
Ingredients: *4 pigeons or quail* ● *olive oil* ● *butter* ● *4 onions, chopped* ● *4 lb/2 kg ceps* ● *1 cup/8 fl. oz/2 dl white wine* ● *1 cup/8 fl. oz/2 dl chicken stock* ● *light (single) cream* ● *fresh tarragon, chopped* ● *1 clove garlic* ● *salt* ● *¼ lb/200 g grapes, peeled and seeded* ● *2 lb/1 kg potatoes.*

● Prepare the woodcock (pluck, clean and singe remaining feathers). ● Stuff each bird with its giblets except for crop and gall. ● Salt, tie the birds up with string and lay the salt pork or bacon slices on them. ● Cook in oil over a moderate heat for 10 minutes or until birds are just tender. ● Take the stuffing out, moisten it with brandy, break it up finely and mix it with a fork. ● Spread the resulting mixture on the bread slices. ● Cut off the string tying the birds and arrange them on separate plates. ● Pour the cooking juices over them and serve with the bread slices.

● Pluck, singe and draw the pigeons. ● Clean them inside and out, and tie them up. ● Heat a little oil and butter in a pan and brown the birds. ● Add the chopped onion. ● Sweat, then put in 3 lb/1½ kg of the ceps, cleaned and sliced (the remaining 1 lb/500 g will serve as a garnish). ● When the ceps are browned sprinkle with wine, bring to a boil and let it evaporate over a low heat. ● Add the chicken stock. ● Take out the pigeons before they are quite done and keep them hot. ● When the ceps are done chop them finely, press through a wire sieve and mix in the cream, tarragon and grapes. ● If it is too thick, dilute the sauce with a little more chicken stock. ● Slice the remaining 1 lb/500 g of ceps and put in an ovenproof dish with oil, chopped garlic and salt to taste. ● Bake in the oven at 475°F/mark 8/250°C for 20–30 minutes. ● Before serving heat up the pigeons in the ceps sauce. ● Place the birds on a serving dish and pour the sauce over, after having removed the grapes and set them aside. ● Slice the potatoes very finely with a potato slicer and fry them. ● Form them into "nests" by pressing against the inside of a large cup. ● Arrange the ceps on the serving dish and beside each bird place a potato nest filled with grapes.

Rellenos de Vergara
Vergara pastries

"Intxausalsa"
Walnut cream

For 6 persons

Time: *preparation 30 min. ● cooking 30 min.*
Ingredients: For the pastry: 6 eggs ● 1 cup/½ lb/200 g sugar ● 2 cups/½ lb/200 g all-purpose (plain) flour ● ½ cup/3 oz/80 g confectioners' (icing) sugar ● cinnamon. For the filling: ¾ cup/6 oz/150 g sugar ● 10 egg yolks ● a little syrup made from sugar and water, to brush tops of pastries.

For 6 persons

Time: *preparation 15 min. ● cooking 50 min.*
Ingredients: 4 cups/1 lb/500 g whole English walnuts (or half that quantity of shelled nuts) ● 3 slices toast ● 4½ cups/1¾ pints/1 liter milk ● 1 cup/½ lb/200 g sugar.

● Beat the whole eggs and the sugar very thoroughly in a bowl. ● When they are well blended add the flour a little at a time and mix with a spatula. ● Put this mixture into a pastry bag (piping tube) with a smooth, rather wide nozzle. ● Form long strips of pastry and place them on a well greased baking sheet or oven tray. ● Sprinkle with confectioners' (icing) sugar. ● Bake in a moderate over (350°F/mark 4/175°C) for 20 minutes, or until nicely browned. ● Take out and cut into sections so as to form small squares. ● Partially split open the squares horizontally and insert the egg filling, which you will have prepared as follows. ● Melt the sugar with a small amount of water and boil till you have a suitably thick syrup. ● In another pan beat the egg yolks. ● Gradually add the syrup to the yolks, stirring constantly. ● Thicken over a low heat, taking care not to let the contents stick to the pan. ● When sufficiently thick pour the mixture on to a plate and leave to cool. ● When you have filled the pastries, brush the pastry tops with a little thick syrup produced by boiling equal amounts of sugar and water to the desired consistency. ● Sprinkle the pastries with cinnamon and put back in the oven for 2 minutes.

● Shell the walnuts and chop them very finely. ● Blend (liquidize) the toast into crumbs. ● Boil the milk with the toast crumbs, sugar and nuts for about 45 minutes. ● Leave to get cold. ● Serve in small bowls.

Pastel de manzana con calvados
Apple pudding with Calvados

Panchineta
Almond tart

For 8 persons

Time: *preparation 25 min.* ● *cooking 50 min. + 15 min. for the custard.*
Ingredients: For the pudding: 2 lb/1 kg Reinette (or similar) apples ●
1 cup/½ lb/250 g sugar ● ½ cup/4 oz/100 g butter ● 6 egg yolks ●
3 whole eggs ● grated lemon rind (peel) ● 4¼ cups/1¾ pints/1 liter milk ●
For the custard: 1 whole egg ● 5 egg yolks ● ¾ cup/6 oz/150 g sugar ●
1¼ cups/½ pint/3 dl Calvados (apple brandy).

For 4 persons

Time: *preparation 20 min.* ● *cooking 30 min.*
Ingredients: 1 tablespoon/½ oz/15 g butter ● 28 in./20 cm rounds of flaky
or puff pastry ● 1 egg, beaten ● 1 cup/8 fl. oz/2.5 dl egg custard
(see p. 187) ● ½ cup/2 oz/50 g chopped toasted almonds ● ½ cup/2 oz/50 g
chopped raw almonds ● confectioners' (icing) sugar.

● Peel and core the apples. ● Cut them into pieces and cook
with ¼ cup/2 oz/50 g sugar and the butter. ● In a small
saucepan caramelize ⅓ cup/3 oz/80 g sugar with a little water,
taking care not to let it burn. ● Spread the caramel over the
inside of a round pudding mould (2 in./5 cm high, 10 in./
24 cm across). ● Chill. ● Beat the eggs and egg yolks in a bowl
with the remaining sugar thoroughly mixed with the finely
grated lemon rind (peel). ● Still beating, add the milk, which
has been brought to a boil beforehand. ● Add the apple pieces
and mix well. ● Pour all into the chilled, caramel-lined mould.
● Cook in a bain-marie in a very hot oven (450°F/mark 8/
230°C) for 20–30 minutes (taking care not to let the water
boil). ● Chill. ● Meanwhile, prepare the custard. ● Put the egg
and egg yolks in a bowl with ¾ cup/6 oz/150 g sugar. ● Beat to
a smooth cream. ● Cook in a double-boiler (double saucepan)
and, stirring continuously, gradually add the Calvados. ●
When the apple pudding is cold turn it out of the mould and
cut it into wedges. ● Cover these with the custard and serve.

● On a buttered baking sheet or oven tray put an 8 in. round of
puff pastry. ● Prick it here and there in the center so that it does
not rise too much, but leave a ½ in./1 cm border round it
unpricked, brushing that with a little beaten egg. ● With the
aid of a spatula, spread the pastry base with the egg custard
and scatter the toasted almonds all over it. ● Cover with the
second round of pastry, pressing it lightly down along the
edge with your fingers. ● Brush the top of this round with the
rest of the beaten egg. ● Sprinkle with the raw chopped
almonds. ● Bake in a moderate oven (325°F/mark 3/160°C)
for 45 minutes to 1 hour, until pastry is well browned and
puffed up. ● Remove tart from oven, sprinkle with
confectioners' (icing) sugar and serve hot.

Gâteau basque
Gâteau Basque

Compota
Compote

For 6 persons

Time: *preparation 15 min. + 30 min. for batter to rest ● cooking 45 min.*
Ingredients: *3 eggs ● 1 cup/$\frac{1}{2}$ lb/200 g sugar ● $\frac{3}{4}$ cup/6 oz/170 g melted butter ● 2$\frac{1}{4}$ cups/10 oz/270 g all-purpose (plain) flour, sifted ● 2$\frac{1}{2}$ teaspoons baking powder ● 1 liqueur glass rum ● 3 drops vanilla essence ● 3 drops essence of bitter almonds (or almond essence) ● juice of 1 orange ● 1 cup/$\frac{1}{2}$ pint/2.5 dl egg custard (see p. 187) ● 10 large dried prunes, soaked overnight and stoned ● 1 beaten egg.*

For 8 persons

Time: *preparation 12 min. ● cooking 35 min.*
Ingredients: *1 lb/500 g dried prunes ● 8 Reinette (or similar) apples ● 1 lb/500 g dried apricots ● 2 cups/1 lb/500 g sugar ● 2 sticks of cinnamon.*

● Beat the eggs in a large bowl. ● Add the sugar and melted butter. ● Mix in, a little at a time, the flour, baking powder, rum, vanilla and bitter almond essences, and orange juice. ● Leave the batter to rest in a cool place for 30 minutes. ● Using a pastry bag (piping tube) with a smooth nozzle, cover the base of a baking sheet or oven tray with some of the mixture. ● The layer should not be too thick. ● With a second bag, filled with egg custard, repeat this operation, leaving a $\frac{1}{2}$ in./1 cm border all round. ● On top of the custard arrange the prunes, and cover them with the rest of the dough. ● Brush with beaten egg, decorate to choice and bake in a hot oven (400°F/ mark 6/200°C) for 45 minutes.

● Soak the prunes overnight. ● Remove stones. ● Peel and quarter the apples. ● Put fruit into a large saucepan with the sugar and cinnamon sticks, cover with water, bring to a boil and simmer until the fruit is cooked. ● Remove the fruit from the pan with a slotted spoon and allow the juice to thicken, but not to the consistency of syrup. ● Pour it over the fruit and serve.

ASTURIAS · GALICIA · SANTANDER

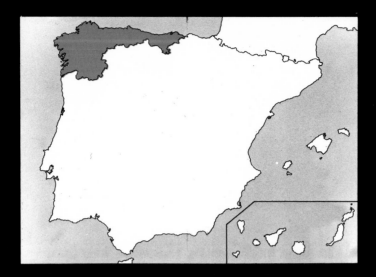

The cooks of Asturias, Galicia and Santander enjoy well deserved renown. Although differing from one another in method, they can be considered together as the great exponents of northern Spanish cuisine. The gastronomical common denominator of their achievements lies in the products of the ocean, for each one of which special dishes and sauces have been created.

Asturias. The Asturias' most celebrated dish is "Fabada," prepared from large beans cooked in the same pot as the meat. Another delicacy is salmon, ranked among the best in Europe. Finally, we must not forget Cabrales, a fermented goat's milk cheese wrapped in fig leaves.

Galicia. Galician gastronomy is justly famous for its seafood and fish, the basis of many excellent recipes. Galicia also produces splendid country cookery, excelling in high-quality meat dishes such as leg of lamb and *empanadas* (savoury ingredients wrapped in flaky pastry), game and a great variety of rich desserts.

Santander. As well as varied recipes based on sea and river fish, Santander offers exquisite country cooking and many ways of preparing snails. The high quality of its meat and vegetables should also be noted.

Fabada
Bean casserole

Pote asturiano
Asturias stew

For 6 persons

Time: *preparation 12 hours for soaking the beans, ham and bacon ●
cooking 3 hours.*
Ingredients: *1 cup/8 oz/250 g navy (haricot) beans ● 1 slice any raw
ham ● 4 oz/100 g salt pork or fat bacon, in 1 chunk ● 6 cloves garlic,
chopped ● 1 onion, quartered ● bay leaf ● 3 Chorizo sausages* ● 1 small
rump steak ● pinch of saffron ● 1 tablespoon paprika ● salt.*

● Soak beans overnight and, in another bowl of water, soak
the ham and bacon. ● Next day put the beans in a saucepan of
cold water with the garlic, onion and bay leaf. ● When the
water comes to the boil add all the other ingredients. ● Half-
cover the pot and simmer for 2½–3 hours. ● Halfway through
the cooking, tip in the saffron and paprika. ● Cook until the
beans are quite tender, not stirring, but shaking the pan
occasionally. ● Add salt at the last moment only if really
necessary, as most of the ingredients are already salty. ● Serve
in soup plates with a little of the stock.

* See footnote page 8.

For 6–8 persons

Time: *preparation 15 min. + 10 hours for soaking the beans ●
cooking 2¼ hours.*
Ingredients: *½ cup/4 oz/100 g navy (haricot) beans ● 1 clove garlic,
chopped ● paprika ● olive oil ● 2 pig's ears and 2 pig's tails ● 4 pork
sausages ● 2 blood sausages or black puddings* ● 1 ham hock (knuckle) ●
1 small Savoy cabbage weighing about 1 lb/500 g and cut into 4 pieces ●
1 lb/500 g potatoes ● salt.*

● Soak the beans for 10 hours or overnight. ● Stir-fry the
chopped garlic with a pinch of paprika in oil. ● Cook the beans
with all the ingredients except the cabbage and potatoes in a
covered pan for an hour. ● Slice the cabbage very finely and
blanch it in boiling water for a few minutes. ● Add to the beans
and other ingredients, which have simmered for an hour, and a
quarter of an hour later add the peeled potatoes. ● Cook all
together for 45 minutes or until all the ingredients are tender. ●
Remove from heat. ● Add salt if required and leave for a few
minutes before serving.

* See footnote page 8.

Caldo gallego
Galician soup

Merluza en "caldeirada"
Hake casserole

For 4 persons

Time: *preparation 20 min. + 12 hours for soaking the beans •*
cooking 1¼ hours.
Ingredients: *1 cup/8 oz/200 g navy (haricot) beans •*
9 cups/3½ pints/2 liters water • ¾ lb/300 g pork back ribs, knuckle or tail •
¼ cup/2 oz/50 g lard • handful of tender turnip (or cabbage) leaves •
1 lb/500 g potatoes peeled and cut in pieces • salt.

For 4 persons

Time: *preparation 15 min. • cooking 35 min.*
Ingredients: *1½ lb/800 g hake (or cod) • salt • 2 lb/1 kg potatoes •*
½ cup/¼ pint/1 dl olive oil • 4 cloves garlic • 1 onion, sliced • 1 tomato cut
into segments • 1 tablespoon paprika • 4 tablespoons wine vinegar.

• Put the beans, water and pork in a pan and bring to the boil. •
Add the lard. • Simmer for 1½ hours. • Halfway through add
the washed and cut-up greens and the potatoes. • Check for
salt. • Continue the slow cooking. • The resulting soup should
be thick: to that end, it is a good idea to take out some of the
potatoes and greens, break them up with a fork and return
them to the soup.

• Cut the fish into equal slices, sprinkle with salt. • Peel and
cut up the potatoes (unless small) and boil in the minimum of
water. • When cooked add the fish. • As soon as the latter is
done remove it from the cooking liquid with a slotted spoon. •
Meanwhile, fry in oil the garlic cloves, sliced onion and tomato
segments. • Add the paprika, then the vinegar and part of the
water in which the fish and potatoes were cooked. • Simmer
for 8–10 minutes. • The resulting sauce should be of a very
liquid consistency. • For best results, cook the potatoes and
fish in sea water.

Fabes con almejas
Beans with clams

Menestra de verduras a la santanderina
Vegetable soup Santander style

For 6 persons

Time: *preparation 12 hours for soaking the beans ● cooking 2 hours.*
Ingredients: *2 lb/1 kg navy (haricot) beans ● 1 slice onion ● 1 clove garlic ● sprig of parsley ● 1 small bay leaf ● olive oil ● 6 clams ● pinch of saffron ● salt ● pepper.*

For 4 persons

Time: *preparation 20 min. ● cooking 40 min.*
Ingredients: *1 quart/1 lb/500 g large clams ● salt ● 2 bay leaves ● 2 potatoes ● 2 sweet red peppers ● 3 carrots ● 1 cup/½ lb/200 g fresh beans, cut into 1 in./2½ cm pieces ● 1 onion ● olive oil ● 1 tomato, peeled and sliced ● flour.*

● Soak the beans in cold water overnight. ● Strain and place in a pan with onion slice, garlic clove, sprig of parsley, bay leaf and a little oil. ● Cover with cold water, set the pan on the heat and put on the lid. ● When the water begins to boil, turn down the heat, partially cover and simmer, making sure that the beans remain under water so that the skins do not split. ● Separately, heat the scrubbed clams in a little boiling water. ● When they start to open add them to the beans with the lightly toasted saffron, mixing all the ingredients very gently. ● Let them just simmer till the beans are tender. ● Check the salt and, if desired, add a little ground pepper. ● Remove from heat and leave for a few minutes before serving.

● Clean the clams and cook in boiling water seasoned with salt and 2 bay leaves just until clams open. ● Remove from water. ● Peel and cube the potatoes, seed and chop peppers and scrape and chop carrots; cook them all in salted water together with the beans. ● When done, strain vegetables, reserving the stock. ● Chop the onion and fry golden brown in oil. ● Add the sliced tomato, fry lightly, and when done add the flour and then, slowly, the clam and vegetable water, stirring all the while. ● Bring to the boil. ● Transfer to a fireproof serving dish and cook for a further 5 minutes. ● Serve.

Tortilla de merluza
Hake omelettes

Caldereta de pescado y mariscos
Fish and seafood casserole

For 4 persons

Time: *preparation 20 min. + 30 min. for the fish ● cooking 20 min.*
Ingredients: *2 fillets hake ● juice of 1 lemon ● 9 eggs ● 2 tablespoons flour ● 4 tablespoons/2 oz/60 g butter ● bunch of chives or a few scallions (spring onions) ● salt ● pepper.*

For 6 persons

Time: *preparation 20 min. ● cooking 20 min*
Ingredients: *6 lb/3 kg lean fish (such as tench, mullet, sea bass or gilthead, but not bluefish) ● 2 lb/1 kg onions ● parsley, chopped ● 2 tablespoons paprika ● pepper (ground and whole) ● grated nutmeg ● $\frac{1}{2}$ hot chili pepper ● 2 lb/1 kg jumbo shrimp (prawns), razor clams and hardshell clams ● $2\frac{1}{4}$ cups/$\frac{3}{4}$ pint/5 dl olive oil ● $2\frac{1}{4}$ cups/$\frac{3}{4}$ pint/5 dl dry white wine ● salt.*

● Wash and dry the hake. ● Skin and remove backbone. ● Cut flesh into small, equal pieces. ● Moisten with lemon juice and leave to marinate for half an hour. ● Beat one of the eggs in a bowl. ● Drain the fish pieces and dip them first in flour and then in beaten egg. ● Melt 3 tablespoons/$1\frac{1}{2}$ oz/40 g butter in a frying pan. ● When it foams put in the fish and brown well, stirring frequently. ● Wipe and chop the chives (or, alternatively, wash, dry and slice the scallions (spring onions)). ● Beat the remaining eggs in a bowl, 2 at a time. ● Add salt, pepper, and the chives or onions. ● Divide both the chopped fish and egg mixtures into 4 portions. ● Mix and fry one after the other till you have 4 individual omelettes.

● Clean the fish carefully and wash under running water. ● Cut into pieces. ● Using a big, wide flameproof casserole dish with a lid, arrange a layer of finely sliced onion on the bottom and above that, a layer of fish. ● Continue with another layer of onions, mingled this time with chopped parsley, paprika pepper, nutmeg, chili pepper, salt and shellfish. ● Alternate layers in this way till the ingredients are used up. ● The top layer must be fish. ● Add the oil, wine and a little water. ● Cover the pot tightly (putting a weight on the lid) and bring quickly to the boil. ● Lower the heat and continue cooking for about 15 minutes. ● When ingredients are just cooked, remove from heat and adjust seasoning.

Chopa a la sidra
Pickerel with cider

Lubina a la asturiana
Sea bass à l'Asturienne

For 4 persons

Time: *preparation 20 min. ● cooking 25 min.*
Ingredients: *2 pickerels (young pikes) of about 1¼ lb/600 g each ● salt ● olive oil ● 2 onions, sliced ● 1 clove garlic ● flour ● 2 apples, peeled and chopped ● chopped parsley ● 2 cups/¾ pint/5 dl cider ● 16 clams.*

For 4 persons

Time: *preparation 15 min. ● cooking 30 min.*
Ingredients: *a 2 lb/1 kg sea bass ● salt ● 1 onion, finely chopped ● 2 cloves garlic, finely chopped ● ½ cup/4 fl. oz/1 dl olive oil ● 1 teaspoon paprika ● ½ glass cider ● 2 tablespoons wine vinegar ● 12 clams ● 1 slice raw ham cut into strips ● 16 shelled jumbo shrimp (prawns) ● ½ cup/4 fl. oz/1 dl light (single) cream ● chopped parsley.*

● Clean, skin and bone the pickerels. ● Half open them and sprinkle with salt. ● Place them in an earthenware oven dish. ● With a little oil in a frying pan sweat the sliced onions and the garlic clove. ● When the onion becomes transparent add a little flour, the peeled and chopped apples, the chopped parsley, the cider and the cleaned and washed clams. ● When the clam shells have opened pour all these ingredients on to the fish and bake in a hot oven (425°F/mark 7/220°C) for 15 minutes. ● Serve in the same dish.

● Clean and wash the sea bass. ● Divide in half, remove the backbone and then cut the fish into 4 pieces. ● Sprinkle with salt and put it under the broiler (grill), skin side downwards, until well browned. ● Sweat the finely chopped onion and garlic in oil. ● When the onion has become transparent take the pan from the fire, add the paprika and let it simmer for a little while. ● Next, pour in the cider and vinegar and cook for several minutes. ● Add the fish, clams (cleaned and washed), ham strips, jumbo shrimp (prawns), cream and chopped parsley. ● Let the liquid reduce somewhat over a low heat, adjust seasoning and serve.

Merluza a la sidra
Hake with cider

Salmón a la ribereña
Salmon riviera

For 4 persons

Time: *preparation 15 min. + 24 hours to soak dried pepper ●*
cooking 16 min.
Ingredients: *1 onion, finely chopped ● 2 cloves garlic, finely chopped ●*
½ cup/4 fl. oz/1 dl olive oil ● flour ● 1 dried chili pepper soaked in water for
24 hours ● 1 tomato, peeled and chopped ● 2 apples, peeled, cored and
chopped ● 1 glass cider ● 1 hake weighing about 2 lb/l kg ● salt ● 2 large
potatoes, peeled and thickly sliced ● 16 clams, cleaned and washed.
To garnish: *chopped parsley ● a few segments of apple.*

For 4 persons

Time: *preparation 10 min. ● cooking 25 min.*
Ingredients: *4 salmon steaks, each weighing ½ lb/250 g ● salt ● flour ● a*
little butter ● 1 slice bacon, chopped ● ½ cup/2 oz/50 g any raw ham,
chopped ● 1 small glass cider or white wine ● ½ cup/4 fl. oz/1 dl heated
stock. As an accompaniment: *steamed potatoes ● fried tomatoes.*

● Sweat the chopped onion and garlic in a little oil. ● When the onion is transparent add 1 tablespoon flour, the soaked chili pepper, the tomato and the apple pieces. ● Mix well and add cider. ● Cook gently for 15 minutes, stirring occasionally. ● Pass through a vegetable mill and keep the stock. ● Clean, skin and bone the hake, cut it into 4 pieces and salt it. ● Coat the pieces in flour and fry them rapidly in sizzling oil. ● Take from the pan, drain and put on one side. ● In the same oil fry the potatoes, rather thickly sliced. ● When cooked, place in an open earthenware dish. ● Add the fish, clams and cider stock. ● Check for seasoning. ● Put the dish in a hot oven (425°F/mark 7/220°C) for 15 minutes. ● Garnish to taste with chopped parsley and apple segments

● Season and flour the salmon steaks. ● Put the butter and chopped bacon and ham in a frying pan and fry gently for a short time. ● Add the salmon and brown lightly on both sides, taking care that the slices stay soft. ● When steaks are done, add the cider (or wine) and stock, which has been heated to boiling point. ● Cover and keep over low heat for 4–5 minutes. ● Remove the salmon skin and bones and arrange the fish on a serving dish to keep warm. ● Put the skin and bones in a saucepan together with the cooking juices. ● Mix well and pass all through a sieve pressing well down to obtain as much liquid as possible. ● Pour this sauce over the salmon slices and serve accompanied by steamed potatoes and fried tomatoes.

Vieiras al Albariño
Coquilles St Jacques (Scallops with white wine)

Rape al coñac
Monkfish with brandy

For 4 persons

Time: *preparation 30 min.* ● *cooking 20 min.*
Ingredients: *3 lb/1½ kg scallops (about a dozen)* ● *salt* ● *pepper* ● *1 small glass Albariño (or other dry white wine)* ● *¼ cup/4 fl. oz/1 dl light (single) cream* ● *2 tablespoons/1 oz/25 g butter* ● *juice of 1 lemon* ● *½ lb/200 g mushrooms* ● *olive oil* ● *chopped parsley.*

For 4 persons

Time: *preparation 10 min.* ● *cooking 25 min.*
Ingredients: *2 lb/1 kg monkfish, or similar,* cut into 4 steaks* ● *salt* ● *pepper* ● *½ cup/2 oz/50 g flour* ● *olive oil* ● *3 cloves garlic or 2 shallots, chopped* ● *1 small glass brandy* ● *3 tablespoons tomato paste* ● *4 tablespoons light (single) cream* ● *chopped parsley.* As an accompaniment: *steamed potatoes.*

● Open the scallop shells with a sharp knife and cut the scallops out with care. ● Wash them and immerse in cold water for a few minutes. ● Drain and place in a saucepan. ● Season, add white wine and cream. ● Poach gently for about 10 minutes. ● In another pan melt the butter with the lemon juice and 2 tablespoons water. ● When the liquid boils add the mushrooms. ● Cover and cook briskly for about 6 minutes, stirring frequently. ● Scrub the scallop shells thoroughly and line the bottom halves with the well drained mushrooms. ● On top of these place the scallops; cover them with their cooking juices and sprinkle with olive oil. ● Garnish with chopped parsley and put in a very hot oven (450°F/mark 8/230°C) for 3 minutes. ● Serve at once.

● Divide each steak into 2 rounds (i.e., cut in half horizontally), after removing skin and bones. ● Season, coat with flour and fry briskly in oil. ● When steaks are cooked, drain off nearly all the oil and add the garlic or chopped shallots. ● When the garlic begins to colour add the brandy, the tomato paste and the cream. ● Allow to thicken, then sprinkle with chopped parsley. ● Serve with steamed potatoes.

* Bluefish may be used.

Ostras fritas
Fried oysters

Polpo a feira
Stewed octopus

For 4 persons

Time: *preparation 30 min. ● cooking 20 min.*
Ingredients: *32 large fresh oysters ● juice of 1 lemon ● 2 eggs, beaten ● cornmeal (maize flour) ● olive oil.*

For 10 persons

Time: *preparation 30 min. ● cooking 3 hours.*
Ingredients: *1 octopus weighing 4–6 lb/2–3 kg ● 1 large onion ● 10–15 cups/4–6 pints/2–3 liters water ● 3 cloves garlic (optional) ● 1 tablespoon paprika ● salt ● pepper ● ½ cup/4 fl. oz/1 dl olive oil.*

● Detach the oysters from their shells. ● Dip them in lemon juice and beaten egg. ● Coat them with cornmeal (maize flour). ● With the help of a fork fry them on both sides in bubbling hot oil. ● Replace the oysters in the shells and serve on separate plates.

● Clean the octopus; turn the body part inside out and remove internal organs, suckers and tips of tentacles. ● Beat the flesh hard to tenderize it. ● Wash thoroughly. ● Bring the onion and water to the boil. ● Dip the octopus into it three times, holding on to the tentacles, then let it simmer for about 3 hours. ● Leave in the cooking water until cold. ● Drain and cut into pieces. ● Chop the garlic and mix with paprika, salt and pepper. ● Dilute with olive oil, pour it over the octopus portions arranged in a serving dish and bring to the table.

Empanada de bacalao
Dried salt cod in pastry

Lenguado al Albariño
Sole with white wine

For 6 persons

Time: *preparation 30 min.+24 hours for soaking the cod ● cooking 50 mins.*
Ingredients: *2 lb/1 kg white bread dough ● 1 lb/500 g dried salt cod ● ½ cup/4 fl. oz/1 dl olive oil ● ½ lb/250 g onions, chopped ● 1 lb/500 g tomatoes, peeled and sliced ● 2 large green peppers.*

For 4 persons

Time: *preparation 15 min. ● cooking 25 min.*
Ingredients: *4 Dover or lemon soles ● 1 small glass Albariño or similar dry white wine ● ½ cup/4 fl. oz/1 dl light (single) cream ● salt ● pepper ● ½ lb/200 g mushrooms ● juice of 1 lemon ● 6 tablespoons/ 3 oz/75 g butter ● 2 egg yolks ● parsley ● 2 cups/1 lb/500 g raw jumbo shrimp (prawns).*

● Soak the dried salt cod for 24 hours, changing the water several times. ● Rinse thoroughly and dry. ● Knead the dough in the usual way, cover it and leave in a warm place. ● While it rises prepare the filling. ● Put the cod in a pan with enough water to cover it, bring to the boil, then take the fish out immediately. ● Bone and cut into small pieces. ● Heat the olive oil in a deep frying pan. ● Add the chopped onions. ● Sweat gently, then add the peeled and sliced tomatoes and seeded, chopped green peppers. ● Leave a little while to gather flavour, then add the fish. ● Divide the dough in half and roll it into two rounds about ¼ in./0.5 cm thick. ● Arrange the fish mixture on one round. ● Top with the second round and pinch down along the edge. ● With the pieces of dough left over form a sort of piping all round the outside border. ● Prick all over the surface with the prongs of a fork and bake in a warm oven (300°F/mark 2/150°C) for 45 minutes.

● Put the cleaned and filleted soles in a buttered oven dish. ● Cover with white wine and cream. ● Season. ● Cook in a moderate oven (350°F/mark 4/175°C) for 12 minutes. ● Wash and cut the mushrooms in strips. ● Mix the lemon juice, 2 tablespoons/1 oz/25 g butter and 2 tablespoons water in a saucepan. ● When they start to simmer add the mushrooms. ● Cover and cook over a brisk heat for 6 minutes, stirring frequently. ● Drain the fish fillets, lay them in a buttered fireproof dish. ● Stud the surfaces with the chopped mushrooms. ● Thicken the liquid in which the soles were cooked with the beaten egg yolks, heating gently and stirring constantly. ● Pour over fish. ● Sprinkle with chopped parsley. ● Place in a very hot oven (450°F/mark 8/230°C) for 3 minutes and serve at once, garnished with the jumbo shrimp (prawns) still in their shells.

Lamprea guisada a la gallega
Stewed eel Galician style

Sardinas a la santanderina
Sardines Santander style

For 4–6 persons

Time: *preparation 15 min. ● cooking 20 min.*
Ingredients: *3 lb/1½ kg eel ● ½ cup/4 fl. oz/1 dl olive oil ●
¼ cup/2 fl. oz/½ dl wine vinegar ● 1 large glass red wine ● white pepper ●
2 bay leaves ● nutmeg ● a few sprigs parsley ● 1 onion, chopped ● 4 cloves
garlic, finely chopped ● salt.* As an accompaniment: *croutons of fried
bread ● boiled rice.*

For 4 persons

Time: *preparation 15 min. ● cooking 30 min.*
Ingredients: *16 very fresh sardines ● 1 cup/4 oz/100 g all-purpose (plain)
flour ● 1¼ cups/½ pint/3 dl olive oil ● 1 onion, chopped ● 5 tomatoes,
peeled and chopped ● 4 cloves garlic, sliced ● chopped parsley ● salt.*

● Wash the eel in warm water. ● Scrape with a knife. ● Suspend from a stout hook. ● Make a circular cut through the skin all the way round just below the head. ● Sprinkle the cut with salt, and firmly pull the skin off in 1 piece from top to bottom. ● Make deep cuts in the fish, without actually cutting it through, and collect the blood. ● In a deep frying pan put the olive oil, blood, vinegar, red wine, white pepper, bay leaves, nutmeg, parsley, chopped onion and garlic. ● Lay the eel on top, bring to the boil and simmer for 20 minutes. ● When cooked, drain the fish and sieve the sauce. ● Add salt if necessary. ● Pour sauce back on to the eel and dish it up accompanied by croutons of fried bread, with the eel curled round a mound of boiled rice in the center.

● Clean, coat with flour and fry the sardines in half the oil. ● When done, place them in a flameproof serving dish. ● In a frying pan, gently fry the onion and tomatoes in the remaining oil, then add them to the sardines. ● Fry the garlic and parsley in the same oil and add them to the pot with the sardines, onion and tomatoes. ● Cook all together for a few minutes. ● Check the seasoning and serve in the cooking dish.

Cachelada gallega
Octopus with potatoes à la Galicienne

Pastel de bonito a la santanderina
Tuna mould à la Santander

For 4–6 persons

Time: *preparation 30 min. ● cooking 2–3 hours to stew the octopus + 30 min.*
Ingredients: *1 octopus of about 2 lb/1 kg ● 2 onions ● 4–5 bay leaves ● 6 large potatoes ● olive oil ● 4 ripe tomatoes, peeled and chopped ● 3 cloves garlic, chopped ● 6 tablespoons flour ● salt. To garnish: 1 sweet red pepper, broiled (grilled) and cut into strips ● parsley.*

For 8 persons

Time: *preparation 30 min. ● cooking 1 hour.*
Ingredients: *8 ripe tomatoes, peeled and chopped ● 1 onion, chopped ● 1 tuna fish (if possible, an albacore, the most delicate variety) weighing some 4 lb/2 kg ● $\frac{1}{2}$ cup/$\frac{1}{4}$ pint/1 dl olive oil ● 13 eggs ● butter ● flour ● 3 scallions (spring onions), chopped ● 4 medium-sized carrots cooked whole ● salt.*

● Clean the octopus. ● Turn inside out and remove internal organs, suckers and tips of tentacles. ● Pound the flesh to soften, then simmer in salted water with 1 onion and 2 or 3 bay leaves for 2–3 hours until tender. ● Drain and cut into pieces about 1 in./2$\frac{1}{2}$ cm across. ● Peel the potatoes, cut into $\frac{1}{4}$ in./0.5 cm slices, and fry to a golden colour in very hot oil. ● Drain and put on one side. ● In the same pan, fry the remaining onion, tomatoes, 2 bay leaves and the chopped garlic, stirring all the while. ● Add flour and dilute with half the octopus stock. ● Cook the sauce for 5 minutes and press through a sieve. ● Put the potatoes, octopus and sauce into a fireproof dish. ● Bring to the boil and cook briskly for a few minutes. ● Adjust seasoning. ● Decorate with strips of red pepper and some chopped parsley. ● Serve immediately.

● Mix the chopped tomato and onion in the blender. ● Clean, skin and bone the tuna, cut it in pieces and brown in oil. ● Add the puréed tomato and onion mixture, season, cover the pan and cook for 30 minutes. ● Remove from heat and put all the contents into the blender. ● Beat the eggs and add them to the resulting purée, mixing well. ● Butter the inside of a rectangular mould or loaf pan, then sprinkle with flour. ● Put half the mixture in the bottom. ● Arrange the chopped scallions (spring onions) and carrots on top. ● Sprinkle with salt. ● Cover with the rest of the mixture. ● Place the mould in a bain-marie and bake in a moderate oven (350°F/mark 4/175°C) for about 40 minutes, until a knitting needle or skewer inserted into the mould comes out clean.

This dish can be enriched by adding boiled lobster at the blending stage. ● Instead of tuna other suitable fish (swordfish, for example) can be used in the same quantities.

Zancarrón o carne gobernada
Chuck beef casserole

Entrecot al Cabrales
Fillet of veal à la Cabrales

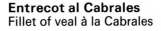

For 4 persons

Time: *preparation 12 min. + 2–3 hours for the meat ● cooking 45 min.*
Ingredients: *1½ lb/750 g chuck beef (steak) ● 1 tablespoon paprika ● 2 cloves garlic, finely chopped ● olive oil ● 1 large onion, chopped ● 1 leek, chopped ● 1 carrot, chopped ● 1 sweet red pepper, seeded and chopped ● 1 tomato ● ¼ lb//100 g mushrooms, coarsley chopped ● 1 glass cider (or white wine) ● salt ● chopped parsley. Accompaniment: 1 lb/500 g new potatoes.*

For 4 persons

Time: *preparation 10 min. ● cooking 15–20 min.*
Ingredients: *¼ cup/2 oz/60 g butter ● 1½ lb/800 g fillet of veal ● ⅓ cup/3 oz/80 g Cabrales* ● dash of brandy ● ½ cup/4 fl. oz/1 dl beef stock ● 1 cup/8 fl. oz/2 dl light (single) cream ● salt. Can be served with: mushrooms ● new potatoes.*

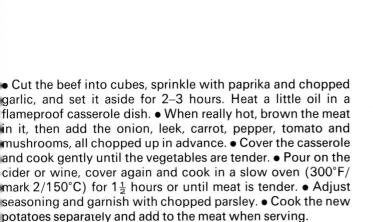

● Cut the beef into cubes, sprinkle with paprika and chopped garlic, and set it aside for 2–3 hours. Heat a little oil in a flameproof casserole dish. ● When really hot, brown the meat in it, then add the onion, leek, carrot, pepper, tomato and mushrooms, all chopped up in advance. ● Cover the casserole and cook gently until the vegetables are tender. ● Pour on the cider or wine, cover again and cook in a slow oven (300°F/mark 2/150°C) for 1½ hours or until meat is tender. ● Adjust seasoning and garnish with chopped parsley. ● Cook the new potatoes separately and add to the meat when serving.

● Melt the butter in a frying pan. ● When foaming add the veal divided into 4 portions. ● Brown on both sides, then add the cheese, brandy, beef stock and cream. ● When the meat is done take it out of the pan and keep it hot. ● Reduce the sauce somewhat, add salt if desired and pour it over the cutlets. ● Serve with mushrooms and new potatoes.

*A goat's milk cheese. If unobtainable, Gorgonzola will do.

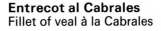

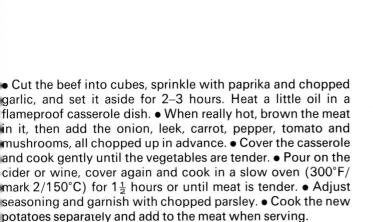

Callos a la asturiana
Tripe Asturias style

Lacón con grelos
Pork with turnip tops

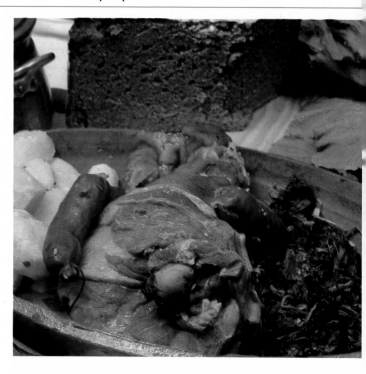

For 10 persons

Time: *preparation 30 min.* ● *cooking 3–4 hours for the tripe + 1¼ hours.*
Ingredients: *4 lb/2 kg tripe* ● *1 calf's foot* ● *1 calf's head* ● *2 pig's feet (trotters)* ● *1 onion, finely chopped* ● *2 cloves garlic, finely chopped* ● *olive oil* ● *½ lb/200 g any raw ham* ● *1 tablespoon paprika* ● *1½ teaspoons ground chili pepper* ● *glass of white wine* ● *½ cup/4 fl. oz/1 dl tomato sauce (see p. 187)* ● *salt.*

For 6 persons

Time: *preparation 20 min. + 24 hours for soaking the pork pieces* ● *cooking 3 hours.*
Ingredients: *3 lb/1½ kg turnip leaves* ● *12 medium or 6 large potatoes* ● *2 lb/1 kg pig's feet (trotters)* ● *½ lb/250 g pig's head (preferably the cheek)* ● *½ lb/250 g pig's ears* ● *salt* ● *1¼ lb/600 g Chorizo sausage*.*

● Clean the tripe scrupulously and blanch it. ● Bring to a boil in one pan the tripe and in another the calf's head and foot and the pig's feet (trotters). ● Simmer gently for 3–4 hours. ● When the tripe is done, cut it into equal pieces about 1 in./2½ cm across. ● Put in a flameproof dish. ● Separately, fry the finely chopped onion and garlic in oil. ● When the onion begins to colour add the ham cut in strips, the paprika and the chili pepper. ● Sweat them gently. ● Moisten with the white wine, add the tomato sauce and fry gently for a few more minutes. ● Add all this to the tripe. ● Then add the calf's head and foot and the pig's trotters, which have been boned and chopped finely, along with the stock in which they were cooked. ● Stew for about 1 hour. ● Test for seasoning and serve.

● Wash and cut up the turnip tops, and cook in boiling water for 5 minutes. ● Drain. ● Peel the potatoes, cutting in half if large, leaving whole if small. ● Scrape the pork pieces with a knife and wash thoroughly (having soaked them for 24 hours previously). ● Put feet (trotters), cheek and ears in a saucepan. ● Cover with boiling water and cook gently for 2½ hours. ● Halfway through cooking season with salt. ● When cooked remove meat from the pan, cut into equal pieces and keep hot till time to serve. ● In the still simmering stock put the turnip tops with the Chorizo sausage and potatoes. ● Simmer gently until cooked. ● Test for seasoning and remove from heat. ● Leave for about 10 minutes before dishing up.

* See footnote page 8.

Pierna de cordero a la orensana
Leg of lamb Orense style

Empanada de lomo
Pork pasty

For 4 persons

Time: *preparation 20 min. ● cooking 1¼ hours.*
Ingredients: *1 small leg of lamb ● salt ● pepper ● ½ cup/¼ lb/100 g butter ● olive oil ● 3 carrots ● 3 onions or 9 shallots ● 2¼ cups/1 pint/5 dl brown stock ● 2 cups/¾ lb/300 g already cooked navy (haricot) beans ● sprigs of parsley.*

For 4–5 persons

Time: *preparation 55 min. ● cooking 35 min.*
Ingredients: For the pastry: *2½ cups/10 oz/300 g all-purpose (plain) flour ● 2 eggs ● 8 tablespoons/¼ lb/100 g lard ● 1 small glass water ● ½ cup/¼ pint/1 dl olive oil ● 1 small glass white wine ● 1 teaspoon salt.* For the filling: *1½ cups/½ lb/200 g onions, chopped ● 2 green peppers, seeded and cut into strips or rings ● ¼ lb/100 g any raw ham (or chopped Chorizo sausage) ● 2 cloves garlic, chopped ● ½ cup/¼ pint/1 dl olive oil ● ½ lb/200 g loin of pork, boned and cut into slices ● salt ● ½ glass red or white wine ● 2 tablespoons tomato paste ● pinch of saffron ● freshly ground pepper ● butter ● 1 egg, beaten.*

● Bone and tie the leg of lamb, or have your butcher do it for you. ● Season with salt and pepper. ● Place in a large open cooking pan or stock pot. ● Baste with butter that has been melted with a little olive oil (to prevent the butter burning). ● Fry gently till the joint is browned on all sides. ● At this point add the carrots and whole onions or shallots. ● Cook over a low heat. ● When meat and vegetables are well browned add the stock. ● Continue cooking gently till the meat is tender. ● If the juices have reduced too much, top up with a little stock or water. ● Some 30 minutes before the joint is done add the cooked navy (haricot) beans, which will absorb almost all the meat gravy. ● Serve the joint on a meat dish surrounded with the beans, the onions quartered and carrots cut into pieces. ● Garnish with sprigs of parsley.

● Melt the lard in a pan, then leave to cool. ● Sift the flour, reserving 4 tablespoons for flouring the pastry board. ● Pile it into a mound with a central depression. ● Into this put the eggs, the melted lard, water, oil, wine and salt. ● Mix these ingredients, blending them gradually into the surrounding flour till you have obtained a smooth pastry. ● Cover with a cloth and leave to rest for 15–20 minutes. ● Meanwhile, fry the onions, peppers, ham (or sausage) and garlic in a little oil, stirring constantly. ● When the onion begins to colour add the lightly salted pork slices and continue frying gently till the onion is golden brown. ● Add the tomato paste, wine, saffron and pepper. ● Continue to cook until the liquid has evaporated and thickened. ● Divide the pastry into two equal parts. ● Roll one half into a very thin layer and from it cut out a circle big enough to line your buttered pie dish and overhang the edges slightly. ● Fill it with the meat and vegetable mixture, now quite cold. ● Roll the rest of the pastry and lay it over the filling. ● Moisten the edges so that the two layers stick together. ● Brush all over with beaten egg and prick the surface. ● Bake in a moderate oven (375°F/mark 5/190°C) for 25–30 minutes.

Lomo de ternera al horno
Roast loin of veal

Callos a la montañesa
Tripe à la montagnarde

For 6 persons

Time: *preparation 15 min. ● cooking 2 hours.*
Ingredients: *3 cloves garlic ● 1 teaspoon paprika ● salt ● juice of 2 lemons ● ½ cup/4 fl. oz/1 dl olive oil ● 5 lb/2½ kg loin of veal in one piece ● ¼ cup/2 oz/50 g lard ● 1 glass white wine ● 36 small new potatoes all the same size ● 2½ cups/1 lb/500 g cooked peas.*

For 6–8 persons

Time: *preparation 15 min. ● cooking 4½ hours.*
Ingredients: *6 lb/3 kg tripe ready for cooking ● 1 ham hock (knuckle) ● 1 medium onion stuck with cloves ● a little muslin bag containing a few peppercorns ● 2¼ cups/1 pint/5 dl white wine ● 1 bouquet garni ● 1 large onion, chopped ● 1 sweet red pepper, seeded and chopped ● 2 cloves garlic, finely chopped ● 1 cup/8 fl. oz/2 dl olive oil ● 1 tablespoon flour ● 1 tablespoon paprika ● salt ● chopped parsley.*

● Pound the garlic, paprika and salt in a mortar. ● Dilute with lemon juice and oil. ● Put the veal in a baking dish (oven tray) containing the lard and baste all over with oil and lemon mixture. ● Roast in a hot oven (425°F/mark 7/220°C) for about 20 minutes, basting with white wine from time to time. ● Scrape the new potatoes and brown them in a pan with a little oil. ● When half cooked take out and put with the meat in the oven and continue to roast, but at a moderate heat (350°F/mark 4/175°C) for another 1¾ hours. ● Add the already cooked peas, leave for a few minutes and serve.

● Clean and wash the tripe. ● Cut in pieces and boil for 3 minutes. ● Drain and transfer to a saucepan. ● Cover with plenty of water. ● Add the ham hock (knuckle), the onion stuck with cloves, the bag of peppercorns, the white wine and the bouquet garni. ● Bring to a boil and skim carefully, then cook gently for about 3 hours. ● By the end of that time the stock should have become rather thick. ● Sweat the remaining onion, red pepper and garlic cloves (all well chopped) in oil. ● When they have begun to turn colour add the flour, stirring over a low heat. ● Gradually add the paprika dissolved in a little of the tripe stock. ● Remove the clove-stuck onion, the bag of peppercorns and the bouquet garni from the tripe saucepan. ● Add the stir-fried mixture and cook for a further hour. ● When done, remove the ham hock (knuckle), adjust seasoning, add a little chopped parsley and serve the tripe very hot.

Venado astur
Venison Asturias style

Pollo campurriano
Chicken Santander

For 4–6 persons

Time: *preparation 20 min. + 4 days of marination ● cooking 2½ hours.*
Ingredients: *1 onion ● 1 leek ● 1 carrot ● 1 stick celery ● 1 tomato ● 1–2 bottles red wine ● 1 bay leaf ● ¼ teaspoon thyme ● ¼ teaspoon oregano ● 1¾ cups/¾ pint/4 dl olive oil ● 1 leg of venison, boned and rolled ● 1 cup/8 fl. oz/2.5 dl light (single) cream.* As an accompaniment: *boiled chestnuts ● fried apple slices.*

For 4 persons

Time: *preparation 15 min. ● cooking 1 hour.*
Ingredients: *One 3 lb/1½ kg chicken ● salt ● pepper ● 1 cup/½ lb/200 g lard ● ¾ cup/6 oz/150 g bacon, finely chopped ● 1 large onion, chopped ● 1 bay leaf ● 1½ teaspoons flour ● 1½ teaspoons paprika ● 1 large glass white wine ● chicken stock or water ● ½ lb/250 g shallots ● 1 cup/½ lb/200 g rice ● 3 green peppers.*

● Clean the vegetables. ● Cut them into pieces more or less the same size and mix with the wine. ● Add the bay leaf, thyme and oregano. ● When the joint of venison has been boned and rolled leave it to steep in this marinade for 4 days. ● Put oil in a fireproof dish and brown the meat on all sides. ● Add the marinated vegetables. ● When they begin to soften put the dish in the oven (350°F/mark 4/175°C) for 2 hours. ● Take the venison out, remove the string and carve the meat into slices. ● Sieve the sauce and mix in the cream. ● Put over low heat to thicken. ● Pour this sauce over the meat. ● Garnish with boiled chestnuts and fried apple slices.

● Clean and joint the chicken. ● Season. ● Melt the lard with the finely chopped bacon in a large skillet (frying pan). ● Quickly fry the chicken portions over a high heat to seal. ● When golden brown add half the chopped onion and the bay leaf. ● Sweat the onion, add flour and paprika. ● Pour in the wine. ● Stir and cover the chicken with heated chicken stock or water. ● Add the shallots. ● Cover and cook gently till the meat is tender. ● Meanwhile, prepare the rice. ● Stir-fry the remaining onion and the peppers peeled and cut into strips* ● Add the rice, stir, and then add hot chicken stock or water to come 1 in./2½ cm above the level of the rice. ● Bring to the boil and cook, uncovered, until most of the liquid is absorbed. ● Remove from heat, cover tightly, and put in a warm place to steam for 30 minutes. ● Dish up the bird on a serving dish and serve the rice separately.

*See footnote page 9.

Casadielles
Fried pastries with walnuts

Frixuelos
Sweet pancakes with honey

For 4–6 persons

Time: *preparation 40 min. ● cooking 30 min.*
Ingredients: *thinly pared rind (peel) of 1 lemon ● 1 cup/7 oz/200 g sugar ● 3 tablespoons hot water ● 2 cups/½ lb/250 g chopped walnuts ● 1 small glass sherry ● 1 tablespoon cinnamon ● 1 tablespoon/½ oz/150 g butter ● 1 cup/½ lb/250 g butter (in a single piece, refrigerated until used) ● 3 cups/¾ lb/350 g all-purpose (plain) flour, sifted ● 1 egg, beaten ● 1 liqueur glass aniseed liqueur such as Pernod ● 1½ teaspoons salt ● confectioners' (icing) sugar. For frying: an equal quantity of butter and sunflower oil.*

For 4–6 persons

Time: *preparation 15 min. ● cooking 30 min.*
Ingredients: *4 eggs ● 4½ cups/1¾ pints/1 liter milk ● ½ teaspoon salt ● about 4 cups/1 lb/500 g all-purpose (plain) flour ● sunflower oil ● honey ● powdered (castor) sugar. To garnish: cooked and sugared apple slices.*

● Make a syrup from the very thinly pared lemon rind (peel), sugar and hot water. ● Simmer for 15 minutes. ● Strain through damp cheesecloth (muslin). ● Mix with the chopped walnuts, sherry, cinnamon, 1 tablespoon/½ oz/15 g butter and a little water. ● Mix well over heat, then leave to cool. ● Now put the refrigerated butter on a floured pastry board. ● Roll it into a rectangular shape less than ½ in./1 cm thick and keep in a very cool place. ● Mix the flour, beaten egg, aniseed liqueur, salt and just enough cold water to form a pastry. ● Cover with a cloth and let it rest for 15 minutes. ● Then roll out into a rectangle less than ½ in./1 cm thick. ● In the center, place the thin butter layer and fold the edges of the pastry over it. ● Roll out to a very thin layer. ● Fold into quarters and roll out again. ● Repeat the operation three times. ● The final layer is very thin. ● Divide into 12 pieces and fill each piece with a little of the walnut filling. ● Moisten the borders and fold the pastry in half. ● Prick all over with a fork and press down and mark the edges to seal the "pasties." ● Fry in equal parts of butter and oil over a moderate heat. ● When cooked, drain and sprinkle with confectioners' (icing) sugar.

● Beat the eggs in a large bowl. ● Add the milk with a little salt and then stir in the flour a little at a time till you have a creamy batter, not too thick. ● Heat plenty of oil in a frying pan until it begins to smoke very slightly. ● Ladle in a little of the batter turning the pan so that it spreads evenly. ● When the underside of the pancake is a golden brown, turn it over so that the other side browns lightly. ● Drain and keep warm while you make the others. ● Spread the pancakes with a little honey and dust with powdered (castor) sugar. ● Pancakes can also be fried using only a little oil for each one and proceeding as before. ● Garnish with sugared segments of cooked apple and serve hot.

Filloas
Sweet crêpes

Tarta de Santiago
Santiago tart

For 6 persons

Time: *preparation 10 min.* ● *cooking 20 min.*
Ingredients: *6 eggs* ● *¾ cup/3 oz/75 g all-purpose (plain) flour* ●
⅓ cup/3 oz/75 g butter ● *2 cups/17 fl. oz/5 dl milk* ● *salt* ● *confectioners'
(icing) sugar* ● *lard.*

For 4–6 persons

Time: *preparation 30 min.* ● *cooking 40 min.*
Ingredients: For the pastry: *1 egg, beaten* ● *1 teaspoon cinnamon* ●
½ cup/4 oz/125 g sugar ● *all-purpose (plain) flour.* For the filling:
1 lb/500 g blanched almonds ● *8 eggs* ● *2 cups/1 lb/500 g sugar* ●
1 teaspoon ground cinnamon ● *grated lemon rind (peel) from 1 lemon* ●
confectioners' (icing) sugar.

● Beat the eggs. ● Stir in the flour, butter and a pinch of salt. ● Mix with the cold milk and strain. ● Grease the crêpe frying pan thoroughly with 1 tablespoon/½ oz/15 g lard. ● When it is sizzling hot pour in a tablespoonful of the batter. ● Spread it evenly over the base. ● When the batter has set and the underside is slightly browned turn it over and brown the other side. ● Drain and keep warm. ● Remember to grease the pan before you fry each crêpe. ● Finally, roll the crêpes up on a plate and sprinkle with confectioners' (icing) sugar. ● They can be served either hot or cold.

● Butter a pie dish (flan tin). ● Prepare the pastry, mixing the beaten egg with a tablespoon water, the cinnamon and sugar, adding the flour till you obtain a smooth mixture. ● Spread it on a floured pastry board and roll out to a very thin layer. ● Chop the almonds finely. ● Beat the eggs for the filling with the sugar, cinnamon and grated lemon rind (peel). ● Mix well. ● Add most of the almonds (keep a few in reserve) and beat once more, really forcibly. ● Line the pie dish with the pastry, spread it with the filling, scatter the top with the remaining chopped almonds and bake in a hot oven (400°F/mark 6/205°C) till well browned. ● Before serving sprinkle liberally with confectioners' (icing) sugar.

Natillas
Egg custard meringues

For 6 persons

Time: *preparation 15 min. ● cooking 50 min.*
Ingredients: *2 cups/¾ pint/4 dl milk ● 6 eggs, separated ● 8 tablespoons powdered (castor) sugar ● rind (peel) of 1 lemon ● confectioners' (icing) sugar ● a few drops lemon juice.*

● Boil the milk in advance and let it get cold. ● Mix the 6 egg yolks with the powdered (castor) sugar, slowly stir in the cooled milk, then, still stirring, add the grated lemon rind (peel). ● Cook the mixture in a double-boiler (double saucepan) over hot but not boiling water, stirring with a wooden spoon. ● When the custard is thick enough to coat the spoon remove the pan from the heat. ● Beat the egg whites until very stiff, then sprinkle them with confectioners' (icing) sugar and a few drops of lemon juice. ● Shape the beaten egg whites into small cones, arrange them on a lightly buttered baking sheet (oven tray) and bake in a slow oven (275°F/mark 1/135°C) until they are firm and crisp, about 50 minutes. ● Pour the custard into little dessert bowls and top each one with a meringue cone.

CATALONIA

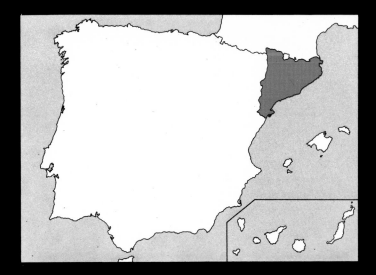

Catalan cooking is mainly country cookery, with a rich choice of dishes. There are four basic sauces to go with it: *sofrito, samfaina, picada* and *allioli*. Thanks to geographical situation of the province, Catalonia enjoys a vast range of products: fish of the highest quality; crustaceans and molluscs, some of which can be found only along the Catalan coast (such as the *espardenyes*, belonging to the Cephalopod family and known solely on the shores of Barcelona and Tarragona); various types of meat, especially pork, which is the main ingredient of numerous dishes and excellent sausages; game, above all partridges. Finally, there is an enormous choice of fruit and vegetables and numerous kinds of edible fungi, the fragrant offerings of woodland and meadow. Catalonia boasts many methods of using all these first-class materials. Beside a number of typical Catalan recipes, there are many others that betray some foreign influence (as is also the case with the exquisite cuisine of Provence) or reflect the cookery of neighbouring regions (the colourful dishes of Valencia, the austerity of central Spain). Catalonia's innumerable specialties make it one of the most important gastronomic areas of Spain.

Sopa de tomillo
Thyme soup

"Patacu"
Pork chops with vegetables

For 4 persons

Time: *preparation 10 min. • cooking 15 min.*
Ingredients: *large sprig of thyme • salt • 9 cups/3½ pints/2 liters water • 3 cloves garlic, finely chopped • 4 tablespoons olive oil • 1 cup/4 oz/200 g sliced stale bread • 4–8 eggs (optional).*

For 6–8 persons

Time: *preparation 20 min. + overnight soaking for beans • cooking 2 hours.*
Ingredients: *2 cups/1 lb/500 g navy (haricot) beans • 1 large cabbage, chopped • 6 tablespoons olive oil • 1 pork chop per serving • 1 lb/500 g onions, chopped • 1 clove garlic, chopped • 1 bay leaf • 1 clove • 1 ripe tomato, peeled and chopped • salt • 1½ lb/750 g zucchini (courgettes), sliced • 2 lb/1 kg potatoes, peeled and sliced.*

• Boil the thyme in salted water for 5 minutes. • Add the chopped garlic. • Heat the oil in a frying pan and fry the bread slices till golden brown. • Pour on the thyme stock, passing it through a fine-meshed sieve. • Simmer for about 10 minutes. • If desired, one or two eggs per person can be added to poach just before removing the pan from the heat. • Sprinkle a few drops of olive oil into each plate of soup before serving.

• Cook the pre-soaked beans and cabbage separately. • Heat the oil in a large saucepan or deep frying pan, and gently fry the chops, chopped onion and garlic, bay leaf, clove and tomato with a little salt. • When all are well browned cover with water and bring to the boil. • Add the zucchini (courgettes) and sliced potatoes. • Leave to cook. • When the potatoes are nearly done put in the cabbage and then, 5 minutes before serving, the beans.

"Escudella i carn d'olla"
Catalan feast

"Trinxat"
Cabbage and potato mould

For 8 persons

Time: *preparation 20 min. + 12 hours soaking for chick peas and beans* ● *cooking 3 hours.*
Ingredients: *1 ham or bacon bone ● 1 beef bone with marrow ● 1 turnip, finely chopped ● 1 carrot, finely chopped ● 1 stick celery, chopped ● 1 lb/500 g stewing veal ● ½ boiling chicken ● ¾ cup/6 oz/150 g fat bacon or salt pork ● 2 pig's ears ● 1 pig's foot (trotter) ● 1 cup/½ lb/250 g chick peas, previously soaked in salted warm water ● 1 cup/½ lb/250 g navy (haricot) beans, also pre-soaked ● ½ cup/¼ lb/100 g ground (minced) veal ● 1 salami sausage ● 1 egg, beaten ● 3 heaped tablespoons stale breadcrumbs ● salt ● pinch of cinnamon ● pinch of pepper ● 1 large clove garlic ● chopped parsley ● 1 tablespoon flour ● ½ lb/250 g blood sausage or black pudding ● 1½ cups/½ lb/250 g potatoes, peeled and finely chopped ● 1 cabbage, chopped. For the escudella: ¼ lb/200 g vermicelli.*

● Put the ham and beef bones and the chopped turnip, carrot and celery in a large saucepan with 12½ cups/5 pints/3 liters water. ● Bring to the boil, skim carefully. ● Add the joint of veal (previously boned, rolled and tied), the half-chicken, bacon, pig's ears and pig's foot (trotter). When the stock comes back to the boil skim once more. ● Add the chick peas and navy (haricot) beans (it is advisable to put these in a muslin bag so that they can be separated from the rest when done). ● Season to taste. ● Simmer gently for 2 hours, or until the chick peas are tender. ● Meanwhile, prepare the *pelota* separately. ● Mix together the ground (minced) veal, salami, beaten egg, breadcrumbs, salt, cinnamon, pepper, garlic and chopped parsley. ● Bind together thoroughly and, with your hands, shape a sort of large sausage, and coat it with flour. ● After the soup has simmered for 2 hours put in the *pelota* together with the blood sausage or black pudding, potatoes and cabbage. ● Check the seasoning. ● If the stock has reduced overmuch, top up with water. ● Simmer for a further 30 minutes. ● Cook the pasta in three-quarters of the soup to produce the *escudella*, which is served as the first course. ● The meat and vegetables are served separately.

For 4 persons

Time: *preparation 15 min.* ● *cooking 40 min.*
Ingredients: *2 lb/1 kg green cabbage ● 4 lb/2 kg potatoes, peeled and sliced ● salt ● ½ lb/200 g bacon ● olive oil.*

● Put 2 large saucepans on the stove, each containing 9 cups/3½ pints/2 litres water. ● Bring to the boil. ● Blanch the shredded cabbage in one pan, then transfer it to the other to cook. ● As soon as it begins to soften put the sliced, salted potatoes in the first pan. ● When both are cooked, drain and put them in the same pan. ● Fry the bacon slices (rashers) in a minimum of oil. ● Remove, drain and cut half of them into pieces. ● Put half the oil on the cabbage and mix thoroughly. ● With a fork mash the cabbage and potato together. ● Pour the rest of the oil in a pan with the chopped bacon pieces. ● Add the vegetables and press well down to form a kind of large pancake or fritter. ● Heat well through. ● When the underside is browned turn the mixture over to brown the other side. ● Decorate the surface with the remaining bacon slices (rashers) and serve hot.

Habas a la catalana
Broad beans à la Catalan

"Mousse d'escalibada"
Cream of vegetable

For 8 persons

Time: *preparation 5 min. ● cooking 40 min*
Ingredients: *1 cup/½ pint/¼ liter olive oil ● bunch of scallions (spring onions) ● 1½ lb/750 g bacon, home-cured and unsliced, if possible ● 2 blood sausages or black puddings* ● 4 lb/2 kg fresh broad beans** ● 1 glass dry white wine ● 1 sprig fresh mint ● 1 bay leaf ● salt ● pinch of sugar ● 2 teaspoons aniseed liqueur such as Pernod ● 2 teaspoons muscatel wine.*

For 3 persons

Time: *preparation 25 min. ● cooking 35 min.*
Ingredients: *2 large green peppers ● 1 red pepper ● 2 eggplants (aubergines) ● 2 large ripe tomatoes ● ½ cup/4 fl. oz/1.5 dl olive oil ● 4 potatoes ● 1 large onion ● 4 cloves garlic ● salt ● pepper ● 4 tablespoons wine vinegar.*

● In a flameproof casserole put a little oil, the finely sliced scallions (spring onions) and half the bacon cut into thick slices (rashers). ● Let them brown lightly, then add one sliced blood sausage or black pudding. ● Put in the shelled broad beans and fry gently for a few minutes. ● Add the white wine, the herbs, the remaining blood sausage or black pudding and the rest of the bacon, left in one piece. ● Stir the beans well with a wooden spoon. ● Season with salt and a pinch of sugar. ● Tightly cover the pot so that no steam escapes. ● Leave to simmer, stirring occasionally, till the beans are tender. ● Check the seasoning. ● Just before removing the pot from the heat add the Pernod and muscatel. ● Remove the bacon and blood sausage in order to slice them and then put them back on top. ● Bring the casserole to table.

* See footnote page 8.
** Lima beans may be used instead.

● On a charcoal grill or in a hot oven (400°F/mark 6/205°C) cook the peppers, eggplants (aubergines), the tomatoes lightly brushed with oil, the potatoes, scrubbed but not peeled, the onion, unpeeled, and the garlic cloves. ● When tender, peel and remove the stalks and seeds from the peppers and tomatoes, then chop them up. ● Peel and slice the onion and potatoes. ● Peel the garlic. ● Season with salt, pepper, oil and vinegar. ● Mix well and put through a blender to produce a smooth cream. ● Refrigerate for about 1 hour. ● Serve very cold.

Tarta gratinada de puerros
Leek flan au gratin

Ensalada de "rovellons"
Mushroom salad

For 6 persons

Time: *preparation 40 min. ● cooking 50 min.*
Ingredients: *4 cups/1 lb/500 g all-purpose (plain) flour ●
¾ cup/6 oz/150 g butter ● salt ● 1 egg yolk ● 2 or 3 leeks ● 4 eggs ●
1¼ cups/½ pint/3 dl light (single) cream ● 1 cup/¼ lb/100 g grated Cheddar
cheese.*

For 6 persons

Time: *preparation 20 min. ● cooking 30 min.*
Ingredients: *2 cups/½ lb/250 g green (French or runner) beans ● 6 baby
turnips ● 1 large carrot ● 1¼ lb/600 g ceps ● ½ lb/250 g button
mushrooms ● 1 red pepper, baked ● 2 cloves garlic ● olive oil ● salt ●
pepper ● white wine vinegar ● chopped parsley.*

● In a mixing bowl put 2 cups/½ lb/250 g flour, ¼ cup/2 oz/
50 g butter in small pieces, a pinch of salt and an egg yolk. ●
Pour in a little cold water and mix until smooth. ● Flour a pastry
board and begin to knead the dough, gradually adding the rest
of the flour and as much water as necessary. ● Knead for at
least 30 minutes. ● Dough should be firm and elastic. ● Form
into a ball, put it in a bowl covered with a cloth and leave in a
warm place for 1 hour. ● Meanwhile, clean the leeks and chop
them up. ● Sweat them in a frying pan with the remaining
butter. ● When they are cooked take them out, drain, leave to
cool. ● Roll the dough out very thin. ● Line a buttered pie dish
(flan tin) with it and fill with leeks. ● Beat the whole eggs,
season; stir in the cream. ● Pour this mixture over the leeks and
scatter with the grated cheese. ● Bake in a moderate oven
(350°F/mark 4/175°C) for about 50 minutes, or until the
surface is an appetizing brown and the filling is set. ● Serve
hot.

● Clean and slice the beans, turnips and carrot. ● Cook them
and the ceps all separately. ● They must be only just done. ●
Arrange all ingredients on a serving plate, as shown above,
and garnish with strips of baked red pepper. ● Dress with a
mixture of the chopped garlic, olive oil, salt, pepper and a
sprinkling of white wine vinegar. ● Sprinkle with chopped
parsley.

Ensalada de habas
Broad bean salad

Ensalada de espinacas
Spinach salad

For 4 persons

Time: *preparation 15 min. • cooking 20 min.*
Ingredients: *mint leaves • 2 lb/1 kg fresh broad beans, shelled* • 1 lettuce heart • $\frac{1}{4}$ lb/100 g any raw ham • 1 teaspoon mild (French) mustard • salt • pepper • 2 tablespoons white wine vinegar • 4 tablespoons olive oil.*

For 4 persons

Time: *preparation 20 min.*
Ingredients: *1 tablespoon French mustard • 4 tablespoons olive oil • 1 lb/500 g spinach • $\frac{1}{4}$ lb/100 g mushrooms • wine vinegar • 1 teaspoon roasted sesame seeds.*

• Put some mint leaves in the water and boil the beans till they are done but still firm. • Leave to cool. • Meanwhile, slice a few lettuce leaves and the ham into thin strips. • Make a dressing with the mustard, salt, pepper, white wine vinegar, olive oil and 2 fresh mint leaves.

* Lima beans may be used instead.

• Put a tablespoon of mustard in a salad bowl. • Dribble the oil on to it, stirring till you obtain a creamy consistency. • Pick over the spinach, then wash it several times under running water to get rid of every trace of soil. • Drain thoroughly. • Put into the salad bowl. • Wash the mushrooms in water with vinegar, dry and slice finely. • Add them to the spinach, scatter with sesame seeds, toss well in the dressing and serve at once.

"Arròs negre"
Rice with cuttlefish ink

Arroz a la marinera
Rice with seafood

For 4–6 persons

Time: *preparation 15 min.* ● *cooking 1 hour.*
Ingredients: *1 pint/300 g mussels* ● *1¼ cups/½ pint/3 dl olive oil* ●
4 crawfish (crayfish) ● *4 jumbo shrimp (prawns)* ● *4 saltwater crayfish
(scampi)* ● *½ lb/200 g onion, chopped* ● *3 cloves garlic, finely chopped* ●
2 green peppers, seeded and finely chopped ● *1 lb/500 g cuttlefish* ●
½ lb/200 g ripe tomatoes, peeled, seeded and sliced ● *2 cups/1 lb/400 g
rice* ● *salt.* As an accompaniment (optional): *allioli (garlic) sauce
(see p. 187).*

For 4 persons

Time: *preparation 30 min. + 1 hour for fish stock* ● *cooking 25 min.*
Ingredients: *½ lb/250 g squid* ● *8 tablespoons olive oil* ● *1 onion,
chopped* ● *2 ripe tomatoes, peeled, seeded and sliced* ● *½ lb/200 g
monkfish** ● *4 pieces (about 1 lb/500 g) conger eel* ● *4 jumbo shrimp
(prawns)* ● *1 cup/½ lb/400 g rice* ● *2 cups/¾ pint/4 dl rich fish stock
(prepared by simmering 1 lb/500 g fish scraps—heads, bones, etc.—with a
sliced onion, parsley, pepper, 2 glasses dry white wine and
½ cup/1¾ pints/1 liter water and salt for 1 hour, then straining)* ● *1 large
green pepper, seeded and chopped* ● *4 tablespoons cooked peas* ●
24 mussels or clams, scrubbed well ● *pinch of saffron* ● *1 clove garlic,
crushed* ● *chopped parsley* ● *salt* ● *pepper.*

● Wash the mussels carefully and put them into a large pan
with 2 large spoonfuls of water. ● Bring to the boil, cover and
wait for the shells to open. ● Free mussels of one of their valves
and return to the hot water. ● Pour a little oil into a large heavy
saucepan and fry the crawfish (crayfish), jumbo shrimp
(prawns) and saltwater crayfish (scampi). ● When cooked
take them out, drain and replace them with the onion, garlic
and peppers. ● Clean cuttlefish: discard tentacles, head and
inner organs but keep the ink sac to one side. ● Remove
cuttlebone from tail section, rub off reddish-brown membrane
under running water, and slice if the cuttlefish are large. ● Add
to the onions and peppers when they have sweated a little. ●
As the contents begin to colour add the tomatoes and fry
gently for a couple of minutes before pouring a ladleful of hot
water over them. ● Simmer for 25 minutes. ● Half an hour
before serving pour in the rice with sufficient water and
mussel stock to equal twice the volume of the rice. ● When the
water comes to the boil, skim. ● Season and slowly add the
cuttlefish ink. ● Lay the seafood on top, cover, and continue to
cook over a low heat for 15 minutes. ● Can be accompanied by
garlic sauce.

● Clean and wash the squid as for cuttlefish (see previous
recipe). ● Cut into rings. ● Place over heat in a wide, shallow
pan with the olive oil. ● Sweat for a while, then add the
chopped onion and stir. ● When the onion begins to colour
add the tomatoes, then the monkfish and conger eel cut into
pieces, and lastly the jumbo shrimp (prawns). ● Stir well
together with a wooden spoon and cook a little longer to
improve the flavour. ● Now add the rice, stir thoroughly again
and pour on the fish stock. ● Cook over a brisk heat at first. ● At
this stage add the green pepper, peas, well-scrubbed mussels
or clams (making sure they are tightly closed—a sign of
freshness), saffron, crushed garlic and chopped parsley. ● Add
salt if necessary and a pinch of pepper. ● Turn down the heat
and cook, covered, for a further 15 minutes. ● Remove the pan,
still covered, from heat and allow the rice to steam for about 5
minutes before serving.

*If unavailable, use bluefish.

Fideos a banda
Vermicelli with fish, potatoes and onions

Canalones a la barcelonesa
Cannelloni à la Barcelona

For 4 persons

Time: *preparation 20 min. ● cooking 1 hour.*
Ingredients: *1 cup/8 fl. oz/2 dl olive oil ● 8 potatoes, peeled and quartered ● 4 onions, sliced ● 6 cloves garlic ● 1 sprig parsley ● pepper ● salt ● cinnamon ● 1 lb/500 g lean fish (e.g., sea bass, mullet, etc.), filleted and cut into pieces ● pinch of saffron ● 1 lb/400 g vermicelli.*

For 4 persons

Time: *preparation 30 min. + 3 hours to cook the calf's brain ● cooking 1 hour.*
Ingredients: *½ cup/¼ lb/100 g butter ● ½ lb/200 g loin of pork, boned and cubed ● ¼ cup/2 oz/50 g any raw ham, chopped ● 4 chicken livers, chopped ● 1 onion, chopped ● 2 ripe tomatoes, peeled and sliced ● 1 egg yolk ● 1 calf's brain, cooked and chopped ● 2 tablespoons pâté de foie gras ● salt ● 12 cannelloni ● 1 cup/8 fl. oz/2 dl white sauce (see p. 187) ● ½ cup/2 oz/50 g grated Cheddar cheese.*

● Heat ½ cup/¼ pint/1 dl olive oil in a flameproof dish or frying pan. ● When sizzling add the potatoes and the sliced onion. ● Fry them gently, stirring continuously with a wooden spatula, then pour in 4½ cups/1¾ pints/1 liter water. ● Add 3 cloves garlic, crushed, and parsley with pinches of pepper, salt and cinnamon. ● Simmer till the potatoes and onions are tender. ● Add the fish pieces, and another 4½ cups/1¾ pints/1 liter water. ● Season; add a pinch of saffron. ● Cook for another 10 minutes or so, then remove from heat. ● In another cooking pot heat the remaining oil. ● Add the remaining 3 cloves of garlic, crushed, and the vermicelli. ● Stir well so that the pasta does not stick together. ● Pour in the stock from the potatoes, onions and fish, together with an equal quantity of hot water. ● Bring rapidly to a boil and cook for 20 minutes. ● Turn the vermicelli into a serving dish and serve the fish, potatoes and onions separately.

● Place half the butter in a frying pan with the chopped pork, ham and livers. ● Season and fry lightly, stirring several times. ● When the meats are browned add the chopped onion; stir again and add the peeled and sliced tomatoes. ● Remove from heat and put the cooked mixture through a food mill. ● Add the egg yolk, the cooked and finely chopped brain and the pâté. ● Mix and season. ● Cook the cannelloni and allow to cool. ● Fill them with the meat mixture. ● Arrange on a bed of half the white sauce in an ovenproof serving dish and cover with the rest of the sauce. ● Sprinkle the grated cheese on top, and dot with a few knobs of butter. ● Brown under the broiler (grill).

Arroz con azul
Rice with fish

Paella Parellada
Paella à la Parellada

For 4 persons

Time: *preparation 15 min. ● cooking 35 min.*
Ingredients: *1 lb/500 g sardines or mackerel ● ½ cup/4 fl. oz/1.5 dl olive oil ● 1 chili pepper ● 1 slice bread ● 4 cloves garlic, chopped ● 1 large tomato, peeled and chopped ● 2 tablespoons/1 oz/30 g butter ● 1½ cups/12 oz/400 g rice ● pinch of saffron ● salt ● pepper.*

● Gut, bone and cut the heads off the fish. ● Fry lightly in half the oil. ● Heat the remaining oil in a pan and sweat the chili pepper; remove from pan and pound it in a mortar. ● In the same oil fry the slice of bread and pound it, too. ● Now in a flameproof serving dish lightly fry the chopped garlic and tomato. ● Add butter, stir and then add the rice, stirring again with a wooden spoon. ● Place the sardines on top of the rice and sprinkle with the oil in which they have been fried. ● Add 3 cups/1¼ pints/7 dl hot water and bring to a boil. ● Add a little powdered saffron to the crushed chili and bread. ● Dilute with a little of the rice stock. ● Add this mixture to the rice dish, season, cook fast for a further 5 minutes, then lower the heat and simmer for 15 minutes more, or until rice is cooked and the liquid absorbed. ● Adjust seasoning. ● Serve in the same dish.

For 6 persons

Time: *preparation 40 mins. ● cooking 60 mins.*
Ingredients: *1 boned chicken cut into 6 pieces ● ½ lb/200 g pork tenderloin (pork fillet) cut into 6 pieces ● ½ lb/200 g squid, cleaned as described on p. 58 and sliced into rings ● 1 cup/8 fl. oz/2 dl olive oil ● 1 tablespoon/½ oz/15 g lard ● 1½ cups/½ lb/200 g chopped onion ● 4 medium-sized artichoke hearts, each cut in half and sprinkled with lemon juice ● 1 cup/½ lb/200 g fresh or canned tomatoes, peeled and sliced ● fish or chicken stock ● 2 cups/1 lb/400 g rice ● ¾ cup/¼ lb/100 g cooked peas ● 4 large green peppers seeded and cut in strips ● ½ teaspoon saffron ● 2 cloves garlic ● 2 tablespoons chopped parsley ● 6 pieces boned monkfish* ● 6 pieces boned lean fish (such as sea bass or wrasse) ● 6 shelled crawfish (crayfish) ● 24 mussels, scrubbed ● 6 Chorizo sausages** ● salt.*

● Using a deep frying pan (if possible a *paella*, the two-handled Spanish pan that has given its name to the recipe), brown the lightly seasoned chicken, pork and squid in sizzling hot oil and lard. ● Add the onion and artichoke hearts; continue frying. ● Lastly, put in the tomatoes. ● A few minutes later add a big ladleful of stock and simmer for a further 10 minutes. ● Turn up the heat and throw in the rice, peas, peppers and 4 cups/1¾ pints/1 liter stock. ● Crush the saffron and garlic together in a mortar; dilute them with a little stock and add to the pot along with the chopped parsley. ● Stir the rice thoroughly and, still stirring, put in the fish pieces and the crawfish (crayfish), which has been fried in advance in a little oil, together with their frying oil. ● Last of all, add the mussels and sausages. ● Cook until rice is cooked and all of the liquid is absorbed. ● Check for seasoning and put the pan in a hot oven (425°F/mark 7/220°C) for a short time just to dry the rice. ● Serve immediately.

* If unavailable, use bluefish.
** See footnote page 8.

"Llenguado amb espardenyes"
Sole with "espardenyes"

"Esqueixada"
Dried salt cod hors d'oeuvre

For 6 persons

Time: *preparation 15 min.* ● *cooking 40 min.*
Ingredients: *6 lemon or Dover soles* ● *salt* ● *pepper* ● *2 tablespoon flour* ● *olive oil* ● *8* espardenyes* ● *1 lb/500 g onions, chopped* ● *3 cloves garlic, finely chopped* ● *1 bay leaf* ● *1 small ripe tomato, peeled* ● *dry white wine* ● *fish stock or consommé (if unobtainable, use water).*

For 4 persons

Time: *preparation 20 min. + 24 hours for soaking the cod.*
Ingredients: *¾ lb/300 g best quality dried salt cod* ● *1 large green pepper* ● *1 onion* ● *a few chives, chopped* ● *⅔ cup/¼ pint/1.5 dl olive oil* ● *4 tablespoons wine vinegar* ● *pepper* ● *salt* ● *3 cloves garlic, crushed* ● *handful of ripe (black) olives.*

● Fillet the soles. ● Season the fillets, coat with flour and fry lightly in oil. ● Put to one side. ● Remove the *espardenyes* from their shells, discard the membrane around the meat and fry in the same way. ● To the oil in which the fish were fried, add the chopped onion, garlic, bay leaf, tomato, a little white wine and some stock or water. ● Cook for a few minutes, then put in the *espardenyes* and fillets of sole. ● Barely simmer for 30 minutes.

Espardenyes are typical shellfish from the Catalan coast. If unobtainable, scallops St Jacques can be used in their place, but these should be cooked for only 2 minutes at the most.

● Soak the dried salt cod for 24 hours, changing the water several times to get rid of all the salt. ● Drain, cut in wide strips and press well to eliminate the last vestige of salt. ● Slice the onion thinly. ● Soften by leaving in cold water for several minutes. ● Cut the pepper into thin, wide strips. ● Put the fish in a salad bowl and dress it with the onion, pepper, a pinch of salt, olive oil and vinegar. ● Mix thoroughly. ● Sprinkle with a little more oil. ● Add the garlic and chopped chives. ● Give the salad one more good stir, arrange the olives on top and serve the *esqueixada* as an appetizer (starter). ● Garnish to taste (with hard-boiled egg, etc.)

"Suquet d'escórpora"
Scorpion fish with potatoes

Langostinos al allioli
Langoustines with garlic sauce

For 4 persons

Time: *preparation 12 min.* ● *cooking 30 min.*
Ingredients: *4 scorpion fish (gurnard*) weighing about 2 lb/1 kg (gross) each (or 1 big scorpion fish weighing 8 lb/4 kg), with their livers ● 6–7 cloves garlic ● 3 tablespoons olive oil ● 1 small onion, finely sliced ● 1 medium-sized tomato, peeled and sliced ● 2 lb/1 kg potatoes, peeled and finely sliced ● salt ● 1 thin slice of toast, grated ● chopped parsley ● scant ½ glass dry white wine. As an accompaniment: allioli (garlic) sauce (see p. 187).*

For 4 persons

Time: *preparation 15 min.* ● *cooking 12 min.*
Ingredients: *2 lb/1 kg langoustines (saltwater crayfish/scampi) ● salt ● allioli(garlic) sauce (see p. 187) ● 1 egg yolk.*

● Clean the fish and cut into pieces. ● Set aside. ● Cut all but one garlic clove into thin slivers and sweat in a little oil. ● When they start to colour add the onion slices. ● As soon as this browns slightly put in the sliced tomato and the fish. ● Continue to fry gently. ● Add the potatoes, cover with water, add salt to taste and cook over a low heat. ● When half cooked add a mixture of chopped fried fish livers, toast crumbs, the remaining garlic clove and parsley, and dilute with a little white wine. ● Continue simmering until all ingredients are cooked. ● The dish is enhanced by garlic sauce.

* The gurnard, or scorpion fish, is caught in the Atlantic and Mediterranean. It has a rather ugly, prehistoric-like head and there are grey, red and yellow varieties. If unavailable, use mullet or whiting.

● Clean the langoustines and remove the shell from the bodies. ● Do not remove the heads. ● Season with salt and lay side by side in a pan, with no space between them. ● Put in a moderate oven (350°F/mark 4/175°C) for 8–9 minutes, by which time they should be cooked. ● Remove pan and discard the remaining liquid. ● Cover with garlic sauce which has been enriched by another egg yolk. ● Put the pan back in the oven to heat for 3 minutes, taking care that the sauce does not scorch. ● Serve very hot.

Lenguado a la "nyoca"
Sole with dried fruit and nuts

Langosta con pollo
Lobster with chicken

For 4 persons

Time: *preparation 10 min. ● cooking 20 min.*
Ingredients: *4 Dover or lemon soles, each weighing about*
½–¾ lb/250–300 g ● flour ● olive oil ● salt ● ½ cup/2 oz/50 g pine kernels ●
½ cup/2 oz/50 g raisins ● ¼ cup/1 oz/25 g blanched almonds ●
¼ cup/1 oz/25 g hazelnuts ● 4 peeled tomatoes.

For 4–5 persons

Time: *preparation 30 min. ● cooking 35 min.*
Ingredients: *a 2 lb/1 kg chicken (with liver) ● ⅔ cup/¼ pint/1.5 dl olive oil ● salt ● pepper ● cinnamon ● 1 cup/5 oz/150 g chopped onion ● 1 bay leaf ● thyme ● oregano ● ½ lb/250 g ripe tomatoes, peeled and chopped ● 1 small glass dry white wine ● 1 small glass brandy ● chicken stock ● a 2 lb/1 kg lobster, cooked ● pinch of saffron ● 1 clove garlic ● ¼ cup/1 oz/20 g shelled and roasted hazelnuts and almonds ● a piece of orange rind (peel) ● 1 oz/30 g baking (unsweetened) chocolate, grated ● chopped parsley.*

● Clean, wash and dry the soles. ● Coat lightly with flour. ● Fry them in hot olive oil until cooked. ● Season. ● Keep warm. ● Heat a little oil in a separate pan and fry the pine kernels and raisins, and the coarsely chopped almonds and hazelnuts until the nuts are browned. ● Distribute this mixture over the fish. ● Place on serving plates and garnish each one with a previously fried tomato.

● Clean the chicken and divide into 8 pieces. ● Heat half the oil in a large frying pan. ● Brown the chicken pieces and chicken liver. ● Season with salt, pepper and a little cinnamon. ● When the meat is well browned take out the liver and add the chopped onion, bay leaf, thyme and oregano. ● Fry lightly, then add the tomatoes. ● Cook them till they have lost their juice. ● Pour in the wine and brandy, raise the heat and allow liquid to evaporate a little. ● Cover with stock, bring to a boil and simmer gently. ● Cut the lobster in two, starting at the tail end. ● Halve the head and clean it. ● Collect and reserve the liquid from the lobster. ● Season and fry the lobster meat briskly in the remaining oil, but do not cook it completely. ● When the chicken is half done after 15–20 minutes, put the lobster in with it. ● Cook for 15 minutes more. ● Five minutes before the meat should be cooked pound the saffron, garlic clove, almonds, hazelnuts, chicken liver and orange peel in a mortar to a paste. ● Add the grated chocolate, dilute with the lobster liquid set aside earlier, and flavour with a few drops of olive oil and a little chicken stock. ● Remove herbs from the casserole, add the sauce and chopped parsley. ● Mix well and serve.

Rape Costa Dorada
Monkfish Costa Dorada style

Samfaina de bacalao a la catalana
Catalan dried salt cod

For 6 persons

Time: *preparation 10 min. ● cooking 30 min.*
Ingredients: *12 slices monkfish* ● 1 tablespoon flour ● 6 tablespoons olive oil ● $\frac{1}{2}$ lb/250 g onions, finely chopped ● 3 cloves garlic, crushed ● 1 bay leaf ● 1 clove ● 1 cinnamon stick ● 2 lb/1 kg ripe tomatoes, peeled and chopped ● brandy ● salt.*

For 4 persons

Time: *preparation 20 min. + 24 hours for soaking the cod ● cooking 50 min.*
Ingredients: *1$\frac{1}{4}$ lb/600 g dried salt cod ● flour ● 1 cup/8 fl. oz/2.5 dl olive oil ● 4 cloves garlic, unpeeled ● 1 sweet red pepper, seeded and chopped ● 1 green pepper, seeded and chopped ● 1 onion, chopped ● $\frac{1}{2}$ lb/200 g zucchini (courgettes) ● $\frac{1}{2}$ lb/200 g eggplant (aubergine) ● 1 lb/500 g ripe tomatoes, scalded and peeled ● $\frac{1}{2}$ teaspoon sugar ● salt.*

● Season and flour the monkfish slices. ● Fry lightly in oil. ● In another pan gently stir-fry the onion, garlic, bay leaf, clove and cinnamon. ● When these are done add the sieved tomatoes, brandy and fish. ● Add salt if desired. ● Complete the cooking.

*Bluefish may be used.

● Soak the dried cod for 24 hours, changing the water frequently. ● Drain, dry and cut in pieces. ● Coat with flour and fry in half the oil. ● Leave in the oil for a few minutes, then remove cod, drain and keep warm. ● Reheat the oil and sweat the garlic cloves in their skins. ● Add the chopped peppers and onion. ● Fry all together. ● Meanwhile, cut the zucchini (courgettes) and eggplants (aubergines) into pieces. ● Season, flour and fry separately in the remaining oil. ● When tender add the fried onion and peppers. ● Add the peeled tomatoes and the sugar. ● Cook for a further 10 minutes or so. ● Add the salt cod and heat up for a few more minutes, taking care that nothing disintegrates. ● Check the seasoning. ● Serve immediately.

Zarzuela
Seafood casserole

Arenques con uvas
Herring with grapes

For 4 persons

Time: *preparation 30 min. ● cooking 45 min.*
Ingredients: *4 medium-sized squid ● 24 mussels (or clams) ● 4 crawfish (crayfish) ● 4 jumbo shrimp (prawns) ● 4 pieces monkfish ● 4 pieces lean fish (e.g., sea bass, black umbra) ● 4 pieces hake ● olive oil ● 1 onion, chopped ● 1 bay leaf ● 3 ripe, peeled (or canned) tomatoes ● 1 small glass dry sherry ● 2 small glasses brandy or rum ● 1 tablespoon flour ● pinch of saffron ● 1 clove garlic ● 1 sprig parsley ● 6 roasted almonds ● 2 slices toast ● juice of 1 lemon ● salt ● pepper.*

For 1 person

Time: *preparation 20 min. + 24 hours to soak herrings ● cooking 5 min.*
Ingredients: *2 smoked herrings ● flour ● butter ● 6–8 muscatel (or other dessert) grapes.*

● Clean, wash and drain all the seafood. ● Discard tentacles, head and inner organs of squid and cut body into rings. ● Put the well-scrubbed mussels into a pan of cold water, bring to the boil and remove from the shells as soon as they open. ● Similarly cook the shellfish and shell them. ● Reserve the cooking liquid. ● Peel and chop the onion and tomatoes. ● Season the filleted fish. ● Fry them lightly in hot oil. ● Take them out one after the other as they are done and transfer to a wide, shallow, flameproof earthenware dish or paella pan in alternating layers of fish, shellfish and mussels. ● Reheat the same oil and sweat the chopped onion with the bay leaf. ● When it begins to colour add the tomatoes. ● Pour in the sherry and brandy or rum. ● Boil briskly to reduce the liquid by half. ● Sprinkle with flour and stir for a minute or two. ● Add the strained mussel stock. ● Bring to a boil and simmer for some 10 minutes. ● In a mortar pound the saffron, garlic, parsley sprig, almonds and toast to a fine paste. ● Dilute with a little oil and stock. ● Check for seasoning and scatter over seafood. ● Remove the bay leaf. ● Return pan to the heat and simmer for a little longer, until all ingredients are tender. ● Add the lemon juice.

● Soak the herrings for 24 hours, changing the water frequently. ● Rinse and pat dry. ● Clean, bone and coat with flour. ● Fry in butter for 2–3 minutes, adding the grapes, also floured, at the last moment. ● Leave the pan on the heat for a minute or two and serve immediately.

"Sèpia amb rossinyols"
Cuttlefish with chanterelles

Sepia con guisantes
Cuttlefish and peas

For 4 persons

Time: *preparation 20 min. ● cooking 1¼ hours.*
Ingredients: *2 onions, coarsely chopped ● ½ cup/¼ pint/1 dl olive oil ● 2 small ripe tomatoes, peeled and mashed ● a 2 lb/1 kg cuttlefish ● 1 lb/500 g chanterelles (Cantharellus cibarius)* ● 5 cloves garlic ● 8 blanched and toasted almonds ● 1 glass dry white wine ● salt.*

For 4 persons

Time: *preparation 30 min. ● cooking 1¼ hours.*
Ingredients: *2 heads of garlic ● a few sprigs parsley ● 2 thin slices bread ● ½ cup/4 fl. oz/1 dl olive oil ● flour ● 3 small ripe tomatoes, peeled and chopped ● 2 lb/1 kg cuttlefish ● 4 lb/2 kg fresh peas ● 1 glass white wine ● salt ● pepper.*

● Fry the coarsely chopped onions in oil in a flameproof earthenware casserole or paella pan. ● When they begin to colour add the tomatoes and fry gently for about 10 minutes. ● Clean the cuttlefish as described on p. 58, cut into rings and add it to the pan. ● Cover with water. ● Simmer for 30 minutes. ● Add the washed and drained chanterelles. ● Cook for 15 minutes more. ● Pound the garlic and almonds with pestle and mortar and dilute with a glass of dry white wine. ● Pour the mixture into the cooking pan, stir and simmer for another 10 minutes or so. ● Add salt if desired and serve immediately.

* Chanterelles, or girolles as they are sometimes called, are an edible fungi found in beech woods throughout Europe. They are the colour of apricots and smell faintly of them. If unavailable, use ordinary mushrooms, but the flavour will not be as good.

● Fry the garlic, separated into individual cloves and peeled, parsley and bread in oil in a fireproof casserole. ● When golden brown drain and set aside. ● Stir a tablespoon of flour into the same oil. ● When it starts to brown add peeled, chopped tomatoes with a little water. ● Pound the fried garlic, parsley and bread in a mortar before adding them to the casserole. ● Bring to a boil and simmer for about 15 minutes. ● If the mixture becomes too thick, add a little water. ● When cooked, pass through a vegetable mill or put in a blender. ● Meanwhile, clean and cut up the cuttlefish as described on p. 58. ● Return puréed mixture to the casserole and add the cuttlefish. ● Bring back to the boil and simmer for 30 minutes. ● Add the shelled peas and a glass of white wine. ● Season. ● Continue to simmer for another 15 minutes.

Buñuelos de bacalao
Dried salt cod fritters

Romesco
Stewed fish with beans

For 4 persons

Time: *preparation 10 min + 1 hour rest time for batter and 24 hours to soak the cod ● cooking 8 min. per fritter.*
Ingredients: *1¼ lb/600 g dried salt cod ● a little cold milk ● 4 tablespoons flour ● ½ cup/4 fl. oz/1 dl olive oil ● For the batter: 1 cup/4 oz/125 g all-purpose (plain) flour ● 1 egg, separated ● salt ● 1 tablespoon olive oil ● ½ cup/4fl. oz/1 dl cold water.*

For 6 persons

Time: *preparation 20 min. ● cooking 25 min.*
Ingredients: *1½ lb/800 g monkfish* ● 1½ lb/800 g sea bream or sea bass ● 1½ lb/800 g Dover or lemon sole ● 4 jumbo shrimp (prawns) ● 1 lb/500 g squid ● 4 cloves garlic, chopped ● 1 ripe tomato, peeled and sliced ● 1 small green pepper, seeded and sliced ● 2 cups/¾ pint/5 dl olive oil ● 1 onion, thinly sliced ● ½ cup/2 oz/50 g toasted almonds ● pinch of saffron ● a few black peppercorns ● sprig of parsley ● 1 chili pepper ● salt. As an accompaniment: boiled navy (haricot) beans.*

● Soak the fish for 24 hours in cold water, changing the water several times. ● Take out, wash and dry. ● Make a mound of flour in a bowl and form a hollow in the center. ● Put the egg yolk, salt and 1 tablespoon olive oil in the hollow. ● Mix thoroughly, then add the water, stirring it in gradually so that no lumps remain. ● Beat the egg white to a stiff froth and blend it with the batter a little at a time. ● Let the batter rest for an hour. ● Remove skin and bones from fish and cut into pieces. ● Moisten with milk, then coat lightly with flour. ● Heat oil in a pan, and when it is very hot but not yet smoking, dip the pieces of fish in the batter and then fry them in the oil. ● Brown well on both sides.

● Clean, wash and bone all the fish, and cut into pieces. ● See p. 66 for how to prepare squid. ● Set all aside. ● Fry the garlic, tomato and green pepper in oil. ● Drain, and use the same oil for frying the onion slices. ● Meanwhile, mix the fried garlic, tomato and pepper with the almonds, saffron and crushed peppercorns. ● When the onion begins to brown add the above mixture and stir thoroughly, then add some water, the parsley, the chili pepper and, last of all, the fish and unshelled shellfish. ● Add more water if needed—fish should be just covered. ● Simmer for 15 minutes. ● When fish is cooked you can add the beans, which should have been cooked separately.

* If unavailable, bluefish may be used.

Espinas de anchoas
Fried anchovy bones

Trucha con salsa de almendras
Trout with almond sauce

For 4 persons

Time: *preparation 30 min. for soaking backbones ● cooking 10–12 min.*
Ingredients: *25–30 anchovy backbones ● 1 cup/8 fl. oz/2.5 dl milk ●*
1 cup/¼ lb/100 g all-purpose (plain) flour ● oil for frying.

For 4 persons

Time: *preparation 15 min. ● cooking 20 min.*
Ingredients: *4 trout ● salt ● flour ● olive oil ● ¼ cup/2 oz/50 g butter ●*
4 cloves garlic ● ½ cup/2 oz/50 g toasted almonds ● 5 sprigs of parsley ●
1 lemon. As an accompaniment: boiled potatoes.

● To prepare this dish you need the backbones of about 30 salted anchovies. ● First let them soak in the milk for 30 minutes. ● Then dip them in flour and deep-fry in sizzling hot oil till golden brown. ● Serve as a snack with aperitifs.

● Gut and wash the trout. ● Drain, dry and season. ● Dip in flour and fry in hot oil in a large frying pan. ● Keep hot. ● In a smaller pan put 4 tablespoons of the oil the fish were fried in and the butter. ● Chop the garlic, almonds and a sprig of parsley. ● When the oil and butter are really hot add this mixture moistened with the juice of half a lemon and stir well. ● Remove the pan from the heat before the contents begin to brown. ● Arrange the trout on separate plates and garnish with a slice of lemon under the head and a sprig of parsley in the mouth. ● Scatter the chopped almond mixture on the fish. ● Serve very hot, with boiled potatoes if desired.

Rodaballo a la salsa de erizos
Turbot with sea urchin sauce

Garum
Fish sauce

For 4 persons

Time: *preparation 15 min. ● cooking 30 min.*
Ingredients: *1 turbot weighing about 1½ lb/750 g ● salt ● pepper ● 1 carrot, cut in rounds ● 1 onion, sliced ● 1 sprig thyme ● 1 bay leaf ● juice of 2 lemons ● 24 sea urchins ● olive oil ● ½ cup/4 fl. oz/1 dl Sauce Hollandaise (see p. 187).*

For 4 persons

Time: *preparation 30 min. + 20 days for marinating.*
Ingredients: *as much olive oil as needed for the marinade ● ½ teaspoon mixed herbs ● pepper ● 5 anchovies ● 5 sardines ● 1 tablespoon capers ● 2 cloves garlic ● ½ teaspoon dried English mustard ● scant half-glass rum ● 4 tablespoons brandy ● 2 cups/1 lb/500 g ripe (black) olives, stoned ● 4 tablespoons olive oil ● 2 hard-boiled egg yolks.*

● Clean the turbot. ● Put it in a large saucepan or fish kettle and cover with cold water. ● Add the salt, pepper, cut-up carrot, sliced onion, thyme, bay leaf and lemon juice. ● Bring to the boil, then cover and simmer for 10–15 minutes. ● Meanwhile, prepare the sauce: open shells and remove sea urchins. ● Dip them in a little oil and mix them with the barely simmering Sauce Hollandaise. ● Divide the turbot into 4 servings; place on separate plates and ladle the sauce over them. ● Garnish to taste.

● Make a marinade with the olive oil, mixed herbs and pepper. ● Soak the anchovies and sardines in it for 20 days. ● When ready to prepare the sauce drain them, chop finely and finally mash them, mixing in a little of the oil, till you have a completely smooth mixture. ● Add the finely chopped capers, garlic, olives, hard-boiled egg yolks and mustard, rum, brandy, and 4 tablespoons olive oil. ● Beat the ingredients together thoroughly till you have a smooth, homogeneous sauce.

Estofado de buey a la catalana
Catalan beef stew

"Botifarra amb mongetes"
Sausages and beans

For 4 persons

Time: *preparation 30 min.* ● *cooking 3 hours.*
Ingredients: *¼ cup/2 oz/50 g lard ● ¼ lb/100 g salt pork or fat bacon ● 1½ lb/600 g beef (shoulder, chuck or shin), sliced ● 1 tablespoon flour ● 1 glass full-bodied red wine ● 4 cloves garlic ● 2 onions, chopped ● 2 tomatoes, chopped ● 1 carrot, sliced ● 1 stick celery, chopped ● 1 leek ● bouquet garni ● 1 oz/30 g baking (unsweetened) chocolate, grated ● pinch of cinnamon ● parsley ● salt ● pepper ● 1¼ cups/½ pint/2.5 dl water or beef stock.*

For 4 persons

Time: *preparation 5 min.* ● *cooking 25 min.*
Ingredients: *¼ lb/100 g Canadian (back) bacon ● 2 tablespoons/1 oz/30 g lard ● 4 Botifarra (Butifara) sausages of about 4 oz/100–125 g each* ● 3 cups/1 lb/500 g cooked navy (haricot) beans ● 1 clove garlic, chopped (optional) ● chopped parsley (optional).*

● Cut the lard and fat bacon or fat salt pork into small pieces and heat in a cast iron pot or flameproof casserole. ● When they begin to colour add the meat cut into slices. ● Fry for 2 or 3 minutes. ● Add the flour, stir for a minute, then add the wine, garlic, onion, tomatoes, carrot, celery, bouquet garni, grated chocolate, cinnamon, parsley, salt and pepper. ● Add the stock or water, cover tightly and simmer for 3 hours. ● Take the meat out, put into a clean flameproof serving vessel, cover with the strained sauce, bring to a boil and cook gently for another 10 minutes or so. ● Serve piping hot.

● Cut the bacon into very small pieces and fry in the lard till they are crisp, well browned morsels. ● Remove from the pan and set aside, but keep the fat they were fried in. ● Scald the sausages in boiling water, dry, prick, baste with the lard used for the bacon and put them in the oven (they can also be fried or broiled (grilled)). ● When cooked drain on paper towels (kitchen roll) and keep hot. ● Heat up the fat still in the pan, add the already cooked beans and stir well till they begin to colour. ● Add the bacon scraps and, if desired, chopped garlic and parsley. ● Serve very hot with the sausages on top.

*This is a Spanish pork sausage with garlic and spices. If unavailable, use any other spicy pork sausage.

Higgado con cebolla
Liver and onions

Manos de cerdo con judías
Pig's feet (trotters) with beans

For 4 persons

Time: *preparation 25 min.* ● *cooking 45 min.*
Ingredients: *1¾ lb/800 g onions* ● *1 slice cooked ham weighing about 3 oz/80 g* ● *1 lb/500 g baby beef (calf's) liver* ● *½ cup/¼ lb/100 g lard* ● *1 small glass dry white wine* ● *salt* ● *pepper* ● *chopped parsley* ● *allioli (garlic) sauce (see p. 187) (optional).*

For 4 persons

Time: *preparation 20 min. + 12 hours for soaking the beans* ● *cooking a good 2 hours.*
Ingredients: *4 pig's feet (trotters)* ● *1 carrot* ● *1 stick celery* ● *pinch of thyme* ● *2 bay leaves* ● *4 black peppercorns* ● *1 cup/½ lb/200 g navy (haricot) beans* ● *flour* ● *oil for frying* ● *2 onions, chopped* ● *4 ripe tomatoes, peeled and chopped* ● *1 liqueur glass brandy* ● *2 cloves garlic* ● *15 roasted almonds* ● *salt.*

● Peel the onions; slice them very thinly. ● Finely chop the ham and cut the liver into thin, wide slices. ● Heat half the lard in a cooking pan. ● Put in the ham. ● When it begins to fry add the onions and fry them, stirring, over a low heat. ● Then moisten with wine, cover the pot and simmer gently for 30–40 minutes, by which time the liquid content should have reduced by half. ● Meanwhile, lightly season the liver and fry in another pan with the rest of the lard. ● When ham and bacon liquid has cooked long enough, add the liver slices. ● Check the seasoning. ● The gravy should be rather thick. ● Sprinkle with chopped parsley. ● If desired the dish can be served with garlic sauce.

● Cut the pig's feet (trotters) in half lengthways. ● Bring them to the boil in a large pan with the carrot, celery, thyme, bay leaves and peppercorns. ● Fill another pan with cold water and cook the beans. ● When the pig's feet (trotters) are cooked drain them, reserving the liquid, dip them in flour and fry them in oil in a large frying pan. ● Remove and keep warm. ● In the same oil sweat the finely chopped onions. ● Add the sliced tomatoes and allow to cook. ● Place the pig's feet (trotters) in a flameproof serving dish. ● Moisten with brandy and *flambé* them. ● Sieve the tomato sauce. ● Pour it over the pig's feet (trotters) with a ladleful of their own stock. ● Add the cooked beans. ● Chop the garlic and almonds. ● Mix these with a little of the stock and add to the trotters. ● Cook for about 20 minutes and serve.

"Turmes i llatons amb all i julivert"
Veal sweetbreads and testicles sautéed

Fricandó con setas
Veal in mushroom sauce

For 4 persons

Time: *preparation 10 min.* ● *cooking 10 min.*
Ingredients: *1 lb/400 g veal testicles and ½ lb/200 g veal sweetbreads ● salt ● pepper ● olive oil ● 2 cloves garlic, chopped ● 1 sprig parsley, chopped.*

For 4 persons

Time: *preparation 10 min.* ● *cooking 1 hour.*
Ingredients: *1¼ lb/600 g boned veal ● flour ● ½ cup/4fl. oz/1 dl olive oil ● 6 cups/6 oz/150 g dried mushrooms ● 1 onion, chopped ● ½ lb/200 g tomatoes, peeled and sliced ● 1 glass dry white wine ● 1 cup/8 fl. oz/2.5 dl stock or water ● salt ● pepper.*

● Clean the testicles by soaking in cold water for a few hours. ● Wash the sweetbreads well in running water, then boil for about 5 minutes. ● Remove the skin and fat. ● Slice the testicles and sweetbreads. ● Season with salt and pepper. ● Brown them slightly in very hot oil, stirring well. ● Add the chopped garlic and fry over a brisk heat till it begins to colour. ● Add the chopped parsley. ● Remove from frying pan and drain well. ● Place on pre-heated plates and serve very hot as a first course.

● Carve the meat into thin slices. ● Dip in flour and fry lightly in oil. ● Drain and transfer to a flameproof casserole. ● Cover with the mushrooms, which have been soaked in hot water for 10 minutes. ● Using the pan in which the veal was fried, sweat the chopped onion. ● Add the sliced tomatoes and fry gently. ● Stir in 2 tablespoons flour and, still stirring, add the glass of white wine. ● Let it boil to evaporate somewhat for about 5 minutes. ● Add the stock or water. ● Season with salt and pepper, and cook for 10 minutes. ● Pass the resulting sauce through a fine sieve. ● Pour it over the meat. ● Bring to a boil and simmer gently for 30 minutes or until the veal is tender.

Morro y oreja de cerdo con judías
Pig's cheek and ears with beans

Pato con higos
Duck with figs

For 4 persons

Time: *preparation 10 min. ● cooking 3½ hours.*
Ingredients: *1¾ lb/600 g pig's cheek and ears ● 2 cloves garlic ● 2 bay leaves ● ½ cup/¼ lb/100 g navy (haricot) beans ● 1 onion stuck with 2 cloves ● 1 cup/8 fl. oz/2.5 dl olive oil ● 1 onion, chopped ● 1 sweet red pepper, chopped ● 1 ham bone ● 2 ripe tomatoes, peeled and sliced ● ½ glass dry white wine ● stock ● salt.*

For 6–8 persons

Time: *preparation 15 min. ● cooking 1¼ hours.*
Ingredients: *2 ducks weighing about 3 lbs/1.5 kg each, ready for cooking ● lard ● 2 onions, chopped ● 1 head garlic, separated into individual cloves and chopped ● a few bay leaves ● 1 sprig parsley ● 1 sprig thyme ● 1 cup/8 fl. oz/2.5 dl dry sherry ● 7 ripe tomatoes, peeled and chopped ● a little stock or hot water ● butter ● 1 lb/500 g dried or fresh (but not overripe) figs ● pepper ● flour ● salt.*

● Place the pig's cheek and ears in a large saucepan. ● Fill with cold water, bring to a boil and add the garlic and bay leaves. ● In another saucepan bring the beans to the boil, then drain, cover with cold water and bring to a boil. ● Add the onion stuck with cloves. ● Cook gently and season when done. ● When the pig's cheek and ears are tender—after 2 hours or even more—remove from heat and leave to cool before cutting into chunks. ● Drain the beans when cooked and rinse in cold water to cool them more rapidly. ● In an aluminum pan put the oil, chopped onion and chopped pepper. ● Add the ham bone and fry. ● When the onion begins to brown add the sliced tomato, stir well and pour in the wine. ● Let it evaporate for a couple of minutes, then put in the cheek and ears. ● Cover with stock. ● Bring to the boil. ● Skim off the fat. ● Add the beans and cook over a low heat for about 30 minutes. ● Season and serve.

● Clean, truss and season the ducks. ● In a large frying pan brown them in the sizzling lard. ● Add the chopped onion and garlic, the bay leaves, parsley and thyme. ● Sweat for a while, then moisten with sherry. ● Place in a moderate oven (375°F/ mark 5/190°C) and roast the ducks till tender, about 1¼ hours. ● Remove from oven and place ducks on heated carving tray in a warm place. ● Add 2 tablespoons flour to the cooking juices in the pan and stir well. ● Add tomatoes, which have been pressed through a sieve. ● Dilute with a little stock or hot water and cook for a few minutes more. ● Carve the ducks in half, put them in a large serving dish. ● Pour the gravy over and keep hot. ● In a pan with a little butter fry the figs (boiled and dipped in flour if dried, peeled and floured if fresh). ● Cook gently for a few minutes. ● Put the figs round the ducks. ● Serve in the casserole.

Perdiz con coles
Partridge with Savoy cabbage

Conejo con peras y nabos
Rabbit with pears and young turnips

For 6 persons

Time: *preparation 15 min. ● cooking 1½ hours.*
Ingredients: *3 oven-ready partridges ● oil ● lard ● 2 large carrots, sliced ● ¾ lb/300 g pork sausages ● ¾ lb/300 g Canadian (back) bacon ● salt ● pepper ● 3 onions, chopped ● 1 head garlic, separated into individual cloves and chopped ● 1 lb/500 g ripe tomatoes, peeled and sliced ● 1 full glass red wine ● 2 Savoy cabbages ● nutmeg ● flour ● ½ cup/4 fl. oz/1 dl olive oil.*

For 4 persons

Time: *preparation 30 min. ● cooking 1 hour.*
Ingredients: *1 rabbit ● salt ● pepper ● flour ● olive oil ● 1 liqueur glass brandy ● 1 glass dry white wine ● stock ● 1 onion ● 1 carrot ● 2 leeks ● 2 cloves garlic ● 1 bouquet garni ● 1 ripe tomato, peeled and quartered ● 8 small turnips ● 2 pears*

● Put the birds in a roasting pan (oven pan) with a little oil and lard. ● Add the sliced carrots, the sausages and the bacon. ● Season and cook in a moderate oven (350°F/mark 4/175°C). ● When the partridges begin to colour add the chopped onions and the garlic. ● Lastly add the sliced tomatoes. ● Finish roasting the birds, basting with the red wine and one or two tablespoons water to stop the onions burning. ● Remove the partridges and bacon from the roasting pan but keep warm. ● Strain the gravy and put to one side. ● Meanwhile, wash the cabbages, taking care not to tear the leaves. ● Boil in salted water for about 10 minutes and drain. ● Keep the outer leaves whole. ● Chop the rest of the leaves finely, flavour with a pinch of nutmeg and shape into egg-size "faggots." ● Wrap a whole cooked cabbage leaf around each faggot. ● Dip them in flour and fry in oil. ● Place the partridges in a serving dish with the faggots, the sausages, sliced, and the chopped-up bacon. ● Add the cooking juices and cook in the oven for another 10 minutes. ● Serve very hot.

● Cut the rabbit into quarters, season with salt and pepper, coat with flour and brown in oil. ● When well coloured transfer the pieces to a flameproof casserole, moisten with brandy and set alight. ● Pour on the white wine, bring to a boil and boil rapidly for a few minutes to let it evaporate. ● Add 2 ladles of chicken or vegetable stock and simmer until tender, about an hour altogether. ● Meanwhile, peel and chop the onion, carrot, leeks and garlic and bring all to a boil. ● Add the bouquet garni, stirring thoroughly, then the quartered tomato, and continue simmering very gently. ● When the vegetables are cooked pass through a sieve or vegetable mill and pour the resulting sauce over the rabbit. ● Add one more tablespoon stock, and continue to simmer. ● Next cook the turnips. ● First boil until they are nearly done, then dip them in flour and fry in oil. ● Add to the rabbit half an hour before the latter is done. ● Peel the pears but leave them whole. ● Stew, drain and halve them, and add to the rabbit shortly before it is ready to serve. ● Make sure the rabbit is well cooked and check for seasoning before serving.

Pollo a la catalana
Chicken Catalan style

Codornices con pasas y piñones
Quail with raisins and pine kernels

For 4 persons

Time: *preparation 15 min. + 4 hours to soak prunes and raisins ● cooking 1 hour.*
Ingredients: *1 cup/6 oz/150 g stoned dried prunes ● ½ cup/3 oz/75 g white raisins (sultanas) ● 2 2½ lb/1.2 kg chickens ● ½ cup/2 oz/50 g pine kernels ● 1 onion, chopped ● 2 ripe tomatoes ● olive oil ● 1 cup/8 fl. oz/2.5 dl water or stock ● ¼ cup/1 oz/25 g toasted almond flakes ● 2 slices toast ● 1 small glass dry white wine ● salt and pepper.*

For 1 person

Time: *preparation 10 min. + ½ hour to soak raisins ● cooking 20 mins.*
Ingredients: *raisins ● 2 quail ● salt ● pepper ● 1 tablespoon olive oil ● pine kernels ● 1 tablespoon/½ oz/15 g butter ● 1 small glass sherry.*

● Soak the prunes and white raisins (sultanas) for 4 hours. ● Clean the chickens, joint, season and brown well in oil in a large pan. ● Transfer the pieces to a casserole. ● Using the oil still in the first pan, sweat the soaked prunes, white raisins (sultanas) and all but 1 teaspoon of the pine kernels. ● Add to the chicken. ● Still in the same pan, sweat the chopped onion. ● When it begins to turn colour add the tomatoes, complete with skin and seeds, and fry for a few minutes, stirring constantly. ● Add the water or stock and cook over a low heat for about 10 minutes. ● Strain this sauce and pour it over the chicken. ● Continue simmering until chicken is cooked and tender. ● Ten minutes before serving add a ground mixture of almonds, the remaining pine kernels and the toast, which has been soaked in the white wine.

● Soak the raisins in cold water for ½ hour. ● Place the quails in a roasting pan (oven pan). ● Season and baste with olive oil. ● Put in a moderate oven (350°F/mark 4/175°C) and bake for 10–12 minutes or until they are appetizingly brown. ● Meanwhile, fry the soaked and dried raisins and the pine kernels in butter. ● When they are done add to the quails, baste with sherry and set alight. ● Eat at once.

"Perdiu amb rovellons"
Partridge with mushrooms

Coca de San Juan
St John's cake

For 4 persons

Time: *preparation 15 min. ● cooking 2 hours.*
Ingredients: *2 partridges ● 1 onion ● 1 stick celery ● 2 carrots ●
2 tomatoes ● 1 bay leaf ● olive oil ● 1 liqueur glass brandy ● 1 large glass
dry white wine ● ½ lb/200 g mushrooms ● salt ● pepper.*

For 6 persons

Time: *preparation 1 hour ● cooking 25 min.*
Ingredients: *3 cups/¾ lb/350 g all-purpose (plain) flour ●
¾ cup/6 oz/150 g sugar ● 3 eggs ● 1 cup/8 fl. oz/2.5 dl milk ● grated rind
(peel) of 1 lemon ● pinch of ground aniseed ● pinch of cinnamon ● pinch
of salt ● ½ cup/¼ lb/100 g butter, melted ● 4½ teaspoons baking powder ●
½ cup/¼ lb/100 g candied orange peel, chopped ● ¼ cup/2 oz/50 g glacé
cherries ● ½ cup/2 oz/50 g pine kernels*

● Clean, truss and season the partridges. ● Clean and chop the
onion, celery, carrots and tomatoes. ● Put partridges in a
casserole dish and baste with olive oil. ● Put them in the oven
to roast at 400°F/mark 6/200°C. ● When they begin to brown
arrange the chopped vegetables and bay leaf all round them
and return to the oven for another 10 minutes. ● Lower the
heat, pour the brandy over and set alight. ● Add the wine with
enough water to cover the birds. ● Cook in a moderate oven
(350°F/mark 4/175°C) for 1 to 1½ hours longer, turning the
partridges now and again. ● Remove from oven, transfer them
to an ovenproof serving dish and pour the strained sauce over
them. ● Keep warm. ● Wash the mushrooms carefully, dry,
season and fry in sizzling oil for 5 minutes. ● Arrange them
around the birds. ● Leave to flavour for about 3 minutes and
make sure partridges are still piping hot before serving.

● Sift the flour into a large bowl and form a hollow in the
center. ● Into this well put ½ cup/¼ lb/100 g sugar, 2 of the
eggs, the milk, grated lemon rind (peel), aniseed, cinnamon
and salt. ● Slowly mix in the flour, a little at a time. ● Mix the
ingredients very thoroughly until you have a smooth,
homogeneous mixture. ● Mix in the melted butter and baking
powder. ● Flour the pastry board and roll out the dough (it
should be twice as long as it is wide, and ½–1 in./1–2 cm
thick). ● Grease a baking sheet (oven tray) with butter. ● Place
the dough on it and dust with flour. ● Let it rest for 15 minutes
in a warm place. ● Brush with a beaten egg. ● Decorate the top
with the chopped candied orange peel, cherries and pine
kernels. ● Sprinkle with the remaining sugar and bake in a very
hot oven (450°F/mark 8/230°C) for 25 minutes. ● When the
cake is cold serve on a paper lace doily.

"Panellets"
Almond sweet potato cakes

Crema de San José
St Joseph's cream

For 6 persons

Time: *preparation 1 hour ● cooking 20 min.*
Ingredients: *½ lb/200 g sweet potatoes or yams ● 4 cups/1 lb/400 g almonds, chopped ● 2 cups/1 lb/400 g sugar ● 2 eggs, separated ● a few drops vanilla essence ● lemon rind (peel) ● ½ cup/2 oz/50 g all-purpose (plain) flour ● 2 oz/50 g baking (unsweetened) chocolate, grated ● ½ wine glass blackcurrant syrup ● ½ cup/2 oz/50 g black cherries, stoned ● 1 cup/¼ lb/100 g pine kernels ● 1 cup/¼ lb/100 g hazelnuts, chopped.*

For 4 persons

Time: *preparation 10 min. ● cooking 10 min.*
Ingredients: *6 egg yolks ● ¾ cup/6 oz/150 g sugar ● ¼ cup/1 oz/25 g cornstarch (cornflour) ● 4½ cups/1¾ pints/1 liter milk ● grated rind (peel) of 1 lemon ● pinch of cinnamon ● confectioners' (icing) sugar.*

● Peel and chop potatoes, bring to a boil and cook until done. ● Drain and sieve. ● Put potatoes, chopped almonds, sugar, egg yolks, vanilla essence and a little grated lemon peel in a large bowl and mix well. ● Knead the mixture on a pastry board dusted with flour, finally rolling it into a cylinder and cutting it in 3 equal parts. ● Mix one third with the chocolate, another with the blackcurrant syrup and leave the third part as it is. ● From each portion of dough form little balls the size of a walnut and shape them like tiny bread rolls. ● Decorate each blackcurrant cake with a black cherry. ● Brush the other two kinds with beaten egg white and garnish the tops with pine kernels and chopped hazelnuts. ● Butter a baking sheet (oven tray), lay the little cakes on it and bake in a very hot oven (425°F/mark 7/220°C) for 20 minutes.

● Beat the egg yolks and sugar together in a heavy-based saucepan. ● Blend the cornstarch (cornflour) smoothly with a little milk. ● Bring the rest of the milk to a boil together with the lemon rind (peel) and cinnamon. ● Strain the milk on to the egg yolk and sugar mixture, stirring all the while. ● Then, still stirring, add the blended cornstarch (cornflour). ● Put the saucepan on the stove and, still stirring, bring the contents to the boil. ● Remove from heat and pour the custard into a dish for the table. ● Let it get quite cold, then sprinkle with confectioners' (icing) sugar. ● Caramelize the sugar quickly under the broiler (grill) or with a salamander or red-hot poker, so that it forms a golden crust.

Sorbete de hierbabuena
Mint sorbet

Helado de crema catalana
Catalan custard ice cream

For 5–6 persons

Time: *preparation 5 min. + 10–12 hours for the syrup ● cooking 10 min.*
Ingredients: *4½ cups/1¾ pints/1 liter water ● 2 cups/1 lb/400 g sugar ● large bunch of mint ● 1 small wine glass lemon juice.*

For 6 persons

Time: *preparation 10 min. ● cooking 10 min.*
Ingredients: *4½ cups/1¾ pints/1 liter milk ● 1 stick cinnamon ● grated rind (peel) of 1 lemon ● 8 egg yolks ● 8 tablespoons sugar ● light brown (demerara) sugar.*

● Prepare the syrup in advance. ● Mix together water and sugar and bring to a boil. ● Add the mint leaves (keeping a few of the tender tips aside) and simmer for about 10 minutes. ● Remove from heat and cover pan. ● Leave the syrup alone for 10–12 hours, then strain and add a small wineglass of lemon juice. ● Put syrup in the freezer. ● Stir freezing mixture several times, and when it has reached the desired consistency garnish with the finely chopped mint tips.

● Boil the milk with the cinnamon and lemon rind (peel). ● Separately, beat the egg yolks and sugar together until smooth and warm the mixture over a low heat, adding the milk little by little, stirring constantly, and never letting it boil. ● Continue to stir over low heat until mixture is thick enough to coat the back of a wooden spoon. ● Allow to cool, then put in refrigerator. ● When it is very cold, bring out, sprinkle with light brown or demerara sugar, and, with a salamander, caramelize the top (or put the dish directly under the broiler (grill) or in a very hot oven to caramelize the surface). ● Put back in the refrigerator. ● Serve very cold in dessert (sundae) glasses.

Buñuelos del Pirineo
Pyrenean profiteroles

"Mel i mató"
Cottage cheese with honey

For 6 persons

Time: *preparation 30 min. ● cooking 30 min.*
Ingredients: *1 cup/8 fl. oz/2.5 dl water ● ¼ cup/2 oz/50 g butter ● salt ● 1 small stick cinnamon ● 1 vanilla pod ● grated rind (peel) of 1 lemon ● 2 teaspoons sugar ● 1 cup/4 oz/125 g all-purpose (plain) flour ● 5 eggs ● oil. For the filling: egg custard (of any flavour desired), or whipped cream. For coating the puffs: 1 cup/½ lb/200 g semi-sweet (plain) chocolate ● ¼ cup/2 oz/50 g butter. For decoration: a handful of chopped almonds.*

For 4 persons

Time: *preparation 6–8 hours for steeping ● cooking 10 min.*
Ingredients: *a handful of cardoon or globe artichoke florets ● 4½ cups/1¾ pints/1 liter whole (full-cream) milk ● 4 tablespoons honey.*

● Heat the water, butter, salt, flavourings and sugar in a saucepan. ● As soon as the water starts to boil remove pan from heat. ● Sift the flour and, stirring briskly, add it to the pan all at once. ● Return to the heat and continue to cook, stirring continously, till you have a smooth, homogeneous paste that detaches itself from the sides of the pan. ● Let it cool for a short while, then stir in 4 of the eggs, one at a time. ● Let the mixture rest for 15 minutes. ● Form the dough into little balls the size of a walnut and fry in moderately hot oil. ● Arrange the little balls on a greased and floured baking sheet (oven tray). ● Brush with beaten egg and bake at a very moderate heat (325°F/mark 3/165°C) for 25–30 minutes. ● When the pastry puffs are done let them get cold. ● Then half-open them and fill with custard or whipped cream. ● For the topping, break the chocolate into pieces then melt in a double boiler (double saucepan). ● When melted remove from heat and stir in the butter. ● Pour the hot topping over the profiteroles just before serving. ● Garnish with chopped almonds.

● Steep the cardoon (or globe artichoke) florets in water just to cover for 6–8 hours. ● Bring the milk to a boil and simmer for 10 minutes. ● Let cool, then add the water (strained) in which the florets have steeped. ● Pour into a large square of cheesecloth or muslin, tie the four corners together and hang it up so that the whey drips through. ● Divide the curds that remain into 4 dessert dishes. ● Pour a tablespoon of honey over each.
Note: this recipe can also be followed using fresh ricotta or cottage cheese bought from a store.

ARAGON · NAVARR
LA RIOJA

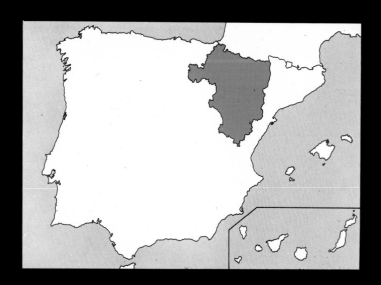

Three hearty types of cookery, individual yet influenced by a
common history, that form part of the great traditions of
Spanish food.

Aragon. The simplicity and excellence of this region's
cookery are exemplified in their roast lamb, fried lamb's feet,
dried cod with eggs and garlic, stewed peppers. . . .
Delicious legumes and green vegetables are a great feature,
to say nothing of the savoury sausages.

Navarre. One of the best known of the regional delicacies
is trout with ham, but other dishes deserve equal praise,
among them "Cordero al chilindrón" (lamb stew),
"Chuletas de ternera" (veal cutlets) and the elaborate
vegetable side-dishes, especially their exquisite asparagus.

La Rioja. Potatoes, tripe and veal cutlets can all be
prepared "in the manner of La Rioja," but best of all,
perhaps, are the dishes based on green vegetables.

Sopas de pastor
Shepherd's soup

Migas de pastor con uva, huevo y longaniza
Eggs, grapes and sausages country style

For 4 persons

Time: *preparation 5 min.* ● *cooking 20 min.*
Ingredients: *½ lb/250 g bread* ● *6 cloves garlic, crushed* ●
1 cup/8 fl. oz/2.5 dl oil ● *4½ cups/1¾ pints/1 liter water* ● *4 eggs* ● *salt.*

For 4 persons

Time: *preparation 20 min. + 24 hours for softening the bread* ● *cooking 30 min.*
Ingredients: *1 medium-sized stale loaf of bread* ● *1 teaspoon salt* ●
olive oil ● *2 cloves garlic, crushed* ● *1 lb/500 g white grapes* ● *¾ lb/300 g spicy pork sausages* ● *4 eggs.*

● Cut the bread into small cubes. ● Fry the garlic in oil. ● Just as it begins to colour put in the bread. ● Bring the slightly salted water to the boil. ● When the bread has browned drop it and the garlic into the boiling water with the oil they have been fried in. ● Let it cook for about 2 minutes. ● Beat the eggs; pour the broth over them. ● Simmer till the eggs are quite set. ● Season and serve.

● The day before the meal cut the bread into very small cubes. ● Put these in a tea towel, dip it in cold water and shake well so that the cubes are evenly wet. ● Drain, and sprinkle them with a teaspoon of salt and leave till the following day. ● Half an hour before serving, heat the oil in a pan and fry the garlic till it is a really dark brown. ● Tip all the croûtons into the pan and fry gently for 12–15 minutes. ● Meanwhile, gently heat the grapes in warm water, then fry the sausages and eggs. ● Distribute croûtons on to four plates, cover with grapes and arrange one fried egg and sausage on each. ● Serve piping hot.

Menestra de verduras
Vegetable soup

Pimientos al chilindrón
Stewed peppers

For 6 persons

Time: *preparation 1 hour ● cooking 45 min.*
Ingredients: *2 lb/1 kg peas ● 2 lb/1 kg lima or broad beans ● 2 lb/1 kg globe artichokes ● 1 lb/500 g carrots ● 1 bunch asparagus ● juice of 1 lemon ● salt ● ½ lb/250 g any raw ham ● ½ cup/4 fl. oz/1 dl olive oil ● 1 onion, chopped ● 6 hard-boiled eggs.*

For 4 persons

Time: *preparation 20 min. ● cooking 1 hour.*
Ingredients: *6 cloves garlic ● 1 large onion ● 1 cup/8 fl. oz/2 dl olive oil ● ¾ lb/300 g any raw ham ● 6 large green, red and yellow peppers ● 1 carrot, finely chopped ● 2 lb/1 kg peeled, seeded tomatoes ● salt ● paprika ● 1 teaspoon sugar.*

● Shell the peas and beans. ● Remove leaves from artichokes, leaving only the hearts. ● Scrape and wash the carrots, cut them in rounds. ● Prepare the asparagus. ● Cook beans, peas and carrots only until they are still slightly underdone. ● Put the artichoke hearts in boiling water with the juice of a lemon and a little salt, and simmer until they are still just crisp. ● Cook the asparagus in the same way. ● Put the water to one side. ● Finely chop the ham and fry gently in olive oil in a large skillet (frying pan with lid). ● After frying gently for a few minutes add the chopped onion. ● Cover the pan and continue cooking over a low heat till the onion is tender but not brown. ● Add the vegetables, and some of the water the artichokes and asparagus were cooked in. ● Stew them for 5 minutes. ● Garnish the soup with hard-boiled eggs and serve.

● Cut the garlic cloves in half, chop the onion and sweat in oil in a frying pan. ● When soft but not coloured add the ham cut in strips. ● Peel* and cut up the peppers, take out the seeds and put the rest in the pan, stirring well. ● Cook for 5 minutes. ● Add the chopped carrot and the tomatoes. ● Season with salt and paprika. ● Add the sugar and simmer till you have quite a thick, stew-like mixture. ● Serve in an earthenware dish.

* See footnote page 9.

Patatas a la riojana
Potatoes La Rioja style

Revuelto de hongos
Mushrooms with scrambled eggs

For 4 persons

Time: *preparation 15 min. ● cooking 30 min.*
Ingredients: *olive oil ● $\frac{1}{2}$ lb/250 g Chorizo sausage* ● 1 onion, chopped ● 2 cloves garlic, crushed ● 2 lb/1 kg potatoes ● salt ● pepper ● 1 bay leaf ● pinch of paprika ● 1 glass dry white wine ● stock.*

For 4 persons

Time: *preparation 12 min. ● cooking 25 min.*
Ingredients: *1$\frac{3}{4}$ lb/800 g mushrooms, sliced ● 2 tablespoons olive oil ● 1 clove garlic ● sprig of parsley, chopped ● 8 eggs, beaten ● salt.* As an accompaniment: *triangular pieces of fried bread.*

● Heat oil in a frying pan. ● Add the sausage cut into 4 pieces. ● Brown, then add the chopped onion and garlic. ● Fry gently. ● Add the potato cut in chunks. ● Season and add bay leaf and paprika. ● Stir; pour in the wine. ● Cover and cook slowly for about 20 minutes, or until potatoes are cooked. ● If necessary during cooking, add a few spoonfuls of stock or water.

*See footnote page 8.

● Fry the sliced mushrooms in hot oil over a low heat. ● When soft add the garlic clove and chopped parsley. ● Leave them to flavour for a short time before removing garlic clove and covering the mushrooms and onions with beaten egg. ● Add a little salt. ● Cook, stirring constantly, till the egg is just set, and serve at once, accompanied by triangular pieces of fried bread.

Huevos carlistas
Eggs Carlist style

Huevos al salmorejo
Meat and egg terrine

For 8 persons

Time: *preparation 15 min. ● cooking 40 min.*
Ingredients: *4½ cups/1¾ pints/1 liter milk ● 12 eggs ● olive oil ● 1 cup/¼ lb/100 g all-purpose (plain) flour ● ¼ cup/2 oz/50 g butter ● salt ● pepper ● pinch of nutmeg ● juice of 1 lemon ● 2 cups/½ lb/200 g dry white breadcrumbs ● sprigs of fried parsley.*

For 4 persons

Time: *preparation 5 min. ● cooking 25 min.*
Ingredients: *3 tablespoons olive oil ● ½ lb/200 g pork loin, chopped ● ½ lb/200 g pork sausages ● 4 oz/120 g any raw ham ● 2 cloves garlic, chopped ● 2 teaspoons flour ● 1 teaspoon paprika ● 1 cup/8fl. oz/2.5 dl asparagus liquid ● 1 cup/8 fl. oz/2.5 dl beef stock ● 8 spears canned asparagus ● 8 eggs ● salt.*

● Bring the milk to a boil and allow to cool. ● Fry 8 eggs in oil (or oil and butter). ● Let them cool slightly. ● Prepare a white sauce by stirring the flour into the butter with a wooden spoon over a low heat. ● Little by little add the cooled milk, stirring constantly. ● Season with salt, pepper and a pinch of nutmeg. ● Simmer for 5 minutes, still stirring, then remove from the heat and mix in 2 beaten egg yolks diluted with the lemon juice. ● (Sauce will still be very thick.) ● Grease a large flat dish, spread it with a tablespoon of the white sauce, put a fried egg on the sauce and cover it with some more of the white sauce. ● Proceed to do the same with the rest of the fried eggs and the remaining sauce, and leave them to get cold. ● Coat with breadcrumbs, dip them in the 2 remaining eggs, beaten, then once more in the crumbs. ● Fry these "rissoles" in plenty of hot oil till deep golden brown. ● Arrange on a paper napkin on a serving dish and garnish with sprigs of fried parsley.

● In 2 tablespoons olive oil fry the pork sausages, the beef sausages and the ham cut in strips. ● Distribute these into individual ovenproof bowls. ● In the same pan, gently fry the garlic, then stir in the flour and finally the paprika. ● Add the asparagus liquid and stock, stirring constantly. ● Bring to a boil and simmer for 3 minutes. ● Pour this into the individual bowls, then break 2 eggs on top of each, garnishing with 2 chopped asparagus spears. ● Sprinkle with salt. ● Put the bowls in a hot oven (425°F/mark 7/220°C) until the eggs have set. ● Serve immediately.

Truchas a la navarra
Trout à la Navarraise

Ajoarriero con bogavante
Dried salt cod casserole with lobster

For 4 persons

Time: *preparation 15 min. + 1 hour for the trout • cooking 20 min.*
Ingredients: *4 trout weighing ½ lb/250 g each • 3 lemons • ¼ lb/100 g small mushrooms • ¼ lb/100 g any raw ham • 1 clove garlic • parsley • flour • olive oil • 2 tablespoons/1 oz/30 g butter • salt.*

For 6 persons

Time: *preparation 25 min. + 24 hours for soaking the cod • cooking 45 min.*
Ingredients: *2 lb/1 kg dried salt cod • 1 live lobster weighing 3 lb/1.5 kg • clear strong stock (consommé) • salt • 1 lb/500 g onions • 4 sweet red peppers • 2 tablespoons paprika • 1 cup/8 fl. oz/2 dl olive oil • chopped parsley.*

• Clean the trout, sprinkle with the juice of 1 lemon and leave for an hour. • Clean the mushrooms and wet with the juice of the second lemon. • Finely chop the ham. • Chop garlic and parsley together. • Drain the trout and coat with flour. • Fry in a little hot oil. • When well browned take out the fish, drain, put on a plate and keep hot. • Add the butter to the same oil. • When melted add the mushrooms, garlic and chopped parsley. • Cook over a mild heat for 5 minutes. • Now add the ham, fry for 1–2 minutes more and turn it all on to the trout. • Sprinkle with salt, garnish with lemon slices and serve at once.

• Soak the dried salt cod for 24 hours, changing the water frequently. • Drain, put the fish in a large pot, cover with cold water and bring to the boil. • Just before the water comes to the boil take the cod out. • Cut it up and remove the bones. • Put the lobster in the cold salted stock, cover and bring slowly to a boil. • Simmer for about 10 minutes. • Take lobster out, drain and cool. • Chop the onions and peppers, mix thoroughly and season with paprika and a pinch of salt. • Smear the bottom of a large deep pan with olive oil. • Arrange a layer of chopped onion and peppers on the bottom and then a layer of salt cod. • Continue with this alternation of layers until all the ingredients are used up. • Detach the lobster's head, extract the flesh from the claws and mix it with the top layer. • Cut the tail into round slices. • Arrange them on the surface. • Moisten with plenty of olive oil. • Put on the lid, bring to a boil and simmer for 30 minutes. • Serve immediately. • Garnish with chopped parsley if desired.

Bacalao al ajoarriero
Dried salt cod with eggs and garlic

Cordero al chilindrón
Lamb stew

For 4 persons

Time: *preparation 10 min. + 24 hours to soak the cod ● cooking 35 min.*
Ingredients: *8 pieces dried salt cod ● 5 tablespoons olive oil ● 6 cloves garlic, chopped ● 1 tablespoon paprika ● 1 tablespoon wine vinegar ● 2 eggs ● parsley sprigs.*

For 4 persons

Time: *preparation 15 min. ● cooking 40–50 min.*
Ingredients: *2 lb/1 kg lean lamb ● 1 clove garlic, chopped ● 1 cup/8 fl. oz/2 dl olive oil ● 1 onion, finely chopped ● ¾ lb/300 g Canadian bacon (back) ● 6 red peppers, seeded and chopped ● 6 large tomatoes, peeled ● salt.*

● Soak the cod in water for 24 hours, changing the water several times. ● Rinse well. ● Place in a saucepan of water and begin to heat. ● Before the water begins to boil, remove from heat, drain the fish, remove the backbone and flake. ● Heat the oil in a frying pan and brown the garlic in it. ● Add the flaked cod, stir a few times, cover and simmer over a low heat for about 20 minutes. ● During the final 10 minutes of cooking add the paprika dissolved in vinegar. ● Beat the eggs, pour them over the cod and cook for 1 minute. ● Remove from the heat and mix well. ● Serve in the same pan and garnish with parsley sprigs.

● Clean the lamb and cut into equal-sized pieces. ● Sweat the garlic in oil, removing it as soon as it begins to colour. ● In the same pan fry the meat and finely chopped onion over a gentle heat till both are browned. ● Add the Canadian bacon (back) cut in strips, the chopped peppers and the tomatoes, peeled and sliced. ● Season. ● Cover and cook gently till the lamb is tender. ● Adjust seasoning.

Chuletas de ternera a la navarra
Veal cutlets à la Navarraise

Manitas de ternasco
Stewed lambs' feet

For 4 persons

Time: *preparation 15 min.* ● *cooking 1 hour.*
Ingredients: *¼ lb/100 g onions ● 3 large ripe tomatoes ● 2 cloves garlic ● 4 cutlets of veal weighing about 6 oz/150 g each ● ½ cup/2 oz/60 g flour ● ¼ cup/2 oz/60 g lard ● 1 cup/8 fl. oz/2 dl olive oil ● 1 glass dry white wine ● salt ● pepper ● 2 large sweet red peppers ● 2 eggplants (aubergines) ● chopped parsley.*

For 4 persons

Time: *preparation 15 min.* ● *cooking 2 hours.*
Ingredients: *24 sucking lambs feet* ● salt ● 1 hot chili pepper ● 4 tablespoons olive oil ● 4 tomatoes, peeled and chopped ● 1 onion, chopped ● 3 cloves garlic, finely chopped.*

● Chop the onions. ● Peel the tomatoes, squeeze the seeds out and chop coarsely. ● Crush the garlic. ● Season the cutlets, but do not beat them; coat with flour. ● Put the lard and half the oil in a big pan and when sizzling hot fry the veal. ● When tender, remove from the pan and keep hot. ● In the same pan fry the onions, tomatoes and garlic, adding the wine a little at a time. ● Sprinkle with salt and pepper and simmer for 15 minutes. ● Meanwhile, prepare the peppers: remove the stem end and extract the seeds. ● Brush with oil and bake in the oven at 350°F/mark 4/175°C for 25 minutes. ● When cool, peel them, cut in half and put them in a warm place. ● Peel the eggplants (aubergines), slice, coat with flour and fry in oil. ● Place on a hot dish. ● Place the cutlets on top and cover with the halved peppers. ● Press the fried onions, tomatoes and garlic through a sieve, making sure to extract as much juice as possible. ● Heat up and pour over the meat. ● Heat in a hot oven or on the hob for a minute or two, then sprinkle with chopped parsley and serve.

● Clean the lambs' feet and cut in three. ● Boil in salted water for 1½ hours. ● When cooked, drain and set aside. ● Put the chili pepper in a pan with the oil and gently fry the tomatoes, chopped onion and chopped garlic. ● When browned add the lambs' feet and simmer for about 10 minutes. ● Remove chili pepper and serve.

* If unavailable, use 16 small pigs' feet (trotters).

Fritada de conejo y caracoles
Fried rabbit with snails

Paletillas de ternasco
Roast lamb

For 4 persons

Time: *preparation 30 min.* ● *cooking 1 hour.*
Ingredients: *1 rabbit weighing about 2 lb/1 kg* ● *olive oil* ● *½ lb/250 g onions, chopped* ● *½ lb/250 g green peppers, seeded and chopped* ● *1 pint/½ lb/250 g snails (already cooked)* ● *2 lb/1 kg tomatoes, peeled and chopped* ● *salt.* Garnish: *1 green pepper cut into rings.*

For 4 persons

Time: *preparation 15 min.* ● *cooking 1–1¼ hours.*
Ingredients: *4 lb/2 kg shoulder of lamb* ● *1 clove garlic* ● *salt* ● *1 cup/¼ lb/200 g lard, melted* ● *paprika.* As an accompaniment: *1 lb/500 g roast or sautéed potatoes.*

● Clean and joint the rabbit. ● Fry in a little olive oil. ● When cooked remove and keep hot. ● In the same oil fry the chopped onion and peppers. ● As soon as they begin to colour add the snails (cooked beforehand) and the chopped tomatoes. ● Stir well and pour all over the rabbit. ● Leave to flavour for 5 minutes. ● Season. ● Serve on a plate garnished with green pepper rings.

● Rub the shoulder of lamb with garlic and sprinkle with salt. ● Cut the garlic into slivers and insert into the fat layer. ● Place the joint on a rack above a roasting pan (oven pan) and put in a very hot oven (450°F/mark 8/230°C). ● When the meat is "sealed" baste it with melted lard, lower the oven temperature to 375°F/mark 6/190°C and bake it for 1–1¼ hours. ● Sprinkle with paprika and serve with roast or sautéed potatoes.

Magras con tomate
Ham with tomato sauce

Callos a la riojana
Tripe La Rioja style

For 4 persons

Time: *preparation 10 min. ● cooking 40 min.*
Ingredients: *8 slices any raw ham ●*
½ cup/¼ lb/100 g lard ● 8 pieces thinly sliced bread ● 1 teaspoon sugar ●
2 tablespoons wine vinegar ● ½ glass dry white wine ● 1¾ lb/800 g ripe
tomatoes ● salt.

For 4–6 persons

Time: *preparation 1 hour ● cooking 4–5 hours for the tripe + 1¼ hours for*
the sauce.
Ingredients: *4 lb/2 kg tripe ● vinegar ● salt ● 2 medium or 3 small onions,*
peeled ● 2 medium carrots, coarsley chopped ● 1 stick celery, chopped ●
1 small head garlic ● bouquet garni. For the sauce: ½ cup/4 fl. oz/1 dl
olive oil ● ¼ cup/2 oz/50 g lard ● 2 cloves garlic, finely chopped ●
¼ lb/100 g any raw ham, chopped ● 1 onion, finely chopped ● 1 bay leaf ●
½ lb/200 g Chorizo sausage ● 1 tablespoon paprika ● 1 teaspoon ground*
chili pepper ● 2 tablespoons flour ● 16 English walnuts ● chopped parsley.

● Fry the ham slices in half the lard. ● Add the bread slices and fry them too. ● When all are done take out the ham and bread and put them on two separate plates. ● Keep warm. ● Add ½ teaspoon sugar to the cooking fat, taking care not to burn it. ● Pour on the vinegar and wine at once. ● Stir well and reduce a little before pouring the mixture over the ham. ● Arrange on a dish, alternating ham slices with fried bread slices till they are used up. ● Moisten with the remainder of the ham sauce. ● Add the tomatoes prepared as follows: peel, remove seeds, chop finely and fry gently in the remaining lard with the addition of a pinch of salt and the rest of the sugar.

● Wash the tripe in abundant water, cut up and put into a large crock or pot. ● Cover with a solution of three parts water to one part vinegar and a handful of salt. ● Leave overnight. ● Next day clean again with salt and vinegar and rinse till the water is clear. ● Put the tripe in a saucepan and cover with cold water. ● Add the onions, carrot, celery, peeled garlic cloves and bouquet garni. ● Cover and cook for 4–5 hours. ● Remove tripe and keep warm. ● Reserve the cooking liquid. ● (Of course, if the tripe is ready cooked, the above operations are unnecessary.) ● Heat oil and lard in a saucepan. ● Add the chopped garlic and finely chopped ham. ● Fry for a short time before adding the finely chopped onion, the bay leaf and the sausage cut into 4 pieces. ● Cover and fry gently. ● When the onion is soft add the paprika, chili pepper and flour, stirring well. ● Pour in 2 cups/1 pint/5 dl of the tripe stock and add the strained tripe. ● Bring to the boil, check seasoning, then add the chopped walnuts and parsley. ● Simmer for 1 hour more and serve. ● (If the tripe is prepared the previous day and heated up at the last moment, the flavour is much improved.)

*See footnote page 8.

Solomillo de buey al vino de Rioja
Fillet of beef with Rioja wine

Chuletas de ternera a la riojana
Veal cutlets and peppers

For 6 persons

Time: *preparation 12 min. + 2–3 hours for marinating the meat ● cooking 40 min.*
Ingredients: *6 fillet steaks weighing about $\frac{1}{4}$ lb/200 g each ● $\frac{1}{2}$ bottle Rioja wine (or other vintage red wine) ● $\frac{1}{2}$ teaspoon mixed herbs ● oil ● butter ● 1 small glass brandy ● 1 cup/8 fl. oz/2.5 dl beef stock (prepared from the scraps if possible) ● 12 shallots ● 12 button mushrooms ● pepper ● salt ● flour ● 6 slices bread ● 1 clove garlic, split ● chopped parsley.*

For 4 persons

Time: *preparation 10 min. ● cooking 15 min.*
Ingredients: *4 veal cutlets ● olive oil ● salt ● pepper ● 4 sweet red peppers ● chopped parsley.*

● Marinate the steaks for a few hours in the wine and herbs. ● Drain very well and season. ● Heat oil and butter in a heavy frying pan and cook steaks until rare or medium-rare and browned on both sides. ● Remove from pan and keep hot. ● Skim the fat off the cooking juices. ● Pour in the brandy and set alight. ● Strain the wine used for the marinade and add to the pan. ● Bring to a boil and cook over high heat to reduce the volume of liquid by more than half. ● Add the beef stock, shallots, mushrooms (the last two sautéed in a little butter beforehand), pepper and salt. ● Cook for 15 minutes, or till the onions are tender. ● Add a roux made from equal amounts of flour and butter creamed together, to thicken the sauce; take care not to let it boil. ● Meanwhile, fry the bread in a mixture of olive oil and butter, then rub with garlic. ● Arrange the bread on individual plates. ● Place on each slice one of the steaks, which have been kept hot. ● Cover with the sauce and sprinkle with chopped parsley.

● Trim the fat from the cutlets and brush with olive oil. ● Heat the broiler (grill) until very hot. ● Then put in the cutlets, lower the broiling pan (turn down the heat) and broil (grill) for 8 minutes on one side and 5 on the other. ● Press the cutlets against the broiling rack (grill rack) with a spatula just enough to give the characteristic lines on the surface. ● Season. ● Arrange the cutlets on the serving plates garnished with de-seeded baked peppers, halved or whole, and chopped parsley. ● (To bake peppers: remove stem, scrape out seeds, and bake at 350°F/mark 4/175°C) for 30 minutes, in a pan to which an inch or so of hot water has been added.)

Perdices a la tudelana
Partridges à la Tudelane

Perdiz con chocolate
Partridge with chocolate

For 4 persons

Time: *preparation 15 min. ● cooking 50 min.*
Ingredients: *lard ● 2 patridges ready for cooking. ● ¼ cup/2 oz/50 g any raw ham ● 2 apples, peeled and chopped ● 1 cup/8 fl. oz/2.5 dl light (single) cream ● salt.* ● As an accompaniment: *sautéed potatoes ● sautéed mushrooms ● croûtons.*

For 4 persons

Time: *preparation 15 min. ● cooking 45 min.*
Ingredients: *4 medium-sized partridges ● salt ● ¾ cup/6 fl. oz/1.5 dl olive oil ● 3 cloves garlic, chopped ● 1 bay leaf ● 6 tablespoons wine vinegar ● 1 cup/8 fl. oz/2.5 dl red or white wine ● 1 cup/8 fl. oz/2.5 dl chicken stock ● 6 peppercorns ● 2 cloves ● ½ lb/200 g white grapes ● 1 oz/30 g baking (unsweetened) chocolate ● 4 slices fried bread (optional).*

● Put lard in a frying pan, heat and brown the partridges very lightly. ● Add the ham cut in strips and the apple segments. ● Simmer until the apples are soft. ● Pour in the cream, stir, remove from heat and leave for several minutes in the covered pan to allow flavours to develop. ● Serve with sautéed potatoes and mushrooms sautéed in butter. ● A few fried croûtons can be added if desired.

● Clean and truss the partridges. ● Season inside and out. ● Heat about two-thirds of the oil in a frying pan and brown the birds evenly over a gentle heat. ● When brown remove from pan and keep warm. ● In the same cooking fat fry the garlic. ● Add bay leaf, vinegar, wine, stock, peppercorns and cloves. ● Cover and cook for 5 minutes. ● Put the partridges back and complete the cooking, which should take about 45 minutes. ● Meanwhile, peel the grapes. ● Remove the birds, untie them and place in another pan. ● Strain the sauce and pour it over the birds. ● Add the melted chocolate, which has first been diluted with a little of this sauce. ● Bring to the boil and simmer for 15 minutes. ● Five minutes before the end add the grapes. ● Serve immediately. ● If you wish, you could put a piece of fried bread on each plate, arrange one partridge on top, garnish with grapes and cover with sauce.

Melocotón con vino
Peaches with wine

Frutas de Aragón
Aragonese chocolate fruit

For 5 persons

Time: *preparation 10 min. ● cooking 30–40 min.*
Ingredients: *5 large fresh peaches ● red wine ● water ● 1 stick cinnamon ● 5 tablespoons sugar.*

For 4 persons

Time: *preparation 20 min. ● cooking 10 min.*
Ingredients: *2 cups/1 lb/500 g candied fruit ● 6 oz/180 g semi-sweet (plain) chocolate ● ⅔ cup/3 oz/80 g sweet (unsalted) butter.*

● Pour boiling water over peaches and leave for 30 seconds–1 minute. ● Plunge into cold water and then you will be able to peel them easily. ● Place in a saucepan that just holds the peaches. ● Pour on two parts wine to one of water till the fruit is covered. ● Add the cinnamon. ● Bring to a boil and simmer till the peaches are tender, 20–30 minutes. ● Add the sugar and simmer for another 10–12 minutes. ● Serve hot or cold.

● Cut the candied fruit into regular shapes. ● Melt the chocolate in a double boiler (double saucepan). ● When quite melted remove from the heat and add the butter, beating until you have a smooth mixture. ● Cool a little. ● When it begins to thicken, impale the pieces of fruit on cocktail sticks and dip each one into the chocolate mixture, turning it round several times to be sure it is completely coated. ● Spear the cocktail sticks into an orange or melon, or in the holes of an upside-down colander, so that the chocolate coating stays even. ● Put in the refrigerator or some cool place till the chocolate has quite solidified. ● Pull out the sticks and arrange the sweets in a little dish.

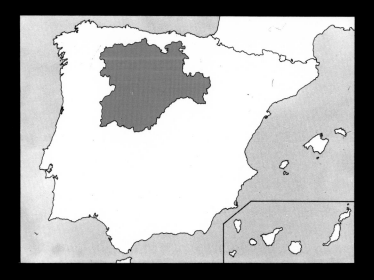

The land of roast meat par excellence—though indeed its gastronomical variety does not stop there.

Old Castile. Best of all are the young lambs and the *tostón* or *lechón*, sucking pigs less than three weeks old, cooked superlatively in the oven or on a spit. Other notable dishes are "Stewed lambs' tongues," "Partridges à la Segovia" and "Pig's ear salad." The freshwater fish deserve a chapter to themselves, among them the trout of the Tiétar and Tormes, as well as the tench and *pececillos*, typical fishlets of the Adaja River. The region's pride and joy are its many types of savoury sausage, especially the famous Chorizos. And not to be forgotten are the exquisite "Cangrejos de rio," freshwater crayfish fried in a pan, a specialty of the area.

León. This is another region rich in gastronomical delights, which bases a number of its dishes on its excellent sausages—best of all the Chorizo and Butillo, made of pork mixed with paprika and bone marrow.

Patatas con setas
Potatoes stewed with mushrooms

Ensalada de orejas
Pig's ear salad

For 4 persons

Time: *preparation 12 min.* ● *cooking 30 min.*
Ingredients: *1 bay leaf* ● *1 onion, chopped* ● *2 cloves garlic, chopped* ● *olive oil* ● *1 lb/500 g potatoes, peeled and chopped* ● *½ lb/250 g mushrooms, sliced* ● *1 liqueur glass brandy* ● *2 cups/7 fl. oz/5 dl stock.*

For 6 persons

Time: *preparation 30 min.* ● *cooking 2 hours, or 30 min. in a pressure cooker.*
Ingredients: *2 pig's ears* ● *1 curly chicory (curly endive)* ● *½ lb/250 g endive (chicory)* ● *pomegranate seeds or a few redcurrants* ● *1 clove garlic, crushed* ● *salt* ● *olive oil* ● *wine vinegar.*

● Lightly brown bay leaf, chopped onion and garlic in oil. ● Add the peeled, chopped potatoes. ● Brown them, too, before adding the cleaned, sliced mushrooms. ● Heat the brandy in a ladle, set it alight and pour over the potatoes. ● Add the stock. ● Cook gently for about 20 minutes.

● Clean and cook the pig's ears. ● This will take about 2 hours, or 30 minutes in a pressure cooker. ● Cool and cut in pieces. ● Wash the chicory and endive. ● Drain well and place on a flat serving dish. ● Arrange the pig's ears on top with the pomegranate seeds or redcurrants. ● Prepare a dressing consisting of the crushed garlic, salt, oil and vinegar: mix all well together, pour over the salad and serve.

Cangrejos de rio
Fried freshwater crayfish

Alubias pintas del Burgo
Stewed beans with sausage

For 4 persons

Time: *preparation 10 min.* ● *cooking 25 min.*
Ingredients: *2 lb/1 kg freshwater crayfish ● 4 cloves garlic, crushed ●*
½ cup/4 fl. oz/1 dl olive oil ● 1 chili pepper (if desired) ● 1 lb/500 g
tomatoes, peeled and chopped ● 1 liqueur glass brandy ● salt.

For 6 persons

Time: *cooking 1½–2 hours.*
Ingredients: *2 cups/1 lb/500 g dried red kidney beans ● ½ lb/250 g*
onions, chopped ● 2 cloves garlic, crushed ● 1 bay leaf ● ¼ lb/100 g bacon,
chopped ● ¼ lb/100 g Chorizo sausage, cut into chunks ● 1 teaspoon*
*paprika ● salt ● ¼ lb/100 g blood sausage (black pudding).***

● Clean the freshwater crayfish but do not shell. ● Brown the
garlic in oil. ● Then add the chili pepper and chopped
tomatoes. ● Fry till done, stirring all the while, then add the
freshwater crayfish. ● Turn them several times and cook till
they have become bright red. ● Moisten the contents with
brandy and set alight. ● Add a pinch of salt. ● Transfer to an
earthenware casserole and serve at once.

● Put all the ingredients except the blood sausage (black
pudding) into a saucepan of cold water. ● Bring to the boil,
then lower heat and simmer for about 2 hours. ● Ten minutes
before serving, add the sliced blood sausage. ● Serve in an
earthenware casserole.

* **See footnotes page 8.

Huevos Virrey
Eggs Virrey

For 6 persons

Time: *preparation 10 min.* ● *cooking 20 min.*
Ingredients: *14 eggs* ● *salt* ● *1 cup/8 fl. oz/2.5 dl wine vinegar* ●
½ cup/2 oz/50 g flour ● *olive oil* ● *1 cup/8 fl. oz/2.5 dl Spanish or tomato sauce (see p. 187).* Garnish (optional): *lemon slices* ● *parsley.*

● Poach 12 eggs in boiling water with salt and vinegar for 2–3 minutes. ● Remove from pan very carefully and set aside. ● Beat the 2 remaining eggs. ● Dip the poached eggs first into the beaten eggs, then into flour. ● Heat the oil in a pan and fry the floured eggs, turning them delicately so that they brown evenly. ● Serve with Spanish or tomato sauce. ● Garnish with lemons and parsley if desired.

Rape castellano
Castilian monkfish

For 6 persons

Time: *preparation 15 min.* ● *cooking 30 min.*
Ingredients: *3 lb/1.5 kg monkfish** ● *salt* ● *pepper* ● *1 egg, beaten* ●
flour ● *olive oil* ● *1 onion, chopped* ● *2 cups/½ lb/200 g pine kernels* ●
1 pint/1 lb/500 g clams ● *1 glass dry white wine.*

● Clean the fish and cut it into round slices. ● Season. ● Dip the slices into beaten egg and then into flour. ● Fry in hot oil. ● In another frying pan brown the chopped onion in a little oil. ● Crush all but 2 tablespoons of the pine kernels to a powder. ● Clean the clams. ● Put the fried monkfish slices and clams into the pan with the onion. ● Add the crushed and whole pine kernels and dilute with white wine. ● Simmer for 10 minutes and serve at once.

* If unavailable, bluefish may be used

Cochinillo asado
Roast sucking pig

Lenguas de lechazo estofadas
Stewed lambs' tongues

For 5–6 persons

Time: *preparation 15 min. ● cooking 2½ hours.*
Ingredients: *1 sucking pig weighing about 6 lb/3 kg ● salt ● pepper ● ½ cup/4 fl. oz/1 dl olive oil ● ½ cup/¼ lb/100 g butter ● 2 carrots ● 1 onion.*

For 4 persons

Time: *preparation 15 min. ● cooking 1½ hours.*
Ingredients: *1 lb/500 g lamb's tongues ● 4 tablespoons olive oil ● 2 medium carrots, chopped ● 1 onion, chopped ● 3 green peppers, seeded and chopped ● 3 cloves garlic, crushed ● salt ● small glass of dry white wine ● 1 cup/8 fl. oz/2.5 dl hot stock ● sprig of thyme.*

● Heat the oven to a high temperature (425°F/mark 7/220°C). ● Season the piglet inside and out. ● Wrap the ears in aluminum (cooking) foil. ● Place the pig in a roasting pan (oven tray). ● Baste with oil and dab with butter. ● Roast, basting often with the cooking fat, for 2½ hours. ● Meanwhile scrape the carrots, peel the onion and slice both into sizeable pieces. ● Five minutes before the end of the cooking time put the carrots and onion in with the piglet. ● When cooked remove piglet from the oven and take the foil off the ears. ● Keep warm. ● Heat up the cooking juices with the vegetables. ● When they start to sizzle skim and immediately add 2 cups/¾ pint/5 dl water. ● Boil rapidly to let this gravy thicken a little, then strain. ● Check the seasoning and serve the sucking pig with the gravy.

● Cook the tongues until tender and remove the skin. ● In a pan with the oil put the carrots, onion, peppers, garlic, and lastly the prepared tongues. ● Check the seasoning. ● Fry until brown. ● Add the wine, stock and thyme. ● Bring to a boil and simmer gently for about an hour. ● Serve hot.

Estofado de ternera a la zamorana
Zamoran veal stew

Caldereta de cordero
Lamb casserole

For 4 persons

Time: *preparation 15 min. ● cooking 45 min.*
Ingredients: *1 lb/500 g lean veal ● 1 onion ● 2 medium carrots ● 3 sweet red peppers ● olive oil ● salt ● 1 glass sherry ● 1 glass dry white wine flavoured with cooking brandy ● 1 cup/8fl. oz/2.5 dl stock ● $\frac{1}{2}$ lb/250 g mushrooms, sliced ● 1 cup/$\frac{1}{2}$ lb/200 g peas, shelled.*

For 4 persons

Time: *preparation 12 min. ● cooking 1 hour.*
Ingredients: *2 lb/1 kg lamb ● 1 head of garlic ● 2 tomatoes, peeled and chopped ● 1 green pepper, seeded and chopped ● 1 carrot, chopped ● 1 onion, chopped ● sprig of parsley ● 1 bay leaf ● salt. For the sauce: 5 peppercorns ● breadcrumbs from 1 bread roll ● 2 cloves ● 1 teaspoon paprika ● pinch of ground cumin.*

● Cut up the veal, chop the onion, carrots and peppers. ● Brown lightly in oil. ● Season. ● Moisten with sherry and white wine, then set alight. ● Bring to a boil and cook briskly for a few minutes. ● When the wine has evaporated pour in the stock. ● After 15 minutes, add the sliced mushrooms and the peas. ● Continue cooking for another 15 minutes or until all is tender. ● Adjust seasoning and serve.

● Cut the lamb into even-sized chunks. ● Place in a large pot, cover with water and bring to the boil. ● Skim. ● Separate the garlic cloves and peel them. ● Add the tomatoes, pepper, carrot and onion, all chopped small, together with the parsley, bay leaf, garlic cloves, salt and oil. ● Simmer for about 50 minutes, or until the meat is tender). ● Pound all the sauce ingredients together in a mortar, dilute with a little of the lamb stock and add the mixture to the stew. ● Cook for another 3 or 4 minutes, then serve.

Lechazo a la panadera
Lamb à la boulangère

Jamón asado con uvas pasas
Baked ham with raisins

For 10 persons

Time: *preparation 15 min.* ● *cooking 2 hours.*
Ingredients: *1 baby lamb* ● *salt* ● *¾ cup/6 oz/200 g lard, melted.*
As an accompaniment: *fried potatoes or salad.*

For 6 persons

Time: *preparation 15 min.* ● *cooking 40 min.*
Ingredients: *3 lb/1.5 kg very mild cured ham in a single piece* ● *olive oil* ●
thyme ● *rosemary* ● *salt* ● *3½ cups/1 lb/500 g raisins* ● *1 lb/500 g raspberry
jam* ● *2¼ cups/1¼ pints/7.5 dl port wine* ● *grated rind (peel) of 1 orange* ●
grated rind (peel) of 1 lemon ● *1 onion, chopped.*

● Clean the lamb. ● Rub with salt. ● Baste well with melted
lard. ● Put in a fairly hot oven (400°F/mark 6/205°C) and
roast, turning and basting occasionally, until the meat is
evenly brown and tender. ● Serve with fried potatoes or salad.

● Tie the ham around with coarse string and place it in a
fireproof cooking pot with a small amount of oil. ● Add the
thyme, chopped rosemary and a little salt. ● Bake in a hot oven
(425°F/mark 7/220°C) for 20 minutes. ● Take out and untie
the ham, then put it back, accompanied by all the other
ingredients, and continue cooking, but in a moderate oven
(350°F/mark 4/175°C), for 20 minutes more. ● Serve hot or
cold.

Cachelada leonesa
Sausage and potatoes León style

Faisán al modo de Alcántara
Pheasant à l'Alcántara

For 6 persons

Time: *preparation 10 min. ● cooking 45–50 min.*
Ingredients: *4 lb/2 kg potatoes ● ½ lb/250 g Chorizo sausage* ● salt ● chopped parsley.*

For 4 persons

Time: *preparation 30 min. + 3 days for marinating the pheasant ● cooking 1 hour.*
Ingredients: *1 large pheasant ● 2 duck livers ● 12 small truffles ● 1 small glass port ● salt ● pepper ● lard. To garnish: mashed potatoes ● a few sprigs of parsley.*

● Peel the potatoes and cut them in quarters. ● Put the potatoes and the whole sausage in a saucepan of lightly salted cold water. ● Cook slowly for 40–50 minutes. ● When the potatoes are done drain them. ● Divide the sausage into 6 portions and arrange with the potatoes in a serving bowl. ● Sprinkle with chopped parsley and serve. ● The stock can be used as a soup.

* See footnote page 8.

● Pluck, clean and gut the pheasant. ● Season and sauté the duck livers, then pound them in a mortar or mash them. ● Simmer 2–3 sliced truffles in the port wine. ● Put the duck livers through a vegetable mill or press through a sieve and add to the truffles. ● Stuff the bird with this mixture and leave it to marinate in the port for 3 days, turning regularly. ● At the end of that time season the pheasant, baste it with lard and bake it in a moderate oven (350°F/mark 4/175°C). ● It will take about an hour to cook. ● Meanwhile, bring the marinating wine with the remaining truffles to a boil, reduce over a brisk heat and pour over the bird shortly before it is done. ● Bake for 5 or 6 minutes more, then transfer it whole to a heated serving dish. ● Pour the wine and truffle sauce over it once more and garnish with a ring of potato purée and some sprigs of parsley.

Perdices a la segoviana
Partridges à la Segovia

Suspiros de monja
"Nun's sighs"

For 8 persons

Time: *preparation 30 min.* ● *cooking 1½ hours.*
Ingredients: *4 partridges ready for the oven* ● *butter* ● *3 carrots* ● *2 leeks* ● *4 green peppers* ● *1 onion* ● *3 tomatoes, peeled* ● *2 cloves garlic* ● *16 shallots* ● *16 button mushrooms* ● *salt* ● *bouquet garni* ● *4 white peppercorns* ● *4 cloves* ● *flour* ● *paprika* ● *5 tablespoons olive oil* ● *2 cups/16 fl. oz/5 dl stock* ● *1 glass dry white wine* ● *1 small glass dry sherry* ● *1 oz/30 g baking (unsweetened) chocolate, grated* ● *parsley.*

For 4 persons

Time: *preparation 10 min.* ● *cooking 25 min.*
Ingredients: *6 egg whites* ● *¾ cup/6 oz/150 g powdered (castor) sugar* ● *ground cinnamon* ● *4½ cups/1¾ pints/1 liter milk* ● *2 scoops vanilla ice cream* ● *6 egg yolks* ● *1 stick cinnamon* ● *rind (peel) of 1 orange* ● *rind (peel) of 1 lemon* ● *whipped cream.*

● Place the partridges in a casserole greased with butter. ● Clean the vegetables and slice all but the mushrooms, which are left whole. ● Season and add the spices, the bouquet garni, the onion, carrots, leeks, peppers and tomatoes. ● Sprinkle the top with a little flour and paprika. ● Dress with a few knobs of butter and the olive oil. ● Put in a hot oven (425°F/mark 7/220°C) for 30 minutes. ● When the flour and paprika start to brown pour on the stock, white wine and sherry. ● Finally, add the grated chocolate, chopped shallots, and mushrooms. ● Lower the oven temperature to 350°F/mark 4/175°C and continue to cook for a further hour. ● Serve very hot with chopped parsley strewn on top.

● Beat 6 egg whites to a stiff froth and fold in ½ cup/¼ lb/100 g powdered (castor) sugar with a pinch of ground cinnamon. ● Heat 2 cups/16 fl. oz/5 dl milk with the vanilla ice cream. ● Just as it begins to boil, dip tablespoonfuls of egg-white froth, one by one, in the simmering liquid and allow them to set. ● Remove with a slotted spoon and set aside. ● Put the milk in which the "sighs" were dipped on one side, allow to cool and stir the egg yolks into it, blending thoroughly. ● Arrange the "sighs" on a serving dish. ● Boil the rest of the milk with the cinnamon stick, the remaining sugar, orange and lemon peel. ● When it comes to the boil add the egg yolk-and-milk mixture. ● Strain and pour over the "sighs." ● Cool and sprinkle with ground cinnamon. ● Decorate with whipped cream and serve.

Higos Villamiel
Figs, walnuts and honey

Costrada soriana
Soria millefeuilles

For 8 persons

Time: *preparation 12 min. ● cooking 1 hour.*
Ingredients: *1 lb/500 g dried figs ● 2 cups/½ lb/250 g shelled English walnuts ● 2 cups/16 fl. oz/5 dl red wine ● 2 cups/16 fl. oz/5 dl port ● 8 tablespoons honey ● 1 small glass orange juice ● 1 cup/8 fl. oz/2 dl whipped cream.*

For 6 persons

Time: *preparation 20 min. ● cooking 15 min.*
Ingredients: *½ cup/4 fl. oz/1 dl water ● 1½ cups/¾ lb/300 g sugar ● 12 egg yolks ● ¾ lb/300 g readymade flaky or puff pastry ● 2 cups/1 pint/5 dl whipped cream ● confectioners' (icing) sugar.*

● Slit each fig and insert a walnut. ● Put stuffed figs in a pan with the wine, port, honey and orange juice. ● Bring to a boil and simmer gently for about an hour. ● Place on a dish and decorate with whipped cream and walnut halves.

● First make the custard. ● Stir the water and sugar together in a saucepan and cook briskly for 5 minutes. ● In another pan beat the egg yolks lightly to a smooth cream. ● Stirring continuously, gradually mix the syrup with the egg yolks. ● Set the pan over heat and beat the custard vigorously until the mixture comes away from the sides of the pan. ● Remove from heat and leave to cool ● Divide the pastry into 3 equal parts and roll out 3 very thin layers. ● Bake them in a hot oven (425°F/mark 7/220°C) for 10–15 minutes. ● When golden brown take out and allow to cool. ● Place one layer of pastry on a plate and spread with whipped cream. ● Cover with the second layer and top that with the custard. ● Put the third layer over the custard and dust with confectioners' (icing) sugar

Not only is Madrid the political capital of Spain; it is also the capital of Spanish gastronomy. In most of the city's restaurants one can enjoy the specialties of various Spanish provinces. The cookery of Madrid itself, say the experts, has the same origin as that of New Castile. It has a pronounced character of its own, tempered by some foreign influences.

Madrid. Madrilene cookery is distinguished by the simplicity of its savoury dishes, chief among them "Cocido madrileño," a kind of rich stew that can, to some degree, be considered as the worthy representative of all Spanish *cocidos.* Some of the recipes have won national acclaim, especially the "tripe à la Madrilène" and the "Sopa de ajo," a tasty garlic soup. Other dishes of particular interest include "Judías blancas" (navy (haricot) beans) "a lo tío Lucas," Uncle Luke being a legendary character who kept an inn in Madrid. Also among the capital's specialities are *churros*, a sort of elongated pancake.

New Castile. This is the land of regal cuisine, of decided and appetizing flavours, closely related to the cookery of La Mancha, from the time when that area included a large part of New Castile. Especially excellent are Castilian veal cutlets, the "Migas canas," a sort of bread pudding with grapes, and chicken with apple.

Aceitunas a la madrileña
Olives à la Madrilène

Potaje de garbanzos y espinacas
Chick pea and spinach soup

For 6 persons

Time: *preparation 30 min. + 1 hour to marinate.*
Ingredients: *2 lb/1 kg large ripe (black) olives ● $\frac{1}{2}$ lb/250 g scallions (spring onions) ● olive oil ● paprika ● wine vinegar ● salt ● oregano ● 1 clove garlic, chopped.*

For 6 persons

Time: *preparation 30 min. + 24 hours soaking ● cooking 3 hours.*
Ingredients: *$\frac{1}{2}$ lb/200 g dried salt cod ● $1\frac{1}{2}$ cups/$\frac{3}{4}$ lb/300 g chick peas ● 2 onions ● 1 clove ● 1 carrot ● 1 bay leaf ● $1\frac{1}{2}$ lb/800 g spinach ● $\frac{1}{2}$ cup/4 fl. oz/1 dl olive oil ● 2 cloves garlic, chopped ● $\frac{1}{2}$ teaspoon paprika ● 2 ripe tomatoes, peeled and sliced ● 2 eggs ● salt.*

● Wash the olives in cold water and dry carefully. ● Put them in a bowl. ● Add the trimmed, washed and sliced scallions (spring onions). ● Dress with oil, paprika, vinegar and salt to taste. ● Stir well. ● Sprinkle with oregano and chopped garlic. ● Mix all the ingredients thoroughly and leave in a cool place for 1 hour before serving.

● Soak the dried salt cod in cold water for 24 hours, changing the water several times. ● Soak the chick peas overnight in salted water. ● Wash the soaked cod in cold water, drain well and chop small. ● Fill a saucepan with 9 cups/$3\frac{1}{2}$ pints/2 litres water and bring to a boil. ● When it begins to boil put in the soaked peas, the cod, one onion peeled and stuck with a clove, the scraped carrot and the bay leaf. ● Bring back to the boil, cover and cook slowly. ● Pick over the spinach and wash it scrupulously. ● Cook in a minimum of water for 5 minutes. ● Drain, squeeze, and chop with a fork. ● Peel and chop the other onion. ● Sweat onion in the olive oil along with the chopped garlic. ● Add the paprika and the peeled and sliced tomatoes. ● Turn the fried mixture and the spinach into the saucepan containing the chick peas and cod and continue to cook. ● When nearly done take out the whole onion, the carrot and the bay leaf. ● Take the clove out of the onion and pass onion and carrot through a vegetable mill with a few of the peas. ● Put the resulting purée back into the soup. ● Simmer until the chick peas are tender. ● Boil the eggs, chop them and add them to the soup. ● Check the seasoning. ● Serve piping hot.

Lombarda de San Isidro
Red cabbage San Isidro style

Migas canas
Savoury bread pudding with grapes

For 4 persons

Time: *preparation 15 min. ● cooking 2¾ hours.*
Ingredients: *a 2 lb/1 kg red cabbage ● 2 onions ● 3 cooking apples ●
¼ lb/200 g Canadian (back) bacon ● 3 large potatoes ●
¼ cup/2 oz/60 g lard ● 4 tablespoons wine vinegar ● ½ bay leaf ● salt ●
pepper.*

For 4–6 persons

Time: *preparation 15 min. ● cooking 15–20 min.*
Ingredients: *1 large (2 lb/1 kg) loaf bread ● 6 oz/150 g Chorizo
sausage* ● ½ lb/200 g fat (streaky) bacon ● ½ cup/4 fl. oz/1 dl olive oil ●
¼ cup/2 oz/50 g lard ● 3 cloves garlic, crushed ● 1 tablespoon paprika ●
2 cups/16 fl. oz/5 dl milk ● salt. To garnish: bunch of black grapes.*

● Clean the cabbage and slice finely. ● Chop the onions. ●
Peel, core, and finely chop the apples. ● Chop the bacon into
small pieces. ● Peel the potatoes and cut each into 8 chunks. ●
Melt the lard in a stew pan. ● When hot, sweat the onion. ●
Add cabbage, apples and bacon. ● A few minutes later add the
vinegar, bay leaf, salt and pepper. ● Stir well to prevent the
ingredients from sticking to the base of the pan. ● Pour in
1 cup/8 fl. oz/2 dl hot water. ● When it comes to the boil,
cover the pot very tightly and put in a moderately hot (350°F/
mark 4/175°C) oven for 2 hours. ● Uncover the pot and add
the potatoes. ● Cover again and cook for a further 30 minutes.
● Serve very hot.

● Remove the crusts from the loaf of bread and make the rest
into crumbs. ● Finely chop the sausage and bacon. ● Heat the
oil and lard in a pan. ● Fry the sausage, bacon and garlic,
stirring to keep from burning. ● While still stirring add the
breadcrumbs. ● Sprinkle with paprika and slowly pour in the
milk and salt, mixing well. ● When the bread pudding is soft
and all the milk is absorbed garnish the top with grapes and
serve.

* See footnote page 8.

Sopa de ajo
Garlic soup

Judías blancas a lo tío Lucas
Uncle Luke's beans

For 4 persons

Time: *preparation 10 min. ● cooking 20 min + 8 min. in the oven.*
Ingredients: *4 thin slices bread ● olive oil ● 3 cloves garlic, chopped ● 1 teaspoon paprika ● salt ● 4 eggs.*

For 6 persons

Time: *4 hours to soak beans ● cooking 2 hours.*
Ingredients: *3 cups/1½ lb/800 g navy (haricot) beans ● ½ lb/200 g fat (streaky) bacon ● ½ cup/4 fl. oz/1 dl olive oil ● 1 onion, chopped ● 1 head of garlic, all cloves peeled and chopped ● 1 bay leaf ● 1 teaspoon paprika ● pinch of ground cumin ● 1 sprig parsley ● salt.*

● Fry the bread slices in a little oil. ● Sweat the chopped garlic in oil in a large pan. ● Before it browns add the fried bread sprinkled with paprika. ● Pour in 4½ cups/1¾ pints/1 liter hot water and salt judiciously. ● Cook gently for about 15 minutes. ● Divide the soup into 4 soup bowls. ● Break an egg into each bowl, then place in a warm oven (325°F/mark 3/165°C) for about 8 minutes to allow the egg whites to set slightly. ● Serve at once.

● Soak the dried beans for 4 hours in cold water. ● Chop the bacon into small pieces and fry in the oil in a frying pan. ● Add the drained beans, onion, garlic, bay leaf, paprika, cumin and parsley. ● Cover with plenty of cold water. ● Simmer over a low heat until the beans are tender, about 2 hours. ● Halfway through the cooking adjust the seasoning. ● Serve in a soup tureen.

Cocido madrileño
Madrilene stew

Tortilla de patatas
Potato omelette

For 6 persons

Time: *preparation 30 min. + 12 hours for soaking the chick peas and pig's foot (trotter)* ● *cooking 3 hours.*
Ingredients: *1 lb/500 g stewing beef* ● *1 beef bone* ● *1 pig's foot (trotter)* ● *¼ lb/100 g fat (streaky) bacon* ● *¼ lb/100 g any raw ham* ● *½ boiling chicken* ● *2 cups/1 lb/500 g chick peas* ● *1 carrot* ● *1 small turnip* ● *½ stick celery* ● *1 small onion stuck with a clove* ● *6–8 potatoes* ● *1 large Savoy cabbage (or Swiss chard), globe artichokes or green beans* ● *1 Chorizo sausage** ● *1½ cups/¾ lb/300 g pasta (or rice)* ● *1 blood sausage (black pudding).** As an accompaniment: *tomato sauce (see p. 187).*

For 4 persons

Time: *preparation 15 min.* ● *cooking 15 min.*
Ingredients: *1¼ lb/800 g potatoes* ● *1 cup/8 fl. oz/2.5 dl olive oil* ● *6 eggs* ● *salt.*

● Soak the pig's foot (trotter) and the chick peas separately in cold water for 12 hours. ● In a large saucepan with 13 cups/5¼ pints/3 liters water put the beef, beef bone, soaked pig's foot (trotter), raw ham. ● Bring to the boil, skim, add the half chicken, the soaked chick peas, carrot, turnip, celery and onion. ● Simmer for about 2½ hours. ● Peel and wash the potatoes. ● Add them to the pot half an hour before the end. ● Cook the cabbage (or other vegetable) separately with the sausages in equal parts of the stew broth and water. ● Now you can make the soup. ● Take as much stock as necessary from the meat saucepan and mix it with an equal amount of stock from the vegetables and sausages. ● Cook the pasta (or rice or bread) in the resulting liquid until tender. ● Serve the soup as a first course. ● On one side of a fairly deep serving dish arrange the well drained chick peas, and on the other the thin slices of beef, the cabbage and the chopped sausages. ● Serve with garlic-flavoured tomato sauce.

* See footnote page 8.

● Peel and wash the potatoes, dry them very thoroughly and slice extremely finely. ● Heat oil in a frying pan. ● When it begins to sizzle put in the sliced potatoes and fry, stirring now and again so that they do not stick. ● In the meanwhile, beat the eggs with a little salt. ● Tip over the potatoes, stir and leave the omelette to swell. ● When it begins to brown on one side turn it over and brown the other side. ● Serve on hot plates.

Chanfaina castellana
Pig's liver à la Castilienne

Pecho de ternera con guisantes
Veal stew with peas

For 6 persons

Time: *preparation 12 min. ● cooking 20 min.*
Ingredients: *1 onion ● ½ chili pepper ● 4 cloves garlic ● ½ cup/4 fl. oz/1 dl olive oil ● 1 lb/500 g pig's liver ● 1 tablespoon paprika ● 2 lb/1 kg pig's blood* ● 2 tablespoons tomato sauce (see p. 187) ● 2 bay leaves ● ½ glass wine vinegar ● chopped parsley.*

For 6 persons

Time: *preparation 10 min. ● cooking 50 min.*
Ingredients: *6 slices of stewing veal weighing about 6 oz/150 g each ● salt ● pepper ● flour ● ¾ cup/6 fl. oz/2 dl olive oil ● 1 onion, finely chopped ● 2 cups/16 fl. oz/5 dl dry white wine ● 2 cups/16 fl. oz/5 dl stock ● 4 cups/1 lb/500 g shelled peas ● chopped parsley ● pinch of thyme ● pinch of saffron.*

● Chop the onion, chili pepper and garlic very finely. ● Fry them in oil, stirring all the while. ● Cut the liver in pieces. ● Add to pan and fry lightly for 10 minutes. ● Add the paprika, the chopped-up blood*, tomato sauce, bay leaves and vinegar. ● Season, cook for another 5 minutes, sprinkle with chopped parsley and serve.

*Pig's blood is sometimes available from pork butchers. It is sold in a congealed form, which is why you chop it up. If unobtainable, use 1¼ cups/ ½ pint/3 dl each of good beef stock and red wine.

● Season the veal slices and dip in flour. ● Heat oil in a frying pan and brown the veal on both sides for 10 minutes altogether. ● Add the finely chopped onion and cook over a low heat. ● Add the wine and cover with hot stock. ● Then put in the peas, chopped parsley, thyme and saffron. ● Bring to a boil and simmer for 30 minutes. ● Check the seasoning and serve.

Chuletas de cerdo a la madrileña
Pork chops à la Madrilène

Callos a la madrileña
Tripe à la Madrilène

For 4 persons

Time: *preparation 15 min.* ● *cooking 25 min.*
Ingredients: *2 cloves garlic* ● *4 sprigs parsley* ● *1 small onion* ● *1 tablespoon paprika* ● *pepper* ● *salt* ● *5 tablespoons olive oil* ● *4 pork loin chops of about 5–6 oz/125–150 g each. As an accompaniment: mashed potatoes.*

For 6 persons

Time: *preparation 1 hour* ● *cooking 4 hours + 1½ hours for stewing.*
Ingredients: *1 calf's foot* ● *2 lb/1 kg tripe* ● *2 lb/1 kg calf's head* ● *vinegar* ● *salt* ● *2 onions* ● *2 heads garlic* ● *1 bay leaf* ● *a few peppercorns* ● *½ cup/4 fl. oz/1 dl olive oil* ● *6 oz/150 g any raw ham* ● *6 oz/150 g Chorizo sausage** ● *1 tablespoon paprika* ● *6 oz/150 g blood sausage (black pudding)*** ● *chili pepper (optional).*

● Finely chop the garlic, parsley and onion and mix together. ● Season with paprika, pepper and a little salt. ● Mix well and moisten with 3 tablespoons oil, keeping it to a fairly thick consistency. ● Grease a roasting pan (oven tray) generously with oil. ● Season the chops, cover them with the chopped herb mixture and cook in a hot oven (425°F/mark 7/220°C) for 5 minutes on each side. ● Serve with mashed potatoes.

● Trim the calf's foot and cut in half. ● Clean the tripe and calf's head. ● Cut into pieces. ● Scrub them in vinegar with a little salt, then rinse several times under running water. ● Place all together in a large saucepan, cover with water and bring to a boil, then transfer the meat to another saucepan of water with 1 onion, all but 1 clove of the garlic, peeled but not chopped, bay leaf and peppercorns. ● Bring to the boil and simmer gently for 4 hours. ● Season, then put on one side till the following day. ● Finely chop a clove of garlic and 1 onion and brown them in oil. ● Then add the raw ham, chopped, and the Chorizo sausage cut in rounds. ● Stir well, take the pan from the heat and add the paprika. ● Put the tripe in a large earthenware casserole, removing the onion, garlic and bay leaf. ● Bone the calf's foot and cut up the meat. ● To the pan containing the raw ham and Chorizo sausage add the blood sausage (black pudding) and 4½ cups/1¾ pints/1 liter of the stock set aside the day before. ● Add salt if necessary. ● Add the hot chili pepper if desired. ● Pour this stock over the tripe and cook in a moderate oven (350°F/mark 4/175°C) for 1½ hours. ● Serve in the same casserole.

* ** See footnotes page 8.

Chuletas de ternera a la castellana
Veal cutlets à la Castilienne

Perdices a la toledana
Partridges Toledo style

For 4 persons

Time: *preparation 25 min.* ● *cooking 30 min.*
Ingredients: *8 veal cutlets ● 24 fat (streaky) bacon strips for larding ● salt ● pepper ● $\frac{1}{4}$ cup/2 oz/60 g lard ● 1 glass dry sherry ● $\frac{1}{2}$ cup/4 fl. oz/1 dl meat stock ● $1\frac{1}{2}$ lb/600 g green (French or runner) beans ● 2 bunches asparagus ● 2 cloves garlic ● 1 cup/8 fl. oz/2 dl olive oil.*

For 4 persons

Time: *preparation 15 min* ● *cooking 2 hours.*
Ingredients: *6 patridges ● 3 heads garlic ● 3 onions ● 2 cups/$\frac{3}{4}$ pint/5 dl olive oil ● 3 glasses dry white wine ● $\frac{1}{2}$ glass wine vinegar ● 2 bay leaves ● 6 peppercorns ● salt ● 12 small new potatoes.*

● Trim the rind and fat from the cutlets. ● Make a few slits in them and carefully lard the cutlets with the strips of fat bacon, using a larding needle. ● Season. ● Heat the lard and brown the cutlets on both sides. ● Heat the sherry in another pan and add the browned cutlets to it. ● Cover and cook over a low heat until the sherry has completely evaporated. ● At this stage add the meat stock and continue to simmer the cutlets until they are cooked. ● Remove from heat but keep warm. ● Meanwhile trim the beans, slice them and cook in salted water. ● Do the same with the asparagus: let it get cold, then cut off the tips and divide the stalks in two. ● Fry the cloves of garlic in the olive oil, then remove them. ● Sauté the asparagus and then the beans in the same pan. ● Serve cutlets on individual plates. ● In the center of each place the meat. ● Garnish with the asparagus and beans round the outside.

● Pluck the partridges, singe the remaining down and draw. ● Wash well and truss. ● Peel and chop garlic and onions. ● Put the birds in a large earthenware ovenproof casserole. ● Add the onion, garlic, oil, wine, vinegar, bay leaves, peppercorns and salt. ● Roast in a moderate oven (350°F/mark 4/175°C) for 2 hours. ● Halfway through add the scraped potatoes. ● Serve in the earthenware cooking pot.

Perdiz en escabeche
Spiced partridge

Pollo con manzanas
Chicken with apples

For 4 persons

Time: *preparation 15 min. ● cooking 30 min.*
Ingredients: *4 partridges ● salt ● ½ cup/4 fl. oz/2 dl olive oil ● 1 large onion, thinly sliced ● 4 cloves garlic, crushed ● 2 bay leaves ● thyme ● oregano ● 1 teaspoon paprika (optional) ● dry white wine ● wine vinegar ● chicken stock ● 6 peppercorns ● 2 cloves.*

For 4 persons

Time: *preparation 20 min. ● cooking 1¾ hours.*
Ingredients: *1 oven-ready chicken weighing about 3½ lb/1.5 kg ● salt ● pepper ● juice of 1 lemon ● 2 cooking apples ● ¼ lb/100 g finely sliced fat (streaky) bacon ● 1 small glass dry white wine ● 1 tablespoon brandy ● parsley.* As an accompaniment: *duchesse potatoes.*

● Clean the partridges, draw, and truss them with coarse string. ● Sprinkle with salt inside and out. ● Fry in the oil till brown, then transfer to a deep cooking pot. ● Using the same oil, brown the thinly sliced onion, the crushed garlic, the bay leaves, thyme and oregano. ● Put this fried mixture onto the partridges, adding the paprika if desired. ● Cover with equal quantities of wine, vinegar and stock. ● Add the peppercorns, cloves and salt. ● Bring to a boil and cook the partridges over a gentle heat in this sauce. ● As soon as they are cooked (about 30 minutes) remove the pot from the stove and let the birds get cold in the broth. ● When cold cut the string and put partridges into an earthenware ovenproof casserole. ● Strain the sauce over the partridges, heat up and serve.

● Clean and dry the chicken. ● Season the interior with salt, pepper and lemon juice. ● Stuff the chicken with 2 unpeeled apples, i.e., first one half-apple, cored, then a whole apple, and finally the other half. ● Push them well in, then sew up the opening with coarse thread. ● Season the outside of the bird, wrap it in the fat bacon and truss it with kitchen string. ● Roast the chicken either on a spit or in the oven at 375°F/mark 5/190°C for 1¾ hours. ● When half cooked baste with wine mixed with brandy. ● Also baste several times with the cooking juices. ● Serve the bird whole. ● Carve it into four quarters at the table. ● Also cut the whole apple in half, so that each diner has a quarter chicken and half an apple on his plate. ● Serve with duchesse potatoes and garnish with parsley.

Yemas
Egg yolk candies

Rosquillas tontas y listas
"Rich and poor" buns

For 8 persons

Time: *preparation 30 min. • cooking 15 min.*
Ingredients: *1 cup/½ lb/250 g sugar • 1 cup/8 fl. oz/2.5 dl water • rind (peel) of 1 lemon or 1 orange • 16 egg yolks • confectioners' (icing) sugar.*

For 6 persons

Time: *preparation 35 min. • cooking 15 min.*
Ingredients: *4 cups/1 lb/500 g all-purpose (plain) flour • 2 tablespoons aniseeds • 6 eggs • ½ cup/¼ lb/100 g sugar • ⅔ cup/5 fl. oz/1.5 dl sunflower oil • 1 small glass anise liqueur (e.g. Pernod) • ⅔ cup/5 fl. oz/1.5 dl water • 1 teaspoon lemon juice • 2 cups/1 lb/400 g granulated sugar • 2 egg whites whipped to a stiff froth • 2 teaspoons confectioners' (icing) sugar.*

• Put the sugar, water and orange or lemon peel in a saucepan.
• Cook to the point of caramelization (to test: a little of the syrup dropped into cold water should form soft pellets). • Beat the egg yolks lightly in another pan. • Pour the liquid caramel slowly into the egg yolks, stirring constantly with a wooden spoon as you do so. • Heat the pan and continue stirring until you obtain a thick paste that comes away from the base. • Cool. • Spread the paste on a marble slab or pastry board and dust with confectioners' (icing) sugar. • Roll the paste into cylinders about 1 in./2.5 cm across and cut them into 1–1½ in./2½–4 cm lengths.

• Sift the flour. • Toast the aniseeds and pound in a mortar. • Beat 5 eggs into the sugar till you have a frothy mixture. • Add the oil, anise liqueur (Pernod), aniseeds and flour to the egg and sugar mixture. • Mix thoroughly and turn the resulting dough on to a lightly greased marble slab or pastry board. • Knead till you obtain a smooth, compact and elastic texture. • Let the dough rest for some minutes. • Form circular buns by twisting lengths of the dough around your finger. • Brush with oil and dust with flour. • Arrange them, not touching one another, on a lightly greased baking sheet (oven tray). • Brush buns with the remaining beaten egg and bake in a very hot oven (450°F/mark 8/230°C) for 15 minutes. • The "poor" buns are now ready, but the "rich" ones must be iced. • Put the water, lemon juice and granulated sugar in a pan, bring to a boil and simmer till the syrup oozes off the spoon in a ribbon. • Let it cool, then gradually fold in the whipped egg whites. • Add the confectioners' (icing) sugar and ice the little cakes, which have meanwhile grown cold.

Mazapán de Toledo
Toledo marzipan

Torrijas
Fried bread dessert

For 10–12 persons

Time: *preparation 50 min.* ● *cooking 15–20 min.*
Ingredients: *2 lb/1 kg blanched almonds* ● *4 cups/2 lb/1 kg sugar* ●
2 eggs, beaten. For the frosting: *2 cups/1 lb/500 g sugar* ● *1 egg white.*

For 4 persons

Time: *preparation 10 min. + 10 min. for soaking* ● *cooking 15 min.*
Ingredients: *1 cup/8 fl. oz/2.5 dl milk* ● *½ cup/¼ lb/100 g sugar* ● *8 slices stale bread* ● *2 eggs, beaten* ● *sunflower oil* ● *cinnamon.*

● Run almonds through a meat grinder (mincer) 3 or 4 times, using the finest cutter. ● Add the sugar very slowly until you have obtained a smooth paste. ● Still stirring, add a few drops of water to make it easier to manipulate. ● Put on a marble slab or chilled platter and knead for 20 minutes. ● Form the dough into rings or other shapes. ● Brush with beaten egg and arrange on a buttered baking sheet (oven tray). ● Bake at 325°F/mark 3/165°C for 15–20 minutes. ● Remove from oven and allow to cool. ● To make the icing, melt the sugar in a pan over low heat and allow to cool. ● Beat an egg white to a stiff froth and mix with the cooled sugar. ● Decorate the marzipan shapes with this mixture.

● Mix the warm milk with 4 tablespoons sugar. ● Soak the bread slices, which can be cut into circles or other shapes if desired, in the milk for about 10 minutes. ● Then dip them in beaten egg and fry in plenty of sizzling hot oil. ● When the slices are golden brown drain them well on paper towels and sprinkle with sugar and a little cinnamon.

Churros
"Cucumber" fritters

Rosquillas de Alcalá
Alcalá cakes

For 3–4 persons

Time: *preparation 15 min. ● cooking 30 min.*
Ingredients: *4 cups/1 lb/500 g all-purpose (plain) flour ● salt ● 8 cups/4 pints/2 liters oil for frying ● 1 cup/½ lb/200 g sugar.*

For 6 persons

Time: *preparation 1 hour ● cooking 15 min. for the buns + 30 min. for the egg glaze + 15 min. for the sugar frosting.*
Ingredients: *4 cups/1 lb/500 g all-purpose (plain) flour ● 3 eggs ● 4½ cups/1¾ pints/1 liter white wine ● pinch of salt ● 2 cups/1 lb/500 g lard. For the egg glaze: 2 cups/1 lb/500 g sugar ● 1 teaspoon glucose powder ● 15 egg yolks. For the sugar frosting: 2 cups/1 lb/500 g sugar.*

● *Churros* are a special kind of fritter shaped like a cucumber, which is produced by using an implement something like a pastry tube (icing bag) called a *churrera*. ● The semi-liquid batter passes through a striated pipe into the hot oil, forming a cylindrical shape that, when fried, can be divided into pieces. ● Heat 2 cups/16 fl. oz/5 dl water with a pinch of salt, and as it comes to the boil add the flour. ● Stir with a wooden spoon for 2 or 3 minutes till the mixture is smooth and without lumps. ● Remove from the heat, cool, and then put into the *churrera*, or pastry tube (icing bag). ● Heat the oil in a deep pan. ● When it reaches boiling point squeeze the *churrera* to force the batter into the hot oil. ● Repeat the process until all the batter is used up. ● When the *churros* are crisp and evenly browned remove from oil. ● Cut the long cylindrical fritters into pieces of equal length, dust with sugar and serve very hot.

● Make a mound of flour on a marble slab or large chilled mixing bowl and hollow out a well in the center. ● Pour in the beaten eggs, wine and a little salt. ● Stir till you have blended all the ingredients to a smooth dough. ● Let it rest for 30 minutes. ● Then roll out on a marble slab or pastry board and spread a third of the lard all over the layer of dough. ● Fold the dough into quarters, roll it flat again and cover with half the remaining lard. ● Repeat the operation, using the remaining lard. ● Roll the pastry out again, fold into quarters as before, and repeat the operation three times. ● Leave it in a cool place. ● After 30 minutes roll it out once more to ½ in./1 cm thickness and cut into ring-shaped cakes. ● Bake in a very hot oven (425°F/mark 7/220°C) for 15 minutes and proceed to the glazing. ● Make a syrup—not too thick—from the sugar, glucose and half a glass of water. ● Put the egg yolks in another pan, stir in the syrup and thicken, stirring continuously, over low heat. ● Dip the cooled cakes into the glaze, then arrange them on a large dish and leave to dry. ● For the sugar frosting, make a syrup from sugar and half a glass of water. ● Cook slowly stirring with a wooden spoon until opaque. ● Dip in cakes.

Leche frita
Fried custard

Arroz con leche
Rice pudding

For 6 persons

Time: *preparation 15 min.* ● *cooking 10 min. for the custard + 10 min. for frying.*
Ingredients: *¾ cup/6 oz/150 g butter* ● *2 cups/½ lb/200 g all-purpose (plain) flour* ● *1¼ cups/10 oz/250 g sugar* ● *2 cups/16 fl. oz/5 dl milk* ● *1 pod vanilla (or stick of cinnamon) for flavouring* ● *4 egg yolks* ● *1 egg, beaten* ● *5 cups/1 lb/400 g breadcrumbs* ● *oil for frying.*

For 4–6 persons

Time: *preparation 10 min.* ● *cooking 1 hour.*
Ingredients: *½ cup/¼ lb/100 g short-grain (pudding) rice.* ● *4½ cups/1¾ pints/1 liter milk* ● *stick of cinnamon* ● *rind (peel) from 1 lemon.* ● *¾ cup/6 oz/200 g sugar* ● *ground cinnamon.*

● Melt the butter in a deep pan. ● Add 1½ cups/6 oz/150 g sifted flour. ● Stir over heat for a short while, then add ⅔ cup/ 5 oz/125 g sugar, beating with an egg whisk. ● Bring the milk barely to the boil, and flavour with vanilla or cinnamon. ● Strain it into the pan. ● Continue to beat the mixture to prevent it from sticking to the pan. ● When it begins to boil remove from the heat and stir in the 4 egg yolks, one by one. ● Mix until thoroughly blended. ● Spread the mixture in a layer about 1 in./2 cm deep on a marble slab or lightly greased chilled platter. ● Leave to cool. ● When cold cut it into quarters and dip each section into the remaining flour, then into beaten egg, then into breadcrumbs. ● Fry in sizzling oil. ● When golden brown take out, drain on paper towels (kitchen roll) and coat with the rest of the sugar. ● The cakes can be eaten hot or cold.

● Boil the rice in 2 cups/16 fl. oz/5 dl water for about 5 minutes. ● Drain, then return to the same pan. ● Add the boiling milk, the stick of cinnamon and the lemon rind (peel) ● Simmer gently for 1 hour. ● Five minutes before it is ready add the sugar. ● Empty the pan into a large bowl and sprinkle with ground cinnamon.

VALENCIA · LA MANCHA MURCIA

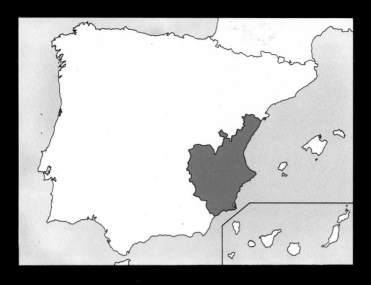

This chapter brings together the most important recipes from three great regional schools of Spanish cookery. That of Valencia is Mediterranean in type, characterized by savoury dishes based on rice. La Mancha represents a cuisine of the interior, Murcia one of coast and hinterland.

Valencia. Valencia's gastronomic horizon is not bound by the universally known paella. There are other notable rice dishes, such as "Arròs amb fesols i naps" (rice with beans, turnips and pork), "Arroz a banda" (rice and fish) and "Fideuà," based on fish and pasta.

La Mancha. Some idea of La Manchan cookery can be gained from the study of two world-renowned figures, Don Quixote and Sancho Panza. In Cervantes' immortal work there are indeed numerous references to the food of this region, so rich in distinguished dishes, with their very individual, even "violent" flavours. Among them we find "Ajo de mataero," a casserole of pork and pine kernels, also "Mojete," a first course of peppers and onions, and "Morteruelo," a tasty hare and chicken hash.

Murcia. Murcian cookery takes full advantage of the rich produce of her fertile soil, but there are other products not to be forgotten: fish and seafood, especially the delicious octopus of the western Mediterranean, sausages, game and savoury soups.

Guiso de trigo
Wholewheat soup

Olla gitana
Gypsy soup

For 4 persons

Time: *preparation 25 min. + 8 hours for soaking the chick peas ● cooking 2 hours.*
Ingredient: *1 cup/½ lb/250 g chick peas ● 1 cup/½ lb/250 g wholewheat grains (or pearl barley) ● 1 slice yellow squash* ● 1 pig's foot (trotter) cut in four ● ½ lb/200 g young turnips, peeled and halved ● 1 cardoon** ● 1 sprig mint ● 1 tablespoon paprika ● salt.*

For 4 persons

Time: *preparation 25 min. + 8 hours for soaking chick peas ● cooking 2½ hours.*
Ingredients: *1 cup/½ lb/250 g chick peas ● ½ lb/250 g green (French or runner) beans ● 1½ cups/6 oz/150 g squash or pumpkin, finely chopped ● 1 onion ● 2 ripe tomatoes ● 3 pears ● salt ● pepper ● 1 slice bread ● 1 clove garlic ● ½ cup/4 fl. oz/1 dl olive oil ● 1 tablespoon paprika ● 10 toasted almonds ● 2 tablespoons wine vinegar ● pinch of saffron ● stock.*

● Soak the chick peas overnight. ● Soak the wheat for 15 minutes. ● Remove rind from squash slice. ● Put the wheat, chick peas, pig's foot (trotter), turnips, squash and cardoon in a saucepan. ● Cover with cold water. ● Bring to the boil and simmer for 2 hours. ● The soup should remain fairly liquid. ● Halfway through add the mint and paprika. ● Check seasoning and finish cooking.

* If unavailable, use 1 courgette (zucchini) or 1 slice vegetable marrow.
** If unavailable, use 1 stick celery.

● Soak the chick peas for 8 hours. ● String and slice the beans. ● Peel and coarsely chop the squash. ● Chop the onion. ● Peel and slice the tomatoes. ● Peel and halve the pears. ● Bring 11 cups/4 pints/2.5 liters water to the boil in a saucepan, throw in the soaked chick peas and simmer. ● After 1 hour add the beans, squash and pears without letting the water go off the boil. ● Season. ● Meanwhile, fry the bread with the peeled garlic in olive oil until browned. ● Fry the onion in the same oil. ● When it begins to colour add the paprika and, immediately afterwards, the tomatoes. ● Continue cooking till the tomatoes are done. ● Crush the garlic, almonds and fried bread to a paste. ● Dilute with the vinegar and a little stock, in which the saffron has been dissolved. ● Mix with the fried onion and tomatoes and add to the soup. ● Check the seasoning. ● Serve very hot in a tureen.

Potaje de garbanzos con rellenos
Chick pea, spinach and cod soup

Judías estofadas con perdiz
Bean and partridge casserole

For 6 persons

Time: *preparation 15 min. + 24 hours for soaking dried salt cod and chick peas ● cooking 2 hours.*
Ingredients: *2 cups/1 lb/500 g chick peas ● ½ lb/250 g dried salt cod ● ½ lb/250 g spinach ● ½ lb/250 g potatoes ● 1 clove garlic, peeled ● 1 slice bread ● ½ cup/4 fl. oz/1 dl olive oil ● pinch of saffron ● salt.*

For 6 persons

Time: *preparation 15 min. + 2 hours soaking for beans ● cooking 2 hours.*
Ingredients: *2 cups/1 lb/500 g navy (haricot) beans ● 2 partridges ● 8 peppercorns ● 3 bay leaves ● salt ● 1 onion, finely chopped ● 4 cloves garlic, peeled ● 1 cup/8 fl. oz/2.5 dl olive oil ● 1 teaspoon paprika ● 4 tablespoons tomato paste.*

● Soak the chick peas and the dried salt cod, which has been cut in pieces, for 24 hours. ● Rinse. ● The next day put together in a saucepan of boiling water and simmer for 2 hours. ● Meanwhile, pick over and wash the spinach. ● Cut into strips and boil in a small amount of water for 5 minutes. ● Drain and squeeze as dry as possible. ● Set aside. ● Peel and chop the potatoes and add to the chick peas half an hour before the end. ● When the chick peas are on the point of becoming tender, fry the garlic and bread in oil. ● Sweat the cooked spinach in the same oil for a minute or two, then add it to the chick peas. ● Crush the fried bread, garlic and saffron with pestle and mortar. ● Dilute this mixture with a little of the cooking liquid and pour it over the chick peas. ● Season and simmer till ready.

● Soak the beans in cold water for 2 hours. ● Drain. ● Simmer the beans, partridges, peppercorns and bay leaves in salted water for 1 hour. ● When the birds are done take them out and bone them. ● Continue simmering the beans until they are tender. ● Fry the very finely chopped onion with the whole cloves of garlic in the oil. ● When they start to colour mash the garlic cloves and add the paprika and tomato paste. ● Add this fried mixture and the partridge meat to the drained beans along with some of the stock they have cooked in. ● Cook all together for about 15 minutes. ● Season and serve.

Ajo de "mataero"
Pork and pine kernel stew

Pipirrana
Lettuce and dried salt cod salad

For 6 persons

Time: *preparation 15 min. ● cooking 35 min. + time to cool and remove fat.*
Ingredients: *1 lb/500 g pig's liver ● ½ lb/250 g fat (streaky) bacon ● ½ lb/250 g tenderloin of pork (pork fillet) ● scant cup/7 oz/200 g lard ● 6 cloves garlic, chopped ● 1 tablespoon paprika ● 8 cups/2 lb/1 kg fresh breadcrumbs ● 1 cup/¼ lb/100 g pine kernels ● salt ● pepper ● pinch of cinnamon.*

For 4 persons

Time: *preparation 24 hours to soak the cod + 35 min.*
Ingredients: *½ lb/200 g dried salt cod (or salted sardines) ● 1 head lettuce ● 1 cucumber ● 2 fresh hot peppers ● 3 cloves garlic ● 2 ripe tomatoes ● ½ cup/4 fl. oz/1 dl olive oil ● salt ● juice of 1 lemon.*

● Fry the liver, bacon and pork in hot lard in a large pot or deep frying pan. ● Remove from the pan and drain. ● In the same fat sweat the garlic. ● Let it brown, then add the paprika and breadcrumbs. ● Mash half the liver in a mortar (or press through a sieve) and add 2 cups/16 fl. oz/5 dl water. ● Add it to the contents of the pan and mix thoroughly. ● Allow to cool. ● When the fat rises to the surface remove it, and return pan to heat. ● Add pine kernels, the pork, cut into pieces, and the rest of the liver. ● Season with salt, pepper and a pinch of cinnamon and serve when heated through.

● Soak the cod in cold water for 24 hours, changing the water several times. ● Wash the lettuce, cut it in pieces and leave in cold water. ● Peel and slice the cucumber. ● Cut the seeded peppers in strips. ● Crush the garlic and moisten with oil. ● Rinse and drain the soaked cod and remove skin and bones. ● Peel and chop the tomatoes. ● Put all these ingredients in a wide shallow salad bowl. ● Dress with oil, salt and lemon juice. ● Mix thoroughly and serve cold.

Berenjenas a la crema con gambas y jamón
Eggplants au gratin with shrimp (prawns) and ham

Zarangollo
Zucchini (courgette) fantasy

For 4 persons

Time: *preparation 20 min. + 1 hour for the eggplants (aubergines)* ● *cooking 40 min.*
Ingredients: *1 cup/8 fl. oz/2 dl olive oil ● 4 cloves garlic, peeled ● 4 eggplants (aubergines), about ½ lb/250 g each, peeled and cut into thick slices ● flour ● 12 shelled jumbo shrimp (prawns) ● 2 oz/50 g any raw ham cut into strips ● 1 small onion, chopped ● 2 cups/16 fl. oz/5 dl milk ● ¾ cup/6 fl. oz/1.5 dl chicken stock ● salt ● pepper ● ½ cup/2 oz/50 g grated Swiss (Gruyère) cheese.*

For 6 persons

Time: *preparation 10 min. ● cooking 40 min.*
Ingredients: *½ cup/4 fl. oz/1 dl olive oil ● 4 cloves garlic, crushed ● 2 onions, very finely chopped ● 4 lb/2 kg zucchini (courgettes) sliced thinly ● salt ● white pepper ● 1 tablespoon fresh oregano or 1½ teaspoons dried. As an accompaniment: 4 slices fried bread.*

● Put oil in a pan and fry the garlic cloves whole (they are for flavouring only), then take them out. ● Slice the eggplants (aubergines); sprinkle with salt and allow to drain for an hour; then pat dry, dip in flour, and fry in the garlic-flavoured oil. ● Drain. ● Arrange them in layers in a casserole dish and strew jumbo shrimp (prawns) and ham on top. ● Put 4 tablespoons of the frying oil into another pan and fry the chopped onion over a low heat, stirring. ● When it begins to colour add 2 tablespoons flour. ● As soon as this starts to brown gradually mix in the milk and stock, stirring with a wooden spoon all the time till you have a smooth sauce (if it becomes too thick dilute with a little more milk). ● Season. ● Strain the sauce over the eggplants (aubergines) and jumbo shrimp (prawns). ● Sprinkle with the grated cheese and brown in a very hot oven (450°F/mark 7/220°C) for about 10 minutes.

● Heat oil in a heavy saucepan. ● Add garlic. ● Before it begins to colour put in the onions. ● Turn down the heat and cook very gently. ● When the onion starts to soften add the zucchini (courgettes), stir, cover and continue cooking very slowly for about 20 minutes. ● Season with salt, pepper and oregano and cook for some 10 minutes more till all is well done. ● Serve on a dish garnished with the fried bread slices.

Pisto murciano
Vegetable stir-fry Murcian style

Mojete
Onion and sweet pepper hors d'oeuvre

For 6 persons

Time: *preparation 20 min. + 1 hour for the eggplants (aubergines)* ●
cooking 50 min.
Ingredients: *2 lb/1 kg ripe tomatoes ● 1 cup/8 fl. oz/2.5 dl olive oil ●*
2 bay leaves ● salt ● pepper ● 1 tablespoon sugar ● 2 lb/1 kg eggplants
(aubergines) ● flour ● 2 lb/1 kg red and green peppers, chopped ●
2 lb/1 kg onions, chopped.

For 4 persons

Time: *preparation 15 min. ● cooking 30 min.*
Ingredients: *2 lb/1 kg medium-sized onions ● 2 lb/1 kg sweet red*
peppers ● 5 cloves garlic ● 2 teaspoons cumin ● juice of 1 lemon ●
6 tablespoons olive oil ● 3 tablespoons wine vinegar. ● salt ● chopped
parsley.

● Peel the tomatoes, cut in pieces and fry in half the oil with the
bay leaves, salt, pepper and sugar. ● When the tomatoes are
cooked, put through a sieve. ● Cut the eggplants (aubergines)
in slices, sprinkle with salt and allow to drain for an hour. ● Pat
dry, dip in flour and fry in the remaining oil. ● Brown them
well, then transfer them to a flameproof serving dish. ● In the
same oil fry the chopped peppers. ● Arrange them on top of the
eggplants (augergines). ● Fry the finely chopped onions very
slowly in the same oil, not allowing them to colour. ● Add
them to the eggplants and peppers. ● Finally, add the sieved
tomatoes. ● Season, stir, serve very hot.

● Peel the onions. ● Wash and dry the sweet peppers. ● Wrap
the onions in foil. ● Bake them in the oven (350°F/mark 4/
175°C) with the whole peppers and 3 of the garlic cloves for
30 minutes. ● When done unwrap the onions and cut the
onions and peppers into strips. ● In a mortar pound 2
teaspoons cumin, 2 garlic cloves and the garlic from the oven.
● Add lemon juice, oil and vinegar. ● Press the mixture through
a sieve and use the liquid to dress the onion-and-pepper
mixture. ● Sprinkle with salt and serve in an earthenware bowl
and sprinkle with chopped parsley.

Paella valenciana
Valencian paella

"Arròs amb fesols i naps"
Rice with beans, turnips and pork

For 6–8 persons

Time: *preparation 30 min. + 2 hours for soaking beans ● cooking 1 hour.*
Ingredients: *1½ cups/¾ lb/300 g navy (haricot) beans ● 1 chicken weighing 2 lb/1 kg ● 1 lb/500 g rabbit meat ● ⅖ lb/200 g green (French or runner) beans ● 1 green pepper ● 1 cup/8 fl. oz/2.5 dl olive oil ● chopped parsley ● 3 cloves garlic, chopped ● 1 chili pepper, chopped ● 3 ripe tomatoes, peeled and chopped ● 2½ cups/1¼ lb/600 g rice ● ½ teaspoon saffron ● salt ● lemon slices.*

For 4 persons

Time: *preparation 1½ hours + 2 hours to soak the beans ● cooking 20 min.*
Ingredients: *1 cup/½ lb/250 g navy (haricot) beans ● 1 lb/400 g leg of pork or other pig meat ● ⅖ lb/200 g pig's ears ● 1 pig's foot (trotter) ● ¼ lb/100 g fat (streaky) bacon ● 2 blood sausages (black puddings*) ● 2 pork sausages ● 6 small turnips, peeled ● ⅓ teaspoon saffron ● 1½ cups/¾ lb/300 g rice ● salt.*

● Soak the navy (haricot) beans for 2 hours. ● Clean and joint the chicken and rabbit. ● Slice the green beans and chop the pepper. ● Pour the oil into the paella pan (or, failing that, a large frying pan). ● When oil begins to smoke put in chicken and rabbit pieces. ● When they have browned add the pepper, green beans and navy (haricot) beans. ● Fry gently, stirring, for a short while, then add the parsley, garlic, chili pepper and tomatoes. ● Mix, then pour in 1 cup/8 fl. oz /2.5 dl water. ● Bring to a boil and simmer for 15 minutes. ● Add the rice and saffron, and turn the heat up so that the rice cooks rapidly for the first 3 minutes. ● Add salt to taste. ● Turn the heat down again and cook slowly for another 15 minutes. ● Serve in the paella pan or in a large, shallow earthenware bowl. ● Garnish with lemon slices if desired.

● First soak the navy (haricot) beans in cold water for 2 hours. ● Put 13 cups/5½ pints/3 liters cold water in a large saucepan. ● Add the beans, meat, sausages and peeled turnips. ● Simmer very gently for 45 minutes. ● Season. ● Take out the meat and sausages. ● Let them cool slightly, then cut into chunks. ● Add the saffron and rice to the saucepan with the beans and turnips. ● Bring back to the boil and simmer for 15 minutes. Then put the meat and sausages back in the pan. ● There should still be sufficient stock to cover the rice. ● Continue cooking until rice is done.

*See footnote page 8.

Arroz al horno
Baked rice

Arroz a banda
Rice and fish

For 6–8 persons

Time: *preparation 15 min.* ● *cooking 40 min.*
Ingredients: *1 cup/½ lb/200 g lard* ● *2 lb/1 kg potatoes, peeled and sliced* ● *¾ lb/350 g Canadian (back) bacon* ● *1 head garlic, separated into individual cloves and peeled* ● *3 blood sausages (black puddings*), sliced* ● *2 Chorizo** sausages, sliced* ● *⅔ cup/¼ pint/1.5 dl tomato sauce (see p. 187)* ● *2½ cups/1¼ lb/600 g rice* ● *5 cups/2 pints/generous liter heated stock* ● *pinch of saffron* ● *3 ripe tomatoes, peeled and chopped* ● *chopped parsley* ● *salt.*

For 4–6 persons

Time: *preparation 10 min* ● *cooking 20 min. for the stock + 25 min. for the rice.*
Ingredients: *2 lb/1 kg fish or seafood according to choice* ● *salt* ● *1 onion, chopped* ● *1 bay leaf* ● *1 clove garlic* ● *pinch of saffron* ● *½ cup/4 fl. oz/1 dl olive oil* ● *1 teaspoon tomato paste* ● *1 teaspoon paprika* ● *2 cups/1 lb/500 g rice.*

● Melt the lard in a flameproof casserole. ● Add the peeled and sliced potatoes, the bacon, garlic, blood sausages (black puddings), Chorizo sausages and tomato sauce. ● Fry all together, stirring all the while. ● Add the rice. ● Stir again very thoroughly and add the hot stock, saffron, tomatoes and parsley. ● Season. ● Cover and bake in a hot oven (425°F/mark 7/220°C) for 20 minutes, or until rice is cooked and all the liquid is absorbed.

* ** See footnotes page 8.

● Put 5 cups/2 pints/1¼ liters water, salt, fish or seafood, onion and bay leaf in a saucepan. ● Bring to the boil and simmer for about 20 minutes. ● Take out the fish and strain the stock (there should be about 4 cups/1¾ pints/1 liter left). ● Pound the garlic in a mortar with a pinch of salt and the saffron. ● Dilute with a little of the fish stock. ● Heat the oil in a flameproof casserole and add the tomato paste, crushed garlic and paprika. ● Simmer for 3 minutes before adding the washed rice. ● Mix thoroughly. ● Add the boiling fish stock and cook briskly for 5 minutes, then lower the heat and simmer for 15 minutes more, or until rice is cooked and the liquid is absorbed. ● Cover and remove from heat. ● Leave for 5 minutes before bringing to the table.

Paella de caza
Paella with game

Arroz con costra
Rice au gratin

For 4 persons

Time: *preparation 30 min.* • *cooking 1 hour for the stock* + *30 min. for the paella.*
Ingredients: *5 ripe tomatoes* • *5 cloves garlic* • *olive oil* • *1 lb/500 g game (hare, partridge, etc.)* • *salt* • *pinch of paprika* • *1 onion, chopped* • *1 small green pepper, seeded and chopped* • *2 cups/1 lb/400 g rice.*

For 4 persons

Time: *preparation 15 min.* + *12 hours to soak chick peas* • *cooking 2 hours* + *1½ hours for the albondiga* + *35 min. for the rice.*
Ingredients: *For the stock: ¾ cup/¼ lb/100 g chick peas* • *½ lb/250 g veal* • *¼ boiling hen or chicken* • *¼ lb/100 g pig's ears* • *¼ lb/100 g fat (streaky) bacon* • *¼ lb/100 g blood sausage (black pudding*)* • *½ lb/200 g potatoes, peeled and chopped* • *1 parsnip, sliced* • *1 carrot, sliced* • *1 turnip, chopped* • *1 stick celery, quartered* • *2 ripe tomatoes, peeled and chopped* • *4 cloves garlic, peeled* • *paprika* • *pinch of saffron* • *salt. For the albondiga (a sort of large rissole): 1¾ lb/800 g ground (minced) pork* • *1 cup/3 oz/80 g crumbled stale bread* • *1 tablespoon/1½ oz/15 g lard* • *1 tablespoon chopped parsley* • *1 egg* • *1 tablespoon pine kernels* • *salt* • *cinnamon* • *blood of 1 chicken (optional). For the rice: ¼ cup/2 oz/50 g lard* • *2 lb/800 g ripe tomatoes, peeled and cut up* • *2 cups/1 lb/400 g rice* • *chopped parsley* • *8 eggs, beat*

• Peel and chop 2 tomatoes. • Add 4 cloves crushed garlic and fry slowly in a little oil. • Clean and joint the game. • Add to the frying pan and cover with boiling water. • Season. • Simmer for 1 hour. • Strain the cooking juices and keep on one side. • Cut the meat off the bone. • Put a little oil in the paella pan (or a big frying pan). • Sweat the chopped onion, 1 clove crushed garlic and the chopped pepper. • When beginning to colour add the game, stir, and add the remaining 3 tomatoes, peeled and chopped. • Fry, stirring, until the tomatoes are cooked. • Season, then pour in the rice. • When this is thoroughly mixed with the rest cover with 4½ cups/1¾ pints/1 litre of the game stock. • Boil rapidly for 5 minutes, then lower the heat and cook slowly for 15 minutes. • Remove from heat and rest for 3–4 minutes before serving.

• Soak the chick peas for 12 hours. • Put 6 cups/2½ pints/ 1.5 liters water into a saucepan and add the various kinds of meat, the vegetables and all the ingredients for the stock. • Season. • Bring to the boil and cook gently for 2 hours (or 45 minutes in a pressure cooker). • Remove from heat, take the meat out and chop finely. • Set aside. • Meanwhile, prepare the *albondiga* by kneading all the ingredients into a big meat roll. • When the stock is ready, strain into another pan, bring to a boil and cook the *albondiga* in it for 1½ hours. • Drain. • Put the *albondiga*, the chopped-up cooked meat and the stock to one side. • Now prepare the rice. • Put the lard in a flameproof casserole and fry the peeled, chopped tomatoes. • Pour in the rice and chopped parsley, stirring well. • Cover with the stock (there should be twice as much stock as rice). • Put the casserole in the oven (350°F/mark 4/175°C) for 15 minutes, or until rice is cooked and liquid absorbed. • Remove from oven and pour over the beaten eggs mixed with the chopped meat. • Replace in oven for a few minutes to allow the eggs to set and form a crisp crust. • Serve hot with the sliced *albondiga*.

*See footnote page 8.

"Fideuà"
Vermicelli with fish

Dorada a la sal
Salted gilthead

For 6–8 persons

Time: *preparation 20 min.* ● *cooking 1 hour + 30 min. for the fish stock.*
Ingredients: *1 cup/8 fl. oz/2.5 dl olive oil ● 1 lb/500 g saltwater crayfish (scampi) ● 1 lb/500 g shrimp (shrimps), shelled ● salt ● 1 lb/450 g monkfish* ● 1 tablespoon paprika ● 4 cloves garlic, crushed ● 1 cup/8 fl. oz/2.5 dl tomato sauce (see p. 187) ● 7½ cups/3 pints/1.5 liters fish stock (made from boiling the head of the monkfish, or other fish) ● 1¼ lb/600 g vermicelli ● ½ teaspoon saffron ● 4 sprigs parsley, chopped.*

For 4 persons

Time: *preparation 5–6 min.* ● *cooking 20 min.*
Ingredients: *4 giltheads (sea bream or porgy) of about ¾ lb/300 g each (or a larger gilthead weighing 2½ lb/1.25 kg before cleaning) ● 4 cups/2 lb /1 kg coarse or cooking salt (with no additives). As an accompaniment: 1 cup/½ pint/2.5 dl garlic sauce (see p. 187).*

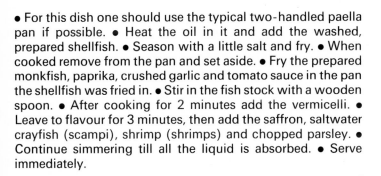

● For this dish one should use the typical two-handled paella pan if possible. ● Heat the oil in it and add the washed, prepared shellfish. ● Season with a little salt and fry. ● When cooked remove from the pan and set aside. ● Fry the prepared monkfish, paprika, crushed garlic and tomato sauce in the pan the shellfish was fried in. ● Stir in the fish stock with a wooden spoon. ● After cooking for 2 minutes add the vermicelli. ● Leave to flavour for 3 minutes, then add the saffron, saltwater crayfish (scampi), shrimp (shrimps) and chopped parsley. ● Continue simmering till all the liquid is absorbed. ● Serve immediately.

*If unavailable, use bluefish.

● Wash the fish but do not gut or scale them. ● Cover the bottom of a large, shallow ovenproof dish with half the salt. ● Lay the fish on it and cover completely with the rest of the salt. ● Place in a hot oven (425°F/mark 7/220°C) for about 20 minutes. ● Clear the salt crust away from the fish and serve it with garlic sauce.

Gazpacho de mero
Grouper gazpacho

"Suc de llobarro"
Sea bass and potato in sauce

For 6 persons

Time: *preparation 20 min.* ● *cooking 1½ hours*
Ingredients: *4 chili peppers* ● *7 cloves garlic* ● *1 cup/8 fl. oz/2 dl olive oil* ● *2 lb/1 kg onions* ● *2 lb/1 kg ripe tomatoes, peeled and chopped* ● *4 bay leaves* ● *salt* ● *pepper* ● *1 head of a grouper or sea bass weighing about 2 lb/1 kg* ● *2 lb/1 kg grouper or sea bass slices* ● *1 cup/¼ lb/100 g toasted almonds* ● *2 large slices stale bread, crumbled.*

For 6 persons

Time: *preparation 15 min.* ● *cooking 25 min.*
Ingredients: *3 lb/1½ kg sea bass* ● *1¼ cups/½ pint/3 dl olive oil* ● *1 head garlic, separated into individual cloves, peeled and chopped* ● *2 chili peppers* ● *1 level tablespoon flour* ● *3 tablespoons paprika* ● *1 lb/500 g potatoes, peeled and sliced* ● *salt.*

● De-seed the chili peppers and put them to soak in some water. ● Put a saucepan containing 9 cups/3½ pints/2 liters water on the heat. ● While waiting for it to boil, sweat 3 sliced garlic cloves in half the olive oil. ● When they begin to colour add half the onions, thinly sliced. ● Fry, stirring, then add the tomatoes, peeled and chopped quite small. ● Fry for 5 minutes, then transfer all to the pan of heating water, plus the bay leaves, salt and pepper. ● Bring to the boil and cook for 30 minutes. ● Add the chopped-up fish head and cook for a further 20 minutes. ● Strain, keeping the stock. ● Drain the chili peppers well and fry in the remaining oil. ● In the same oil lightly brown 2 very finely chopped cloves of garlic, then the rest of the thinly sliced onions. ● Fry gently for 5 minutes. ● Add the slices of fish, cleaned and cut into small pieces, and the flesh obtained from the fish head. ● Continue to simmer for 5 minutes more. ● With pestle and mortar pound the almonds, the last 2 garlic cloves and a pinch of salt. ● Put this pounded mixture, the chili and fish mixture and the stock into a large saucepan. ● Bring to a boil and cook for 10 minutes. ● Add the breadcrumbs and simmer for a further 10 minutes.

● Clean, wash and slice the sea bass. ● Heat the oil in a frying pan. ● Gently fry the chopped garlic and chili peppers till they begin to brown, then add the flour and paprika. ● Stir vigorously, and slowly pour in the water, continuing to stir. ● Add the sliced potatoes. ● When almost done put in the floured slices of sea bass. ● Cook them for just 2 minutes each, sprinkle with salt and serve. ● Arrange so that the sauce does not conceal the slices of fish.

Atascaburras
Dried salt cod with potato and pine kernel sauce

Tiznao
Savoury dried salt cod

For 6 persons

Time: *preparation 15 min + 24 hours to soak the cod ● cooking 25 mins.*
Ingredients: *1 lb/500 g dried salt cod ● 1 lb/500 g potatoes ● 5 cloves garlic ● 2 cups/½ lb/200 g pine kernels ● 2 cups/16 fl. oz/5dl olive oil ● 3 hard-boiled eggs ● 2 cups/½ lb/250 g shelled English walnuts.*

For 4 persons

Time: *preparation 15 min. + 24 hours to soak cod ● cooking 40 min.*
Ingredients: *½ lb/250 g dried salt cod, boned ● olive oil ● 6 onions, chopped ● 1 head garlic, all cloves peeled and chopped ● 2 dried chili peppers ● paprika.*

● Soak the dried salt cod in water for 24 hours, changing the water several times. ● Rinse and drain. ● Boil the peeled potatoes in unsalted water. ● Put the cod in another pan over a low heat. ● When the water begins to boil let the cod simmer until it is tender, about 15 minutes. ● Remove from the water, drain and chop. ● Keep warm. ● When the potatoes are also cooked you are ready for the finishing touches. ● Pound the garlic, pine kernels and potatoes in a mortar. ● Add the oil, fish stock and stock from the potatoes and mix everything thoroughly. ● Add it to the chopped codfish, and garnish with hard-boiled eggs and walnut halves.

● Soak the dried salt cod in water for 24 hours, changing the water several times. ● Rinse and pat dry. ● Cut the cod in pieces and brown it in olive oil along with the chopped onions, garlic and dried peppers. ● When the cod is well browned, remove it from pan, break it up into smaller pieces and then return to the frying pan. ● Place over a very low heat, adding more oil if necessary to keep from sticking. ● Season with a little paprika. ● Stir well, add a minimum of water and bring to the boil. ● Serve.

"All i pebre" de anguilas
Eels in piquant sauce

For 4–6 persons

Time: *preparation 15 min. ● cooking 15–20 min.*
Ingredients: *4 lb/2 kg eels ● salt ● ½ cup/4 fl. oz/1 dl olive oil ● 1 tablespoon paprika ● pinch of saffron ● 3 cloves garlic ● a few sprigs parsley ● 12 toasted blanched almonds.*

● Clean and skin the eels (for instructions see p. 41). ● Cut them in pieces about 1½ in./3–4 cm. long. ● Season. ● Put the oil in a frying pan, and when heated add the paprika. ● Sweat it, being careful not to let it burn. ● Stirring, pour in 3½ cups/ 1¼ pint/7.5 dl hot water. ● Let it boil for a few minutes before adding the sections of eel, which must be covered by the water. ● Simmer gently. ● Add a flavouring mixture made up of saffron, garlic, parsley and almonds, pounded together with pestle and mortar and made into a smooth paste with a few drops of olive oil and then diluted with some of the eel stock. ● Continue cooking until the eels are done, about 15–20 minutes altogether.

Rape al horno
Baked monkfish

For 6 persons

Time: *preparation 12 min. ● cooking 35 min.*
Ingredients: *2½ lb/1.2 kg monkfish* ● 1⅔ cups/¾ pint/4 dl olive oil ● 4 cloves garlic and a sprig of parsley, chopped and mixed together ● 1 chili pepper ● 2 tablespoons flour ● 1 cup/8 fl. oz/2.5 dl tomato sauce (see p. 187) ● 1 tablespoon ground black pepper ● 3½ cups/1¼ pints/7.5 dl fish stock ● ½ lb/250 g shelled peas ● 2 green peppers (baked, peeled and cut into thin strips) ● salt ● chopped parsley.*

● Cut the monkfish into slices about ¾ in./1.5 cm thick. ● Season and flour the slices. ● Heat oil in a frying pan until it is faintly smoking and put in the fish. ● Fry the slices for a minute each, remove and drain. ● Add the chopped garlic and parsley mixture, the chili peppers and 2 tablespoons flour and stir together. ● Add the tomato sauce, black pepper, fish stock, peas, baked green pepper strips and salt. ● Pour into a casserole and place the fish slices on top. ● Put the dish in a hot oven (425°F/mark 7/220°C) for 15 minutes. ● Remove from oven, sprinkle with chopped parsley and serve.
Note: The secrets of success for this recipe are that the fish should not be overcooked and the fish slices should not be covered by the cooking juices.

*If unavailable, use bluefish.

Cordero a la almendra
Lamb with almonds

Pastel di carne
Meat pie

For 4 persons

Time: *preparation 15 min.* ● *cooking 1 hour.*
Ingredients: *a 2 lb/1 kg boned leg of lamb* ● *1 head garlic, all peeled and chopped* ● *½ lb/200 g onions, finely chopped* ● *1 cup/½ lb/250 g lard* ● *flour* ● *½ lb/200 g ripe tomatoes, peeled and chopped* ● *1 small glass brandy* ● *1 glass dry white wine* ● *1 cup/¼ lb/100 g almonds, blanched, toasted and chopped* ● *pinch of saffron* ● *1 tablespoon chopped parsley* ● *pinch of dried thyme* ● *salt* ● *white pepper.*

For 4 persons

Time: *preparation 40 min.* ● *cooking 35 min.*
Ingredients: *For the pastry: 4 cups/1 lb/500 g all-purpose (plain) flour* ● *1 teaspoon salt* ● *4 tablespoons olive oil. For the filling: ¼ lb/100 g Chorizo sausage, sliced* ● *¼ lb /100 g any raw ham* ● *1 calf's brain* ● *a few thin slices veal* ● *2 green peppers, cut in strips* ● *2 tomatoes, peeled and chopped* ● *2 hard-boiled eggs* ● *1 egg, beaten.*

● Cut the lamb into finger-thick slices. ● Sweat the finely chopped garlic and onion in lard in a frying pan. ● Flour the lamb steaks and add them to the pan. ● Brown gently for 10 minutes, turning once. ● Add the tomatoes. ● Moisten with brandy and wine. ● One minute later add 4½ cups/1¾ pints/ 1 liter water. ● When it comes to the boil add a mixture of half the chopped almonds with saffron, chopped parsley and thyme. ● Season. ● Cook till the lamb is tender, about an hour altogether, then add the rest of the almonds. ● Remove from heat and let it rest for a few minutes. ● Serve very hot.

● Pile the flour on to a marble slab and make a hollow in the center. ● Drop the salt, oil and ⅔ cup/¼ pint/1.5 dl water into the hollow. ● First work the ingredients in with a wooden spoon, then, on the marble slab or pastry board, knead by hand to obtain a smooth, homogeneous pastry. ● Roll the pastry out and fold it into quarters. ● Repeat the process several times. ● Roll out finally to a thickness of about ¼ in./ 0.5 cm. ● Divide it into 2 unequal portions, one slightly larger than the other. ● Line a deep pie dish with the larger piece, making sure that the sides are sufficiently high all round. ● Fill it with slices of Chorizo sausage, finely chopped ham and brain, and the slices of veal. ● Next lay the peppers, cut in strips, the sliced tomatoes and the chopped hard-boiled eggs. ● Place the other piece of pastry over the top, pressing the two parts together all round with a fork. ● Brush the surface with beaten egg and bake in a hot oven (400°F/mark 6/200°C) until the pastry is nicely browned (about 35 minutes). ● These ingredients will make a single pie, as described above, or several individual pies baked in small bowls.

Chuletas de cordero al ajo cabañil
Lamb cutlets with garlic

Pimientos rellenos
Stuffed peppers

For 4 persons

Time: *preparation 15 min. ● cooking 30 min.*
Ingredients: *2 lb/1 kg potatoes, peeled and sliced ●*
½ cup/4 fl. oz/1 dl olive oil ● 2 lb/1 kg lamb cutlets ● 1 head garlic ●
4 tablespoons white wine vinegar ● sugar ● salt ● pepper.

For 6 persons

Time: *preparation 25 min. ● cooking 1½ hours.*
Ingredients: *2 onions, finely sliced ● 2 eggplants (aubergines) ●*
¾ cup/6 fl. oz/2 dl olive oil ● 2 lb/1 kg veal ● ¼ lb/100 g fat (streaky)
bacon ● 1 tablespoon brandy ● ½ cup/2 oz/50 g pine kernels ● 2 hard-
boiled eggs ● 2 tomatoes, peeled and sliced ● 1 cup/8 fl. oz/2.5 dl beef
stock ● 2–2½ cups/6–8 fl. oz/150–200 g breadcrumbs ● salt ● pepper ●
paprika ● 12 sweet red peppers.

● Using half the oil, gently fry the sliced potatoes. ● Put the remaining oil in another pan and, when very hot, add the cutlets. ● Fry briskly to brown well on both sides. ● Crush the peeled garlic cloves in a mortar and mix well with the vinegar and ½ cup/4 fl. oz/1 dl water. ● Put one half of this mixture with the frying potatoes and the other with the cutlets. ● Drop a pinch of sugar in both pans. ● Season the cutlets and potatoes and give them both another 10 minutes over a low heat, shaking the two pans occasionally. ● Serve cutlets and potatoes in the same dish.

● Fry the finely sliced onions and chopped eggplants (aubergines) in half the oil. ● Finely chop the veal and bacon and fry them in another pan with the rest of the oil: when brown pour in the brandy and set alight. ● Add the well drained onion and eggplants (aubergines) plus the rest of the oil, the pine kernels, chopped hard-boiled eggs, tomatoes, beef stock, breadcrumbs, salt, pepper and paprika. ● Mix well. ● Slit the peppers longitudinally, remove the seeds, and stuff them with this mixture. ● Bake in a hot oven (400°F/mark 6/205°C) for 1 hour.

Migas ruleras de pastor
Country pie

Duelos y quebrantos
Egg and brain hash

For 6 persons

Time: *preparation 15 min. ● cooking 35 min.*
Ingredients: *2 potatoes, peeled and sliced ● 2 tablespoons/1 oz/ 60 g lard ● 2 cups/½ lb/250 g all-purpose (plain) flour ● salt.*

For 4 persons

Time: *preparation 10 min. + 30 min. for soaking the brains.*
Ingredients: *¼ lb/100 g lamb's brains ● salt ● 1 onion ● ½ bay leaf ● olive oil ● ¼ lb/100 g any raw ham ● ¼ lb/100 g Chorizo sausage* ● ¼ lb/100 g Canadian (back) bacon ● 8 hard-boiled eggs, chopped ● pepper ● chopped parsley.*

● Fry the sliced potato in lard. ● Mix the flour with the salt and water to a fairly loose consistency. ● Beat very thoroughly to eliminate all lumps and spread the dough on to the previously fried potatoes. ● Cook, browning well on both sides.

● Soak the brains in warm water for about 30 minutes. ● Remove membranes, skin and any blood clots. ● Simmer in salted water flavoured with half an onion and the bay leaf segment for 5 minutes. ● Drain and cool, then cut into large pieces or slices and brown lightly in a little oil. ● Cut the ham in strips; finely chop the sausage and bacon. ● Brown them and the other half onion, sliced, over low heat, stirring continuously, till the ham and bacon have shed all their fat. ● Pour this excess fat away. ● Now add the chopped hard-boiled eggs, brains, salt and pepper. ● Mix well. ● Sprinkle with chopped parsley and serve at once.

*See footnote page 8.

Guiso de pavo con albóndigas
Stewed turkey with rissoles

Gazpacho manchego
Gazpacho La Mancha style

For 8–10 persons

Time: *preparation 40 min. ● cooking 3 hours.*
Ingredients: *a turkey weighing about 6½ lb/3 kg ● olive oil ● salt ● 4 lb/2 kg potatoes, peeled ● 2 tomatoes, peeled and chopped ● 4 cloves garlic, chopped ● 2–3 sticks celery, chopped ● 1 tablespoon flaked almonds ● 1 tablespoon pine kernels ● 1 glass dry white wine. For the rissoles: turkey breast and giblets ● ½ lb/200 g ground (minced) pork ● 2 cups/½ lb/250 g breadcrumbs ● fresh turkey blood (optional) ● 1 veal or pork sausage ● 1 tablespoon pine kernels ● chopped parsley ● 1 egg ● salt ● pepper.*

For 6 persons

Time: *preparation 20 min. ● cooking 1 hour.*
Ingredients: *½ lb/250 g hare meat ● ½ lb/250 g rabbit meat ● 1 partridge ● ½ lb/250 g chicken meat ● 2 cups/16 fl. oz/5 dl olive oil ● 1 large onion, chopped ● 1 head garlic, all peeled and chopped ● 1 green pepper, chopped ● 1 sprig thyme ● 2 bay leaves ● salt ● 1 heaped tablespoon paprika ● 8 oz/250 g can of tomatoes ● 2 cups/6 fl. oz/150 g fresh breadcrumbs.*

● Cut the turkey into small pieces, setting aside the breast, giblets and blood. ● Brown the rest of the meat in a little oil and transfer to a large stock pot containing 5–7 quarts/9–10 pints/ 5–6 liters water. ● Season and bring to the boil. ● Simmer for 1½ hours, then add the potatoes, tomatoes, garlic, celery, almonds, chopped pine kernels and white wine. ● Continue cooking for another 1½ hours. ● Meanwhile, prepare the rissoles. ● Chop the turkey breast and giblets and combine with the pork. ● Mix these with the breadcrumbs, turkey blood (if used), sausage meat, pine kernels, chopped parsley, egg, salt and pepper. ● From this mixture form rissoles the size of small bread rolls and add them to the stew, about half an hour before the end. ● Continue cooking over low heat. ● When everything is tender check the seasoning and serve immediately.

● Cut the hare, rabbit, partridge and chicken in pieces. Lightly brown the meat in sizzling oil. ● Add the chopped onion, garlic, pepper, thyme and bay leaves. ● Season. ● When all are browned add the paprika and the canned tomatoes. ● Simmer for 15–20 minutes. ● Add 7½ cups/3 pints/1.5 liter water and cook till the meat is tender, about an hour. ● Transfer the mixture to a *gazpachera* (or a large flameproof casserole). ● Bring contents to the boil. ● Add the breadcrumbs and leave to thicken. ● Adjust seasoning and serve at once.

Estofado de conejo
Rabbit stew

Morteruelo
Hare and chicken hash

For 6 persons

Time: *preparation 15 min.* ● *cooking 2 hours.*
Ingredients: *1 rabbit weighing 4 lb/2 kg, or 2 young rabbits* ●
⅓ cup/3 oz/75 g lard ● *4 cloves garlic, finely chopped* ● *2 onions, sliced* ●
1 large leek, sliced ● *4 ripe tomatoes, peeled and sliced* ● *1 bay leaf* ● *1 sprig
tarragon* ● *1 sprig thyme* ● *1 stick celery* ● *1 liqueur glass brandy* ●
2 cups/16 fl. oz/5 dl white wine ● *½ cup/4 fl. oz/1 dl thin stock* ● *salt* ●
pepper ● *parsley, chopped.* As an accompaniment: *boiled new potatoes.*

For 10 persons

Time: *preparation 25 min.* ● *cooking 3½ hours.*
Ingredients: *1 hare* ● *1 chicken, jointed* ● *1 pig's liver* ● *1 ham or bacon
hock* ● *salt* ● *3 cups/12 oz/300 g breadcrumbs* ● *2 cups/1 lb/500 g lard* ●
cumin ● *paprika* ● *cinnamon* ● *pepper* ● *1 clove, crushed* ● *6 English
walnuts, chopped.*

● Clean the rabbit and cut in small pieces (3–4 to a person). ●
In a frying pan brown the pieces lightly in lard over a brisk
heat. ● Remove and set aside. ● In the same fat sweat the finely
sliced garlic, onion, leek and tomatoes for 4 minutes. ● Add the
bay leaf, tarragon, thyme and chopped celery. ● Return the
rabbit to the casserole, pour in the brandy and set alight. ● Add
the white wine (1 cup/8 fl. oz/2.5 dl) to every 2 lb/1 kg of
rabbit. ● Bring to a rapid boil and reduce the cooking juices by
two-thirds, then add the stock. ● Cover the pan and continue
to simmer gently until cooked, about 2 hours altogether. ●
Season. ● Sprinkle with chopped parsley and serve very hot in
individual bowls. ● Accompany with boiled new potatoes.

● In a saucepan, simmer the hare, chicken, liver and ham or
bacon hock with a little salt for about 3 hours. ● When all are
cooked bone the meat and remove the skin and sinews. ●
Grind (mince) all the meat in a meat grinder (mincer) or
blender and mix with the toasted breadcrumbs. ● Mix with a
bit of the cooking stock to bind. ● Add the lard, cumin, paprika,
cinnamon, pepper and clove. ● Season and let the mixture
thicken over a gentle heat. ● Just before removing it from the
stove add the chopped walnuts.

Hijuelas u orejuelas
Fried honey cakes

Alajú
Nut and honey cake

For 4 persons

Time: *preparation 15 min. ● cooking 20 min.*
Ingredients: *2 cups/½ lb/200 g all-purpose (plain) flour ● 1 egg ● ½ teaspoon cinnamon ● ½ teaspoon grated lemon rind (peel) ● ½ teaspoon grated orange rind (peel) ● 2 tablespoons sugar ● 1 liqueur glass brandy ● 5 tablespoons/2¼ oz/65 g lard ● ½ teaspoon baking powder ● 1 cup/8 fl. oz/2.5 dl sunflower oil. To decorate: sugar ● heated honey.*

For 8 persons

Time: *preparation 10 min. ● cooking 10 min.*
Ingredients: *1 lb/500 g honey ● 2 cups/½ lb/250 g breadcrumbs ● 1½ cups/¾ lb/300 g blanched almonds or English walnuts ● a little orange essence (or grated orange rind (peel)) ● 8 round sheets of rice paper 8 in./20 cm across.*

● Pile the flour on a marble slab or into large mixing bowl; put all the ingredients except the oil into a hollow in the center. ● Mix well together by hand till you have a fairly loose dough. ● Sprinkle with flour, cover and leave to rest for 5 minutes at room temperature. ● Knead lightly. ● Now roll it out to a depth of ¼ in./0.5 cm. ● With a pastry cutter or small knife cut out a number of triangular and diamond-shaped pieces. ● Fry them on both sides in plenty of hot oil, drain and place on a cake rack. ● Sprinkle with sugar. ● At the moment of serving, pour hot honey over the cakes.

● Heat a pan containing the honey. ● Add the breadcrumbs, halved almonds or walnuts, and finally the orange essence or rind (peel). ● Mix thoroughly and cook over a low heat, stirring continuously so that the mixture does not stick to the pan, for about 10 minutes. ● Remove from heat. ● On a circular sheet of rice paper put as much mixture as will make a sort of tart 1 in./2 cm thick in the center, sloping down to nothing at the edges. ● Cover with a second wafer, making sure that the "tart" is completely covered and the edges of the two sheets meet. ● Do the same with the remaining cake mixture and rice paper. ● Leave to cool, cut into slices and serve.

Arrope
Squash in wine must

Buñuelos al aguamiel
Honey syrup fritters

For 6 persons

Time: preparation 15 min. + 3–4 hours for soaking the squash ● cooking 1 hour.
Ingredients: 1 lb/500 g sliced squash (or pumpkin) ● 4½ cups/1¾ pints/1 liter lime-water* ● 3¼ cups/1¼ pints/¾ liter wine must (or black grape juice).

For 4–6 persons

Time: preparation 15 min. + 20 min. for soaking the bread ● cooking 30 min.
Ingredients: 6 cups/1½ lb/750 g fresh breadcrumbs ● 1 cup/8 fl. oz/2.5 dl white wine ● 6 eggs ● ½ cup/4 oz/100 g sugar ● 1 tablespoon cinnamon ● 1 tablespoon grated orange rind (peel) ● juice of 1 lemon ● 4½ cups/1¾ pints/1 liter sunflower oil. For the syrup: 1½ cups/1 lb/500 g honey ● grated rind (peel) of 1 orange ● grated rind (peel) of 1 lemon ● 1 stick cinnamon. To decorate: confectioners' (icing) sugar ● cinnamon.

● Soak the peeled slices of squash or pumpkin in 3¼ cups/1¼ pints/7.5 dl lime-water for 3–4 hours. ● Make a mixture of the wine must or grape juice and the rest of the lime-water. ● Boil until it reaches the right consistency: let a drop of the boiling liquid fall into a glass of cold water; if the drop does not dissolve, the correct point has been attained. ● This will take 45–55 minutes. ● Then add the soaked slices of squash or pumpkin. ● Continue cooking till the squash is tender, another 10–15 minutes, then remove from the heat. ● Allow to cool.

*To prepare lime-water, put 2 or 3 limes, sliced, into 4½ cups/2 pints/ a generous liter cold water and bring to a boil. When the lime slices have sunk to the bottom, remove from heat and leave it to get cold, by which time the water will have become quite clear. Strain through a fine cloth.

● Put the breadcrumbs into a big bowl. ● Cover with wine and leave it to soak for 20 minutes. ● Drain and squeeze thoroughly to get rid of all the wine. ● Beat the eggs together with the sugar, cinnamon, grated orange rind (peel) lemon juice and breadcrumbs. ● Work all these ingredients well together till you have a fairly firm mixture. ● Put the oil in a sufficiently deep pan and when it is really hot, form balls of the mixture with a wooden spoon and drop them in the sizzling oil. ● Brown well. ● Drain on paper towels placed over a cake rack. ● Now make the syrup. ● Heat together the honey, grated orange and lemon rind (peel), cinnamon stick and 4½ cups/1¾ pints/1 liter water. ● When the fritters are well drained lower them into the syrup and simmer over a very low heat for 5 minutes. ● Leave them to cool in the syrup. ● Serve cold, dusted with confectioners' (icing) sugar mixed with cinnamon.

Flores manchegas
Flowers of La Mancha

Frutas en sartén
Honey buds

For 6 persons

Time: *preparation 15 min. ● cooking 20 min.*
Ingredients: *6 eggs ● 4 cups/1 lb/500 g all-purpose (plain) flour ● sunflower oil ● confectioners' (icing) sugar.*

For 4 persons

Time: *preparation 20 min. ● cooking 30 min.*
Ingredients: *1 cup/$\frac{1}{4}$ lb/120 g potato flour* ● $\frac{1}{2}$ cup/3 oz/80 g all-purpose (plain) flour ● 1 egg ● 1 egg yolk ● cinnamon ● 3 tablespoons sugar ● $\frac{1}{2}$ liqueur glass brandy ● $\frac{1}{2}$ teaspoon grated orange rind (peel) ● $\frac{1}{2}$ teaspoon grated lemon rind (peel) ● 3 tablespoons/1$\frac{1}{2}$ oz/40 g lard ● $\frac{1}{2}$ teaspoon baking powder ● 2 cups/16 fl. oz/5 dl sunflower oil ● a few tablespoons honey ● confectioners' (icing) sugar.*

● Beat the eggs well. ● Add 2$\frac{1}{4}$ cups/1 pint/6 dl water. ● Sift the flour into a bowl and gradually stir in the egg mixture. ● Beat until well blended. ● Heat the oil in a large pan and immerse in it a timbale iron—a little flower-shaped cake mould with a long handle. ● When it has become very hot drain it and dip it in the batter, then back into the faintly smoking oil. ● Brown the dough "flower" well, then remove it from the mould and drain it on paper towels (kitchen roll).● Repeat the process till all the dough is used up. ● Sprinkle the "flowers" with confectioners' (icing) sugar.

● Pile the flours on a marble slab or into a large mixing bowl and mix in all the ingredients except the honey, oil and confectioners' (icing) sugar. ● Knead into a fairly loose dough. ● Form into little globes the size of a pea and fry in the hot oil. ● See that the oil does not burn and that the tiny balls are well browned. ● Drain on paper towels (kitchen roll) and sprinkle with a little confectioners' (icing) sugar. ● Put the honey in a copper or stainless steel saucepan and heat, stirring continuously with a wooden spoon. ● Put a few droplets of honey in iced water to prove it crystallizes, if ready remove pan from heat. ● Immerse the little fritters in the honey and then put them all together in a shallow serving bowl to form a sort of tart about 2 in./5 cm deep. ● Cool and serve. ● This delicacy goes very well with sweet wine or liqueurs at the evening meal.

*Available from health food shops.

Turrones de Alicante y Jijona
Nougat from Alicante and Jijona

For 6–8 persons

Time: *preparation 20 min. ● cooking 20–30 min.*
Ingredients: *1 cup/$\frac{3}{4}$ lb/350 g honey ● $\frac{1}{2}$ cup/$\frac{1}{4}$ lb/200 g sugar ● 2 egg whites ● 6 cups/1$\frac{1}{2}$ lb/650 g blanched chopped almonds ● grated rind (peel) of 1 lemon ● rice paper.*

For 6–8 persons

Time: *preparation 30 min. ● cooking 15–25 min.*
Ingredients: *2 cups/$\frac{1}{2}$ lb/230 g blanched almonds ● 2 cups/$\frac{1}{2}$ lb/230 g hazelnuts ● 5 egg whites ● $\frac{2}{3}$ cup/$\frac{1}{2}$ lb/230 g honey ● 1 cup/$\frac{1}{2}$ lb/230 g sugar ● rice paper ● cinnamon ● melted semi-sweet (plain) chocolate (optional) ● English walnut halves (optional).*

Alicante nougat
● Gently heat the honey and 3 tablespoons water in a saucepan till all the water has evaporated. ● Add the sugar, mixing with a wooden spoon, then delicately fold in the egg whites (whisked to a stiff froth) and continue to heat until the honey reaches the right stage of caramelization. ● Then immediately add the chopped almonds and grated lemon rind (peel). ● Stir thoroughly till well blended, then turn the mixture into shallow rectangular moulds lined with rice paper laid over wax (greaseproof) paper. ● Put a second layer of rice paper on top of the nougat and cover it with a suitable wooden board pressed down by weights. ● Cool, slice and serve.

Jijona nougat
● Toast the almonds in the oven. ● Scorch the hazelnuts in a frying pan and remove the skins by rubbing them strenuously together in a cloth. ● Pound both kinds of nut to a fine consistency in a mortar. ● Gently fold in the egg whites beaten to a stiff froth. ● Put the honey and sugar in a saucepan, bring to the boil, then immediately add the nut and egg white mixture. ● Cook for 10 minutes, stirring continuously with a wooden spoon. ● Remove the pan from the heat and pour the nougat mixture into moulds lined as described in previous recipe. ● Cool and sprinkle with powdered cinnamon. ● If desired, cinnamon can be omitted and the coated nougat covered in melted chocolate and decorated with walnut halves.

ANDALUSIA · EXTREMADURA

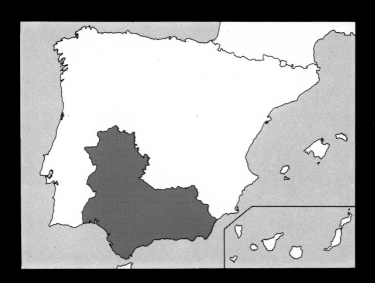

In spite of being geographical neighbours, the cuisines of
Andalusia and Extremadura are quite distinct. However,
they have one extraordinary product in common: "Jamón
serrano," a delicious sort of highland ham prepared from the
meat of a very special breed of pigs. The three capitals of the
areas producing this incomparable ham are Trevélez and
Jabugo in Andalusia, and Montánchez in Extremadura.

Andalusia. Gazpacho, the excellent cold soup prepared in
various ways, represents, together with paella, the dish for
which Spanish cookery is best known abroad. But it is not
Andalusia's only speciality. There are also "Berza andaluza,"
based on pork and vegetables, "eggs à la flamenca," oxtail,
goat kid fried with garlic, and numerous fish dishes from
baked pargo to fish mousse, from "Monkfish Pedro
Ximénez" to "Tortillitas de camarones," little shrimp
(prawn) fritters. The cooks of Andalusia know how to fry
fish like no other cooks in Spain, fish that go so well with
Spain's masterpiece of oenology: sherry.

Extremadura. This is a land of monasteries that once
produced an important cuisine, now forgotten. It is still
possible, however, to find, all over the region, dishes that
excel in their simplicity, such as *Caldereta* (lamb stew),
"Pies de cerdo al pan" (pig's feet (trotters) in breadcrumbs)
and various kinds of pork sausage.

Gazpacho andaluz
Andalusian gazpacho

Menestra de acelgas a la extremeña
Extremaduran Swiss chard timbale

For 4 persons

Time: *preparation 20 min. + 2–3 hours to chill.*
Ingredients: *1 onion* ● *1 small green pepper, seeded* ● $\frac{1}{2}$ *cucumber* ●
1 clove garlic ● *4 ripe tomatoes, peeled* ● *1 teaspoon salt* ● *1 teaspoon
paprika* ● $\frac{1}{2}$ *cup/2 oz/50 g breadcrumbs soaked in water and squeezed
out* ● $\frac{3}{4}$ *cup/6 fl. oz/2 dl olive oil* ● $\frac{1}{3}$ *cup/3 fl. oz/1 dl wine vinegar* ●
$\frac{1}{2}$ *teaspoon pepper (optional).* As an accompaniment: *bread* ● *onion,
tomatoes, cucumber and peppers chopped small and served separately, or
hard-boiled eggs and sliced ham.*

For 6 persons

Time: *preparation 12 min.* ● *cooking 1 hour.*
Ingredients: *1$\frac{1}{2}$ lb/750 g potatoes* ● *1 large onion, sliced* ●
2 cups/16 fl. oz/5 dl olive oil ● *1$\frac{1}{2}$ lb/750 g Swiss chard* ●
$\frac{1}{4}$ *lb/100 g Chorizo sausage* any raw ham* ● *2 cloves garlic, chopped* ●
chopped parsley ● *salt* ● *paprika* ● *3 eggs.*

● Pound all the ingredients, or put through a vegetable mill or
sieve, to procure a smooth mixture. ● If too thick, dilute with a
little water. ● Place in the refrigerator for a few hours. ● When
ready to serve, put bread slices, chopped onion, tomatoes,
pepper and cucumber in the individual soup bowls. ● Or the
gazpacho can be accompanied by hard-boiled eggs and finely
sliced ham.

● Peel the potatoes, cut in pieces and season. ● Fry together
with half the sliced onion in a little olive oil. ● Turn them over
now and again with a wooden spatula. ● Wash and cut up
the Swiss chard. ● Cook till tender, drain and set aside. ●
Sweat the rest of the onion in a frying pan with the rest of
the oil. ● Add the Swiss chard and fry gently for a few
minutes with the onion. ● Add the potato, the rest of the onion
and the chopped Chorizo sausage or raw ham. ● Mix well
together, add the chopped garlic, parsley, salt and paprika
diluted with a little water, and cook all for some minutes. ●
Transfer to an earthenware casserole, stirring lightly about
with a wooden spatula. ● Beat the eggs and pour over the
mixture. ● Put the casserole into a hot oven (450°F/mark 8/
230°C) until the eggs have set and formed a crisp crust.

* See footnote page 8.

Berza andaluza*
Andalusian pork and vegetables

Sopa de picadillo
Ham and egg soup

For 4 persons

Time: *preparation 15 min. + 12 hours for soaking chick peas ● cooking 2–3 hours.*
Ingredients: *1 cup/½ lb/250 g chick peas ● 1 lb/500 g green (French or runner) beans ● 1 stick celery ● 1 tablespoon paprika ● 2 pig's feet (trotters), split in half ● 1 pig's tail ● ½ lb/250 g fat (streaky) bacon ● salt ● ½ lb/200 g blood sausage (black pudding)** ● 1 cup/½ lb/200 g shelled peas ● 4 small globe artichokes or cardoons.*

For 4 persons

Time: *preparation 10 min. + 12 hours to soak chick peas ● cooking 3½ hours.*
Ingredients: *For the stock: ½ lb/250 g chick peas ● 2 raw ham bones or 1 gammon hock ● 2 lb/1 kg veal or beef bones ● 3 carrots ● 2 sticks celery ● 3 leeks ● ½ boiling chicken ● ¾ lb/300 g whole peeled potatoes. For the soup: ¾ cup/6 oz/150 g rice ● ¼ lb/100 g any raw ham ● 2 hard-boiled eggs ● sprig of mint.*

● Soak the chick peas overnight. ● Next day drain them and put in a saucepan with the well washed and sliced green beans, the artichokes or cardoons without the fibres and prickles, the celery, paprika, halved pig's feet (trotters), pig's tail, bacon and a little salt. ● Cover with cold water and cook for 2–3 hours, stirring occasionally. ● Ten minutes before serving add the blood sausage (black pudding) and peas and check the seasoning. ● (If a pressure cooker is used, cooking time will be reduced to 30 minutes. ● After that time open the cooker and simmer for a while till the stock is reduced by half and all the ingredients are tender.)

*Berza is a typical Andalusian dish made with the vegetables listed above or with other vegetables in season.
**See footnote page 8.

● Soak chick peas overnight. ● Rinse and drain. ● Put all the ingredients for the stock into a large saucepan and cover with water. ● Cook for 2 or 3 hours to produce a really good stock. ● Remove chicken from the bone and grind up (mince). ● Set aside. ● Strain the stock. ● For the soup: add the rice and finely chopped raw ham to the stock. ● Bring to a boil and simmer for 15 minutes. ● When about to pour into the tureen add the chopped chicken, chopped hard-boiled eggs and a sprig of mint.

Salmorejo con huevos
Tomato soup with egg and ham

Alcachofas a la montillana
Artichokes with Montilla wine

For 4 persons

Time: *preparation 10 min.*
Ingredients: *1½ lb/750 g stale bread with the crusts removed ●*
⅔ cup/¼ pint/1.5 dl olive oil ● 1 lb/500 g ripe tomatoes, peeled ● 2 cloves
garlic ● salt ● wine vinegar. As an accompaniment: 2 hard-boiled eggs ●
¼ lb/100 g any raw ham.

For 6 persons

Time: *preparation 15 min. ● cooking 40 min.*
Ingredients: *4 lb/2 kg globe artichokes ● 6 lemons ● 4 tablespoons flour ●*
salt ● 4 cloves garlic, chopped ● ½ cup/4 fl. oz/1 dl olive oil ● 1 sprig mint,
chopped ● 1 cup/8 fl. oz/2.5 dl Montilla wine (or other dry white wine) ●
½ lb/200 g roast pork ● pinch of saffron ● 2 cups/16 fl. oz/5 dl meat sauce.

● Soak the bread in water and squeeze as dry as possible. ● Put in a blender with the other ingredients and blend to a smooth, homogeneous mixture. ● Add as much iced water as needed to give it the desired consistency. ● Serve cold with pieces of hard-boiled egg and ham.

● Trim the artichokes, leaving only the hearts. ● Rub them with half a lemon and cook in water to which the juice from all the lemons has been added, along with 2 tablespoons flour and a little salt. ● When tender plunge into cold water to cool and set aside. ● Sweat the chopped garlic in a frying pan with oil and fry the drained artichokes. ● Add 2 tablespoons flour and blend well. ● Then, slowly, add the mint, a little salt, the white wine, the pork cut into strips, saffron and the meat sauce, stirring all the while. ● Bring to boil and cook for about 10 minutes. ● Check the seasoning before serving.

Cazuela de espárragos trigueros
Casserole of wild asparagus

Huevos a la flamenca
Eggs à la Flamenca

For 4 persons

Time: *preparation 10 min. ● cooking 15 min.*
Ingredients: *2 lb/1 kg wild asparagus (or garden variety) ● salt ● 1 slice bread ● 4 cloves garlic, crushed ● 4 tablespoons olive oil ● 1 tablespoon paprika ● 4 tablespoons wine vinegar ● 1 egg.*

For 4 persons

Time: *preparation 15 min. ● cooking 15 min. + 5 min. in oven.*
Ingredients: *3 cloves garlic ● 1 large onion ● olive oil ● $\frac{1}{2}$ lb/200 g peas (shelled) ● $\frac{1}{2}$ lb/200 g lima or broad beans ● $\frac{1}{2}$ lb/200 g green (French or runner) beans ● $\frac{1}{2}$ lb/200 g carrots ● $\frac{1}{2}$ lb/200 g globe artichoke hearts ● 4 tablespoons tomato sauce (see p. 187) ● salt ● 8 eggs ● 8 slices any raw ham ● 8 slices cooked Chorizo sausage*.*

● Trim the asparagus and boil gently in salted water for only a few minutes. ● Drain and set aside. ● Fry bread and crushed garlic in oil. ● Pound together in a mortar. ● Add the paprika and vinegar and mix well. ● Put into an earthenware casserole with the asparagus and stir. ● Break an egg on top and heat in a hot oven (425°F/mark 7/220°C) for 5 minutes, until egg is set.

● Chop the garlic and onion. ● Sweat in oil in a large pan. ● Add the peas, lima or broad beans, green beans, sliced carrots and quartered artichoke hearts. ● Fry, stirring, for about 3 minutes. ● Add the tomato sauce and cook gently for 13 minutes. ● Divide into 4 individual ovenproof dishes. ● Sprinkle with salt. ● Break 2 whole eggs on top of each one and arrange 2 slices ham and 2 slices sausage all round. ● Bake in a very hot oven (450°F/mark 8/230°C) for 5–6 minutes so that the eggs set hard.

*See footnote page 8.

Huevos a la extremeña
Eggs à l'Extremadura

Urta a la roteña
Baked pargo

For 4 persons

Time: *preparation 10 min. ● cooking 50 min.*
Ingredients: *8 eggs ● 4 large green peppers, halved and seeded ●*
2 onions ● ¼ cup/2 oz/60 g lard ● 3 tablespoons flour ●
1 cup/8 fl. oz/2 dl milk ● salt ● pepper ● 1 tablespoon paprika ●
1 tablespoon/½ oz/15 g butter ● chopped parsley ● 1 tomato, peeled,
seeded and cut in strips.

For 4 persons

Time: *preparation 25 min. ● cooking 1 hour.*
Ingredients: *olive oil ● 4 cloves garlic ● 2 large onions ● 3 green peppers,*
seeded and sliced ● 4 ripe tomatoes, peeled and chopped ● salt ● pepper ●
pinch of nutmeg ● 2 bay leaves ● 1 pargo* weighing about 3 lb/1.3 kg,
cleaned and filleted ● flour ● ½ lb/250 g new potatoes.

● Simmer the eggs in water for 12 minutes. ● Cool, shell and slice. ● Put the eggs in an earthenware casserole interspersed with the halved peppers. ● Put aside in a warm place. ● Slice the onions in rings; fry lightly in a frying pan with lard. ● Add the flour, stir for a minute or so, then slowly add the milk, stirring all the while. ● Season, and add the paprika. ● Remove from heat and add the butter. ● Stir once more and add, spoonful by spoonful, to the eggs and peppers. ● Bake the casserole in a moderate oven (350°F/mark 4/175°C) for 10 minutes. ● Sprinkle with chopped parsley and garnish with tomato strips. ● Serve at once.

● First make the sauce. ● Put into a saucepan 2 tablespoons olive oil, the garlic, 1 onion sliced in thin rings and the peppers cut in strips. ● Sweat thoroughly, taking care that the onion does not brown. ● Add the chopped tomatoes and season with salt, pepper and a pinch of nutmeg. ● Add bay leaves. ● Cook gently till well done, about 30 minutes. ● Strain the sauce. ● Grease a flameproof casserole with a little oil and add the other onion, cut into julienne strips. ● Fry lightly so that it does not colour. ● Lay the floured fish fillets on top and cover with the strained sauce. ● Add the potatoes. ● Place in a moderate oven (350°F/mark 4/175°C) and cook until fish becomes tender, about 30 minutes.

* Pargo is a kind of snapper. If unavailable, use red snapper or sea bream.

Soldaditos de Pavía
Little soldiers of Pavia

Rape al Pedro Ximénez
Monkfish Pedro Ximénez

For 4 persons

Time: *preparation 1 hour + 24 hours for soaking the dried salt cod ● cooking 20 min.*
Ingredients: *1 lb/500 g dried salt cod (the front part) ● juice of 1 lemon ● 1 teaspoon paprika ● pepper ● 2 tablespoons olive oil ● 1 cup/¼ lb/100 g all-purpose (plain) flour ● pinch of saffron ● ½ small glass cooking brandy ● salt ● 1½ teaspoon baking powder ● oil for frying. Accompanied by: ½ lb/250 g green (French or runner) beans ● potatoes.*

For 4 persons

Time: *preparation 10 min. ● cooking 20–30 min.*
Ingredients: *1¾ lb/800 g monkfish* ● 1 onion, chopped ● ½ cup/4 fl. oz/1 dl olive oil ● ½ cup/2 oz/50 g raisins ● ½ cup/4 fl. oz/1 dl Pedro Ximénez (or other) sweet sherry ● salt ● ½ cup/4 fl. oz/1 dl fish stock ● ½ cup/4 fl. oz/1 dl asparagus stock.*

● Cut the dried salt cod into small pieces about 1 in./2 cm wide and 2 in./5–6 cm long. ● Soak in cold water for 24 hours, changing the water 2 or 3 times. ● Then drain the fish pieces, dry, and cut in half lengthwise. ● Make a dressing from the lemon juice, paprika, pepper and 1 tablespoon oil. ● Soak the fish "fingers" in it while you make the batter. ● Pile the sifted flour on to a marble slab or in a large bowl and make a well in the center. ● Into this hollow drop 1 tablespoon oil, the saffron, brandy, salt and baking powder. ● Mix the ingredients well, gradually adding enough water to make a thinnish batter. ● Let it rest for about an hour. ● When the batter is ready dip the fish pieces in it one by one, making sure they are evenly covered. ● Fry in boiling oil until they are well browned all over. ● Serve with green beans and boiled potatoes.

● Slice the monkfish. ● In frying pan lightly fry the chopped onion in oil. ● When it begins to colour add the slices of fish and the raisins. ● When the fish is browned, moisten it with the sherry, then season and add the fish and asparagus stocks. ● Cook gently for 15 more minutes.

* If unavailable, use bluefish.

Molde de pescadilla
Fish mould

Caballa asada a la gaditana
Mackerel Gaditana style

For 4–6 persons

Time: *preparation 10 min.* ● *cooking 1¼ hours.*
Ingredients: *2 bay leaves* ● *1 onion* ● *4 cloves* ● *salt* ● *1½ lb/600 g fish (cod, monkfish, salmon, etc.)* ● *½ lb/250 g jumbo shrimp (prawns)* ● *1½ cup/12 fl. oz/3.5 dl milk* ● *1 cup/¼ lb/100 g breadcrumbs* ● *1 pint/1 lb/500 g mussels, scrubbed* ● *pepper* ● *nutmeg* ● *3 egg whites* ● *1 tablespoon/½ oz/15 g butter* ● *1 cup/8 fl. oz/2.5 dl mayonnaise* ● *2 tablespoons tomato paste.*

For 1 person

Time: *preparation 15 min.* ● *cooking 10 min.*
Ingredients: *½ lb/250 g mackerel* ● *olive oil* ● *2 tomatoes, peeled and chopped* ● *1 onion, chopped* ● *1 green pepper, seeded and chopped* ● *vinegar* ● *salt* ● *pepper.*

● Heat 4½ cups/1¾ pints/1 liter water in a saucepan together with the bay leaves, the onion stuck with 4 cloves, and salt. ● When it comes to the boil add the cleaned fish. ● After 5 minutes put in the jumbo shrimp (prawns). ● When both are cooked drain them and leave to cool (the stock can be used in a fish soup). ● Boil the milk and pour over the breadcrumbs. ● Put the cleaned mussels in a large saucepan with a little water, cover and bring to the boil. ● Remove from pot when shells have opened. ● Leave to cool. ● Free the fish of skin and bones. ● Put aside half the shrimp (prawns) for garnishing. ● Remove the mussels from their shells and chop up with the fish. ● Squeeze the milk out of the breadcrumbs and mix the latter with the fish. ● Check the salt content and season with pepper and nutmeg. ● Whip the egg whites to a stiff froth and fold in. ● Grease a rectangular mould or loaf tin with a little butter and line the bottom with wax (greaseproof) paper. ● Turn the mixture into the mould and cook in a bain-marie in a gentle oven (350°F/mark 2/150°C) for 40–50 minutes. ● Let it cool before turning out. ● When the mould has cooled cover with mayonnaise mixed with tomato paste. ● Garnish to taste.

● Clean, wash and season fish. ● Brush with oil and bake—if possible over a charcoal grill, otherwise in the broiler (under the grill). ● When cooked place on a serving plate accompanied by a mixture of the chopped tomatoes, onion, green pepper and some extra slices of tomato. ● Dress on the plate with oil, vinegar, salt and pepper.

Tortillitas de camarones
Shrimp (prawn) fritters

Bacalao monacal
Dried salt cod with spinach and potatoes

For 6 persons

Time: *preparation 15 min. + 3 hours for the batter to rest ● cooking 25 min.*
Ingredients: *¾ lb/300 g onions or shallots, finely chopped ● large bunch parsley, chopped ● 1 pint/¾ lb/300 g shelled jumbo shrimp (prawns) ● salt ● 3 cups/¾ lb/300 g all-purpose (plain) flour ● 1 cup/¼ lb/100 g chick pea flour* ● olive oil.*

For 4 persons

Time: *preparation 20 min. + 24 hours for soaking the cod ● cooking 1 hour.*
Ingredients: *2 lb/800 g dried salt cod (the front part), cut into 4 ● 1 lb/400 g spinach ● salt ● 4 cloves garlic ● 1¾ cups/¾ pint/4 dl olive oil ● 1 tablespoon milk ● ¾ lb/300 g potatoes ● 2 tablespoons flour ● 2 tablespoons stock.*

● In a saucepan mix the chopped onion and parsley with the chopped shrimp (prawns), salt and flour plus enough water to obtain a batter of the right consistency, neither too thick nor too thin. ● Let it rest for 3 hours before frying. ● Heat oil in a pan to a temperature of (320°F/160°C), then drop in the batter spoonful by spoonful. ● When the fritters are brown on one side turn them over with a fish slice or spatula to brown the other. ● Remove when crisp, drain and serve immediately.

*If unavailable, use potato flour, which is available from health food shops.

● Soak the dried salt cod for 24 hours, changing the water several times. ● Rinse, drain and dry. ● Pick over the spinach and wash it several times in running water. ● Cook in a little salted water for about 10 minutes, then drain thoroughly. ● Peel the garlic. ● Pound it vigorously in a mortar with some salt and a few drops of oil. ● Dilute with milk. ● Peel the potatoes and cut into thinnish slices. ● Season and fry in 1 cup/8 fl. oz/ 2 dl of the oil. ● Flour the 4 pieces of cod and fry them in the remaining oil. ● Put the potatoes in a flameproof casserole. ● Arrange the cod on top and pour over the oil in which the fish was fried, then the stock. ● Give the spinach a quick stir-fry in the same oil in which the potatoes were fried and add it to the casserole. ● Cover all with the pounded garlic mixture. ● Place in a moderate oven (350°F/mark 4/175°C) for 10 minutes to finish cooking.

Cordero en caldereta
Lamb casserole

Riñones a la jerezana
Kidneys in sherry sauce

For 4 persons

Time: *preparation 15 min. ● cooking 1 hour.*
Ingredients: *2 onions ● 3 cloves garlic ● parsley ● $\frac{1}{4}$ lb/100 g any raw ham ● 1 bay leaf ● 2 green peppers ● 2 lb/1 kg boned lamb in pieces ● 1 glass red wine ● $\frac{1}{2}$ cup/4 fl. oz/1 dl olive oil ● 1 teaspoon flour ● salt ● pepper.*

For 2 persons

Time: *preparation 15 min. ● cooking 20 min.*
Ingredients: *1 veal kidney (or 6 lamb kidneys) ● $\frac{1}{4}$ cup/2 oz/50 g lard ● 2 cloves garlic ● 1 slice bread ● 1 onion, chopped ● 2 teaspoons chopped parsley ● pepper ● $\frac{1}{2}$ glass sherry ● salt.*

● Chop the onions, garlic, parsley, ham, bay leaf and green peppers. ● Put a third of this mixture in a stewing pot or similar. ● Cover with a layer of lamb, then with another layer of the chopped ham and herbs, another layer of lamb and a final layer of ham and herbs. ● Pour in the wine, $\frac{1}{2}$ cup/4 fl. oz/1 dl water and olive oil. ● Cover and simmer until the meat is tender, about 1 hour. ● Moisten the toasted flour with a little of the meat stock, blend and add to the lamb stew. ● Season with salt and pepper. ● Leave on the heat for a minute to flavour and then serve.

● Clean the kidney and slice rather thinly. ● Scald in boiling water to eliminate the somewhat pungent smell. ● Put lard in a frying pan and when it is very hot fry half the kidney slices with 1 clove garlic and the slice of bread. ● When cooked remove the contents from the pan and put them in a mortar. ● In the same pan put the remaining kidney slices, the onion, 1 teaspoon parsley, the remaining garlic clove, finely chopped, the pepper and the sherry. ● Simmer, adding a glass of water and the salt. ● Pound the ingredients left in the mortar to a paste and dilute with a little water before pouring them over the kidneys in the pan. ● Check the seasoning. ● Continue cooking over a low heat till the kidney is tender and the sauce has thickened. ● Sprinkle with the rest of the chopped parsley and serve at once.

Jamón al jerez
Ham with sherry

Rabos de toro
Oxtail

For 4 persons

Time: *preparation 5 min. ● cooking 5 min.*
Ingredients: *8 slices any raw ham, each about 2 oz/50–60 g ●*
½ cup/4 fl. oz/1 dl sherry ● 1 cup/8 fl. oz/2.5 dl light beef stock ● 1 teaspoon
cornstarch (cornflour) ● 1 tablespoon caramel sauce (see p. 187). To
garnish: potato purée ● parsley.

For 6 persons

Time: *preparation 15 min. ● cooking 1 hour in pressure cooker + 2 hours'*
rest + 15 min. to heat up.
Ingredients: *4 lb/2 kg onions ● 1 cup/8 fl. oz/2.5 dl olive oil ●*
6 lb/3 kg oxtail ● 6 ripe tomatoes, peeled and chopped ● 8 cloves garlic,
chopped ● pinch of saffron ● 2 lb/1 kg carrots, sliced ● salt ● pepper ●
3 cups/1½ pints/¾ liter Montilla, Moriles or other white wine. As an
accompaniment: fried potatoes.

● Arrange the slices of ham in a fireproof dish, moisten with the sherry, cover with buttered aluminum foil or greaseproof paper and put in a very hot oven (450°F/mark 8/230°C) for 1 minute. ● Pour off the sherry and let it cool while keeping the ham warm. ● Heat the beef stock, meanwhile dissolving the cornstarch (cornflour) in the cold sherry and blending it with the stock. ● Let it boil for 1 minute. ● Add a tablespoon of caramel sauce and pour the whole over ham slices arranged on a serving dish. ● Garnish with whirls of potato purée and a few sprigs of parsley.

● Peel and slice onions thinly. ● Fry in the oil, drain and set aside. ● Remove the fat from the oxtail, and put it in a pressure cooker. ● Add the fried sliced onion, the chopped tomatoes garlic, saffron, carrots, salt and pepper. ● Heat the oxtail in the cooker without the lid for 15 minutes, stirring often so that it is browned all over. ● Add the wine and put on the lid. ● Seal. ● When steam begins to emerge lower the heat and cook gently for 45 minutes. ● After that let the oxtail rest for 2 hours. ● When nearly time to serve arrange it in an ovenproof dish together with fried potatoes and heat in a moderate oven (350°F/mark 4/175°C) for about 15 minutes.

Fritada de cabrito con ajos tiernos
Fried kid with garlic

Caldereta extremeña
Lamb Extremaduran style

For 6 persons

Time: *preparation 15 min.* ● *cooking 30 min.*
Ingredients: *3¼ cups/1¼ pints/7.5 dl olive oil* ● *3 lb/1.5 kg kid meat** ● *1 lb/500 g garlic cloves* ● *salt.*

For 6 persons

Time: *preparation 15 min.* ● *cooking 1 hour.*
Ingredients: *3 lb/1½ kg lamb, boned* ● *salt* ● *½ cup/4 fl. oz/1 dl olive oil* ● *4 cloves garlic, peeled* ● *1 lamb's liver* ● *½ lb/200 g onions, chopped* ● *1 carrot, chopped* ● *1 bay leaf* ● *1 tablespoon paprika* ● *2 cups/¾ pint/5 dl dry white wine* ● *1 tablespoon flour* ● *2 cups/16 fl. oz/5 dl beef stock* ● *4 peppercorns* ● *1 fleshy sweet red pepper* ● *chopped parsley.*

● Put the oil in a large pan and set on the heat. ● When the oil faintly smokes add the jointed kid meat. ● Brown evenly and season. ● When the meat is done, after about 30 minutes, add the peeled cloves of garlic. ● Stir well, season and serve after 3 minutes.

*A kid is a young male goat. Lamb may be used as a substitute.

● Cut the lamb into small pieces and season. ● Put oil in a cast iron pot and heat. ● Fry the whole cloves of garlic. ● When browned take them out and put on one side. ● Now put the lamb and liver in the pot. ● Sauté briskly, stirring till all are browned. ● Remove the liver and set aside. ● Add the chopped onions, carrot and bay leaf. ● Fry gently. ● Sprinkle with the paprika. ● Pour in the wine and turn the meat round and round in it until the wine has evaporated. ● Add the flour and fry gently with the lamb. ● Pour on the stock, stirring constantly to blend. ● Cook for 45 minutes. ● In a mortar crush the garlic set aside earlier, the peppercorns, a little oil and the sweet pepper seeded and cut in pieces. ● To the resulting mixture add the fried liver. ● Mash and stir till you have a fine, smooth sauce. ● Dilute with a little of the cooking stock. ● Pour this sauce over the lamb and cook for another 10 minutes. ● Sprinkle with parsley and serve.

Pierna de cabrito al estilo de Badajoz
Kid à la Badajoz

Pies de cerdo al pan
Pig's feet (trotters) in breadcrumbs

For 4 persons

Time: *preparation 10 min.* ● *cooking 1 hour.*
Ingredients: *3 cloves garlic* ● *2 or 3 legs of kid** ● *salt* ●
⅓ cup/3 oz/80 g lard ● *1 glass white wine.* As an accompaniment: *roast new potatoes.*

For 4 persons

Time: *preparation 12 min. + 12 hours for the pig's feet (trotters)* ● *cooking 5 hours.*
Ingredients: *4 pig's feet (trotters)* ● *bouquet garni* ● *1 onion stuck with 2 cloves* ● *1 cup/8 fl. oz/2.5 dl dry white wine* ● *salt* ●
¼ lb/2 oz/50 g butter ● *pepper* ● *½ cup/2 oz/60 g dry breadcrumbs.* As an accompaniment: *mashed potatoes* ● *sprigs of parsley.*

● Peel the garlic cloves, cutting in strips if large, leaving whole if small. ● Make little incisions in the meat and insert the garlic with the help of a pointed knife. ● Sprinkle the meat with salt and place in a large roasting pan. ● Cover with lard and place in a hot oven (425°F/mark 7/220°C). ● When brown on both sides pour the white wine over. ● Roast for about an hour, basting the meat occasionally with the cooking juices. ● When ready arrange on a serving dish and surround with roast new potatoes.

*A kid is a young male goat. Lamb may be used as a substitute.

● Carefully wash and dry the pig's feet (trotters). ● Singe them if necessary and cut in half lengthwise. ● Prepare a clear stock with 6½ cups/2½ pints/1.5 liters water, the bouquet garni, onion with cloves, wine and a little salt. ● Simmer the feet in this for 4½ hours. ● Remove them from the stock, drain, dry and press between two boards with a weight on top. ● Leave them there for 12 hours. ● At the end of that time melt the butter over a high heat and dip the pig's feet in it. ● Then cover them in pepper and breadcrumbs, making sure that they are evenly coated. ● Grease and heat the broiler (grill) and place the pig's feet under it. ● Brown well on both sides and serve at once, accompanied by mashed potatoes and garnished with sprigs of parsley.

Pepitoria de gallina
Chicken fricassee

Pato a la sevillana
Seville duck

For 4–6 persons

Time: *preparation 15 min.* ● *cooking 1½ hours.*
Ingredients: *1 oven-ready chicken weighing about 3 lb/1½ kg ● salt ● pepper ● flour ● olive oil ● 1 onion, finely chopped ● 1 glass dry white wine ● 1 bay leaf ● sprig of parsley ● 12 blanched almonds, chopped ● 1 clove garlic, crushed ● 2 hard-boiled egg yolks ● 1 raw egg yolk ● 1 cup/ 8 fl. oz/2.5 dl chicken stock.*

For 4–5 persons

Time: *preparation 15 min.* ● *cooking 1¼ hours.*
Ingredients: *¾ lb/400 g green olives ● 1 glass dry white wine ● ¼ cup/2 oz/50 g lard ● ¾ cup/6 oz/150 g fat (streaky) bacon cut in pieces ● 1 duck weighing 4 lb/1.8 kg, cleaned, trussed and dusted with pepper inside ● bouquet garni ● ½ lb/200 g onions, chopped ● 3 medium carrots, chopped ● ½ lb/200 g large ripe tomatoes, peeled and sliced ● 2 cloves garlic, chopped ● a few peppercorns ● 2 cloves ● 1 glass sherry ● 1 cup/8 fl. oz/2.5 dl hot chicken stock ● 1 glass white wine. As an accompaniment: fried potatoes ● strips of sweet red pepper.*

● Joint the chicken. ● Season, coat with flour and brown in oil. ● Drain and transfer to a flameproof casserole. ● In the same oil fry the finely chopped onion. ● When it begins to colour put with the pieces of fowl. ● Pour the wine over the chicken plus enough water to cover, add bay leaf and a sprig of parsley. ● Cover, bring to a boil and simmer for about 45 minutes, till the meat is well done. ● Meanwhile prepare a mixture of the chopped almonds, crushed garlic and hard-boiled egg yolks. ● Pound in a mortar until smooth, then moisten with the raw yolk and the hot stock. ● Add this sauce to the fowl and leave to cook a few more minutes. ● Serve very hot.

● Stone the olives and cook in a glass of white wine for 8 minutes. ● Drain and reserve. ● Heat the lard and bacon in a large pan. ● When the fat is hot put in the duck. ● Brown on all sides. ● Add the bouquet garni, onions, carrots, tomatoes, garlic, peppercorns and cloves. ● Cover and fry gently for a few minutes. ● Put in a moderate oven (350°F/mark 4/175°C) and cook the duck, turning it over from time to time, for 1¼ hours. ● Shortly before the end take all the cooking juices from the bird and mix them with the sherry, then reduce the volume over the heat. ● Keep warm. ● Pour hot chicken stock over the duck, cover and finish cooking. ● Take out the bird and place it on a heated serving dish. ● Moisten it with the sherry gravy. ● Keep warm. ● Remove the bouquet garni from the cooking pot. ● Put the vegetables from the pot through a vegetable mill. ● Skim fat off the top. ● Add the carefully drained olives. ● Meanwhile, degrease the pan containing the cooking juices by adding the white wine and bringing it to a boil. ● Cook rapidly for a few minutes to reduce the wine and then add the olives-and-vegetable purée. ● Heat, and pour over the duck. ● Serve garnished with fried potatoes and strips of sweet pepper.

Gallo de campo a la jerezana
Chicken in sherry

Yemas de San Leandro
St Leander's sweet egg yolks

For 4–6 persons

Time: *preparation 30 min. + 3 days for the chicken to hang ● cooking 1¼ hours.*
Ingredients: *chicken weighing about 3 lb/1.5 kg ● olive oil ● 1 large onion, chopped ● 3 cloves garlic, peeled ● parsley ● ½ bottle sherry ● salt ● black peppercorns. As an accompaniment: fried potatoes.*

For 8 persons

Time: *preparation 30 min. ● cooking 35 min.*
Ingredients: *1¼ lb/600 g egg yolks without a trace of white ● 4 cups/2 lb/1 kg sugar ● juice of 1 lemon.*

● Pluck, gut and wash the bird. ● Singe to remove remaining down and then hang in a cold room for 3 days. ● Wipe it well over with a damp cloth inside and out. ● Cut into 4 or 8 pieces. ● Gently heat a little oil in a frying pan. ● Sweat the chopped onion, the whole garlic cloves and a handful of parsley. ● When they turn colour, remove from the pot and put on one side. ● Brown the pieces of chicken in the same oil. ● When well browned drench with sherry. ● Add the fried onion and garlic. ● Season, add some peppercorns and tip in a little water just to stop the ingredients sticking to the casserole. ● Bring back to the boil, lower the heat and simmer until meat is cooked, about 1¼ hours. ● Serve garnished with fried potatoes.

● Put egg yolks through a fine sieve. ● Make a syrup with the sugar, 2 cups/16 fl. oz/5 dl water and the remnants of egg yolk left in the sieve. ● Put the syrup over heat, and when it has reached a temperature of (90°F/33°C) drop the egg yolks in very carefully, bit by bit, (using if possible the special 5-lipped funnel intended for making spun eggs). ● Stir with a slow, continuous action (the syrup must never quite go off the boil). ● When all the yolks are in, strain out the strands that will have formed and drain. ● Taking a little at a time, form the reassembled ''yolks'' into the shape of eggs. ● Let them get cold, then dip them in the glaze. ● To prepare the glaze, strain the syrup in which the yolks were cooked and add a few drops of lemon juice. ● Heat it up again in a saucepan, and when it reaches 90°F/33°C take it from the stove and beat the glaze mixture with a wooden spoon. ● Pour it on to a marble slab or chilled meat platter and continue beating till it becomes white and firm, then knead it with your hands, wet with cold water. ● Put the glaze in a double-boiler (double saucepan) and heat it. ● When it becomes fluid dip the ''yolks'' in, one by one. ● Leave to dry.

Polvorones
Cinnamon biscuits

Piñonate
Pine kernel biscuits

For 6–8 persons

Time: *preparation 40 min. + 1 hour for pastry to rest ● cooking 15 min.*
Ingredients: *4½ cups/1¼ lb/500 g flour ● 1 cup/½ lb/250 g refined lard ● 1½ cups/½ lb/250 g confectioners' (icing) sugar ● 1 tablespoon cinnamon ● grated rind (peel) of ½ lemon ● a few drops lemon juice ● 1 egg yolk (optional).*

For 4 persons

Time: *preparation 10 min. ● cooking 20 min.*
Ingredients: *2 cups/½ lb/250 g pine kernels ● 1 cup/½ lb/250 g sugar ● juice of 1 lemon ● 1½ cups/6 oz/150 g almonds, lightly toasted and chopped ● grated rind (peel) of 1 lemon ● 1 teaspoon cinnamon (optional) ● a little cooking wine.*

● Toast the flour: cover a baking tin (oven tray) with aluminum foil or greaseproof paper and distribute the flour over it. ● Bake in a moderate oven (350°F/mark 4/175°C) for 10–15 minutes, stirring occasionally with a spoon to ensure that the flour toasts evenly. ● Remove from the oven and sift. ● Now pile 4 cups/1 lb/450 g of the flour on a marble slab, hollow out the center and put in the lard, 1 cup/6 oz/200 g confectioners' (icing) sugar, cinnamon, grated rind (peel) and lemon juice. ● Mix all the ingredients and knead the dough. ● Form into a ball and leave to rest in a cool place for 1 hour. ● Then dust the marble slab or pastry board with the remaining flour and roll out the dough to a fairly thin sheet. ● Cut out circles about 2 in./5 cm across with a pastry cutter. ● Arrange these on a slightly damp baking tray and bake them in a fairly hot oven (400°F/mark 6/205°C). ● Leave to cool, still on the baking tray, sprinkle with the remaining confectioners' (icing) sugar and wrap in tissue paper.

A way of making these biscuits richer, and not so friable that they have to be wrapped, is to add one egg yolk to the ingredients.

● Toast the pine kernels lightly in the oven or broiler (under the grill). ● In a copper saucepan mix the sugar with lemon juice. ● Put the saucepan on a brisk heat and, stirring continuously with a wooden spoon, melt the sugar. ● When it begins to caramelize, or turn brown, add the pine kernels, almonds, grated lemon rind (peel) and, if desired, the cinnamon. ● When the mixture is golden brown remove from heat. ● Wet your hands with wine and make the mixture into little cakes shaped like croquettes. ● Allow to cool, then serve.

Pestiños
Honey fritters

Brazo de gitano
"Gypsy's arm"

For 4–6 persons

Time: *preparation 20 min. ● cooking 20 min.*
Ingredients: *¾ cup/¼ pint/1.5 dl sunflower oil ● grated rind (peel) of 1 lemon ● 1 teaspoon aniseeds ● ½ teaspoon sesame seeds ● 3½ cups/14 oz/400 g flour ● salt ● ¾ cup/¼ pint/1.5 dl sherry ● ⅔ cup/½ lb/200 g honey ● confectioners' (icing) sugar.*

For 4 persons

Time: *preparation 15 min ● cooking 10 min.*
Ingredients: *5 eggs ● 1 cup/4 oz/125 g flour ● ½ cup/¼ lb/125 g sugar ● grated rind (peel) of 1 lemon ● chocolate egg custard or whipped cream ● confectioners' (icing) sugar.*

● Heat oil in a frying pan. ● When hot put in the grated lemon rind (peel) and let it brown a little. ● Take the pan from the heat. ● Add the aniseeds and sesame seeds. ● Leave to cool. ● Meanwhile make a mound of the flour on a marble slab or pastry board and pour into a hollow in the center the salt, sherry and the oil previously used (cooled and strained). ● Stir and knead till you have a smooth dough. ● Flatten it with a roller, then cut it into strips, roll them up and fry them in abundant oil. ● Drain on paper towels (kitchen roll). ● Put the honey in a saucepan with 5 tablespoons water. ● Bring to the boil. ● Remove from the heat and immediately dip the cakes in this syrup. ● Drain them on a wire cake rack. ● Before serving sprinkle with confectioners' (icing) sugar or powdered (castor) sugar.

● Cover a baking tray (oven tray) with flour-dusted aluminum foil or greaseproof paper. ● Separate the eggs and whisk the egg whites to a stiff froth. ● Slowly mix them with the yolks, sugar and lemon rind (peel). ● Incorporate the flour, stirring slowly but thoroughly with a wooden spoon. ● Lay the dough on the baking tray and roll it to a thickness of ¼ in./0.5 cm. ● Place in the oven and bake at (350°F/mark 4/175°C) for 10 minutes. ● Remove from oven and place on aluminum foil or greaseproof paper dusted with flour. ● Spread with chocolate egg custard or whipped cream and roll it up. ● Dust with confectioners' (icing) sugar. ● Serve cold.

Suspiros de moro
Moor's sighs

Tocino de cielo
Crème caramel delight

For 4–6 persons

Time: *preparation 30 min. ● cooking 15 min. + 10 min. for the chocolate icing.*
Ingredients: *4 eggs, separated ● ½ cup/¼ lb/100 g sugar ● grated rind (peel) of 1 lemon ● 1 cup/¼ lb/100 g flour ● 2 cups/¾ pint/4.5 dl whipped cream, sweetened if desired ● 7 oz/200 g semi-sweet (plain) chocolate ● 6 tablespoons milk.*

For 8 persons

Time: *preparation 15 min. ● cooking 35 min.*
Ingredients: *3½ cups/1¾ lb/800 g sugar ● 1 cinnamon stick ● grated rind (peel) of 1 lemon ● 5 whole eggs ● 11 egg yolks.*

● Beat the egg yolks with the sugar and grated lemon peel. ● In another bowl, whisk the egg whites to a very stiff froth. ● Work the egg yolks into the flour, then gently fold in the whites. ● Turn the batter into a rectangular cake tin, buttered and sprinkled with flour. ● Bake in a pre-heated moderate oven (350°F/mark 4/175°C) for about 15 minutes. ● Cool, then cut the cake into strips 4 in./10 cm wide. ● Using a pastry bag (icing bag), cover these strips with whipped cream. ● Place in refrigerator. ● While they are chilling cut the chocolate into pieces and melt it in a double-boiler (double saucepan) with the milk. ● When the cake is thoroughly cold pour the chocolate icing on top. ● Cut the strips into more or less regular rectangles and arrange on a serving dish.

● Melt 1 cup/½ lb/200 g sugar in a heavy frying pan rubbed lightly with butter and set the pan over moderate heat. ● Stir constantly until the sugar melts. ● Continue to stir until you have a clear brown syrup. ● Line one large mould, or several smaller ones, with this mixture and set aside. ● Place the remaining sugar in a saucepan. ● Add just enough water to wet the sugar, then add the cinnamon and lemon rind (peel). ● Melt the sugar completely over a low heat. ● Beat the eggs and egg yolks to a smooth cream in a mixing bowl. ● Add the syruped sugar slowly, stirring all the time. ● Strain the mixture into the mould or moulds. ● Cooking the crème is a most delicate operation, and may be done only by steaming, and not in a bain-marie. ● If you do not possess a special steamer, put a trivet or 3 large stones at the bottom of a deep saucepan (about 10 in./25 cm high), add a little water—it must not cover the trivet or stones—and arrange the mould on top of these. ● Cover the pan very tightly and lay a cloth over the lid. ● Bring water to a boil and steam for 35 minutes. ● Let the mould get quite cold before turning it out.

Pastel cordobés
Córdoba pie

Pastel Gloria
Gloria's dessert

For 6 persons

Time: *preparation 30 min.* ● *cooking 35 min.*
Ingredients: *4 cups/1 lb/500 g flour ● vinegar ● ½ cup/¼ lb/100 g lard ●*
1 rounded teaspoon salt ● 1½ cups/¾ lb/300 g margarine ●
2 cups/1 lb/500 g cabello de angel* ● 1 egg, beaten ● sugar ● cinnamon.

For 4 persons

Time: *preparation 25 min.* ● *cooking 40–50 min.*
Ingredients: *24–36 egg whites ● 2 cups/1 lb/400 g sugar ●*
½ cup/¼ lb/100 g potato flour* ● 1¾ cups/½ lb/200 g ground almonds. For
the filling: 4¼ cups/1¾ pints/1 liter milk ● 1 stick cinnamon ● 1 grated lemon
rind (peel) ● 1½ cups/¾ lb/300 g sugar ● ½ cup/2 oz/50 g flour ● 4 egg
yolks ● 1 cup/½ pint/2.5 dl light (single) cream ● 4 sheets gelatin, or
1 packet unflavoured gelatin ● confectioners' (icing) sugar.

● Make a smooth paste with the flour, 2 cups/16 fl. oz/5 dl water, a very little vinegar, the lard and the salt. ● Roll out and place the margarine in the center, as for puff or flaky pastry. ● Fold the pastry 6 times, then divide it into 2 halves. ● Taking one of the halves, roll out into a circular shape and spread it with *cabello de angel**. ● Roll the other half in the same way and lay it on top of the first, brushing the edges with a little beaten egg. ● Press down the edges and shape them like a ring of rope. ● Bake in a very hot oven (450°F/mark 8/230°C) for 35 minutes. ● Remove from oven, brush the surface with beaten egg and sprinkle with sugar and powdered cinnamon.

*To make *cabello de angel*: cook pieces of peeled squash or pumpkin until tender and drain well. ● Push through a sieve. ● Take 1 cup/½ lb/250 g of the pulp and mix it with an equal amount of sugar. ● Cook in a saucepan with the grated rind (peel) of 1 lemon and stir until fairly thick.

● Whisk the egg whites to a stiff froth. ● Fold in first the sugar, then the potato flour and ground almonds. ● Line a baking sheet (tin) with aluminum foil or greaseproof paper. ● Fill a pastry bag (icing bag) with the mixture and make 2 large, flat square or circular meringues. ● Bake them in a very cool oven (250°F/mark ½/120°C) for 40–50 minutes. ● Meanwhile prepare the cream filling. ● Bring to a boil the milk with the cinnamon and lemon rind (peel), then remove from heat. ● In another pan put the sugar, flour, egg yolks and cream. ● Mix well and dilute with the strained warm milk. ● Still stirring, bring this mixture to the boil. ● Remove from the heat and then incorporate the gelatin, previously soaked in cold water. ● Leave to cool. ● When the meringues are baked and cooled, spread the chilled cream over one of them and cover it with the other. ● Sprinkle liberally with confectioners' (icing) sugar.

* Can be bought from most health food shops.

Helado de pasas al Viña 25
Ice cream with dessert wine and currants

Pudding de pasas
Raisin pudding

For 8 persons

Time: *preparation 10 min. + 1 hour to marinate the currants ● cooking 20 min.*
Ingredients: *½ cup/¼ lb/100 g currants ● 1 cup/½ pint/2.5 dl Viña 25 or other dessert wine ● 4½ cups/1¾ pints/1 liter milk ● 1½ cups/¾ lb/300 g powdered (castor) sugar ● 1 vanilla pod ● 6 egg yolks ● 4 egg whites.*

For 4–6 persons

Time: *preparation 15 min. + 1 hour for soaking raisins ● cooking 50 min.*
Ingredients: *1 cup/¼ lb/100 g raisins ● 2 cups/16 fl. oz/5 dl milk ● 1 cup/½ lb/200 g sugar ● rind (peel) of 1 lemon ● ½ stick cinnamon ● 1 cup/¼ lb/100 g breadcrumbs ● 4 eggs, separated ● flour ● lemon juice ● ½ cup/2 oz/50 g pine kernels.*

● Marinate the currants in the sweet wine for 1 hour. ● Meanwhile, prepare the ice cream. ● Take ½ cup/4 fl. oz/1 dl of the milk and set it aside. ● Boil the rest with the sugar and vanilla. ● Beat the egg yolks with the milk that was set aside. ● The moment the milk in the pan comes to the boil, add the egg yolk mixture and bring all back to the boil, stirring continuously. ● Strain the resulting custard and cool it to room temperature as quickly as possible. ● Then place in the freezer. ● When half frozen, take out and beat in an electric mixer to produce a smooth, rich cream. ● Add the well marinated raisins and 4 egg whites, whisked to a stiff froth. ● Mix very delicately with a wooden spoon to achieve a homogeneous texture. ● Return to the freezer till the ice cream is properly frozen.

● Soak the raisins in warm water for 1 hour. ● Boil the milk with ¾ cup/6 oz/150 g sugar, the lemon rind (peel) and the cinnamon stick. ● Remove from the heat and strain over the breadcrumbs. ● Cool. ● When cold add the beaten egg yolks, stirring vigorously. ● Drain the raisins, dip them in flour and add them to the mixture. ● Finally, fold in the egg whites, beaten to a stiff froth. ● Melt the remaining sugar with 2 tablespoons water and a few drops of lemon juice and let it caramelize. ● Line a rectangular mould with the caramelized sugar. ● Now add the pudding mixture, put the mould in a bain-marie and bake in a warm (325°F/mark 3/165°F) oven for 30–40 minutes. ● Turn out on to a serving dish and decorate with toasted pine kernels.

BALEARIC ISLANDS
CANARY ISLANDS

The Spanish archipelagos, one in the Mediterranean, the
other in the Atlantic, have very different cooking traditions,
united though they are by the effects on those traditions of
their island heritage.

Balearic Islands. The traditional cookery of these islands
has to some extent been forgotten, but it now seems
destined to be revived. It is a cookery of substantial soups,
such as the "Sopa dorada" or the "Sopas mallorquinas de
matanza," of the "Sofrito ibicenco" (Ibiza casserole), and of
eggplants (aubergines), one of the principal crops of the
local market gardens. Some of the fish and crustaceans native
to the surrounding sea would provide a chapter in themselves
(headed by the great "Majorcan seafood" or the "Fillets
of John Dory with mussels"). Minorca has a rather individual
cuisine when compared with that of Majorca and Ibiza, partly,
no doubt, because of its historical connections with Great
Britain, and is also an interesting center for sampling
particular kinds of seafoods as well as excellent soups.

Canary Islands. The Atlantic archipelago provides the grand
and varied mosaic of Spanish cookery with its most exotic
touches. The island cuisine derives mainly from that of Spain,
but reflects also some influences from Latin America and the
nearby regions of North Africa. The excellent local fish go
particulary well with "Mojo," the most characteristic sauce.
Among the most notable dishes are "Sancocho canario,"
made from fish and potatoes, "Sama frita con mojo verde y
'papas' arrugadas" (sea bream with green sauce and baked
potatoes), and "Truchas canarias" (Canary Islands doughnuts).

Sopa dorado
Cream of veal and onion soup

Potaje de berros
Watercress soup

For 4 persons

Time: *preparation 15 min. + 2 hours for stock • cooking 1½ hours in an ordinary saucepan or 40 min. in a pressure cooker.*
Ingredients: *5½ cups/2¼ pints/1¼ liters meat stock (prepared by boiling beef bones together with various vegetables, such as carrots, celery, onions, for 2 hours) • ¾ lb/300 g stewing veal • 7–8 onions • ¼ cup/2 oz/50 g lard • 2 tablespoons tomato sauce (see p. 187) • ½ cup/2 oz/50 g Cheddar or other firm cheese, grated • a handful of vegetables cooked in the stock • salt • pepper • 4 slices bread • 3 egg yolks • chives.*

For 4 persons

Time: *preparation 10 min. • cooking 1 hour.*
Ingredients: *½ lb/250 g stewing pork or veal • a bare 6 cups/2½ pints/1.5 liters water or stock • 3 large potatoes, peeled and coarsely chopped • 3 bunches watercress • 1 cob of corn (sweetcorn) • 1 onion • 2 cloves garlic • 2 ripe tomatoes, peeled and seeded • ¼ cup/2 oz/50 g lard • salt • pepper.*

• First make the stock, as described above. • Cut the veal into small cubes. • Peel and halve the onions, place in a large saucepan with the melted lard, and brown over a gentle heat. • As soon as it is ready add the stock, tomato sauce, grated cheese and the handful of vegetables cooked in the meat stock. • Cook slowly for 1½ hours (or 40 minutes in a pressure cooker). • Strain the soup. • Season with salt, pepper and other flavourings to taste. • Toast the bread and lay it at the bottom of the tureen. • Dilute 3 beaten egg yolks with a little of the cooled stock. • Bring the rest of the soup to the boil, pour it over the toast in the tureen and add the diluted egg yolks. • Stir, and garnish with chopped chives.

• Trim the meat and cut into cubes. • Bring the stock or water to the boil. • Add the meat, potatoes, watercress (without stalks) and corn on the cob, cut into four. • Cook slowly for 1 hour. • Meanwhile, chop the onion, garlic and tomatoes finely. • Melt the lard in a frying pan and sweat this chopped mixture. • When soft, add it to the soup. • A quarter of an hour before the end check the seasoning.

Caldo de pescado
Stewed fish with potatoes

Sopas mallorquinas de matanza
Majorcan vegetable soup

For 4–6 persons

Time: *preparation 25 min. ● cooking 40 min.*
Ingredients: *2 lb/1 kg of any suitable fish ● salt ● olive oil ● 2 onions, chopped ● 4 tomatoes, peeled and sliced ● 1 head garlic, peeled and chopped ● parsley ● 1 green pepper seeded and sliced ● 1 teaspoon paprika ● 2 bread rolls ● juice from 2 bitter oranges or lemons ● 1 sprig coriander ● 1 sprig mint ● 2 lb/1 kg potatoes, peeled and chopped ● 12 blanched almonds ● pinch of saffron ● pinch of cinnamon ● pinch of nutmeg.*

For 4 persons

Time: *preparation 15 min. ● cooking 1½ hours.*
Ingredients: *1 lb/450 g stewing pork ● 4 cloves garlic ● ½ cup/4 fl. oz/1 dl olive oil ● ¼ lb/100 g blood sausage (black pudding)* ● a few scallions (spring onions), sliced ● handful of parsley, chopped ● 1 tablespoon paprika ● 3 or 4 tomatoes, peeled and chopped ● ¾ lb/300 g vegetables in season (preferably of the cabbage family) ● salt ● 1 lb/500 g stale wholemeal bread.*

● Clean the fish. ● Cut in two or more pieces according to size. ● Season and leave for a while, then brown in a large saucepan with hot oil, and transfer to a casserole. ● Keep warm. ● In the frying pan sweat the chopped onions and let them begin to colour. ● Add the tomatoes. ● Soon afterwards add all but 1 clove of garlic, chopped, the parsley, and the green pepper cut into strips. ● Stir well. ● Add the paprika, 2 cups/¾ pint/5 dl water, sliced bread rolls, orange or lemon juice, coriander and mint. ● Bring to the boil, then add the potatoes. ● Simmer for about 30 minutes, or until potatoes are cooked. ● Meanwhile, with pestle and mortar crush the remaining clove of garlic, the almonds and saffron. ● Mix in cinnamon and nutmeg. ● Add this flavouring to the saucepan and cook for several minutes more. ● Pour it all over the fish in the casserole, heat up and serve immediately.

● Trim the pork and cut into cubes. ● Gently fry the garlic cloves in oil. ● When nearly black take them out and discard. ● In the same oil fry the pork cubes and the whole piece of blood sausage (black pudding). ● When both are done remove them from the pan and put on one side. ● Still using the same oil, fry the sliced scallions (spring onions) and the chopped parsley ● Add the paprika and chopped tomatoes. ● Cook for a few minutes, then add the chopped-up seasonal vegetables. ● Cover with water, season, and cook over a low heat for about 45 minutes. ● Cut the stale bread into very thin slices and put on the bottom of a flameproof pot. ● Pour the meat and vegetable stock over the bread. ● Add the meat, vegetable and the blood sausage (black pudding) chopped small. ● Scatter with a little fresh olive oil. ● Heat the soup without letting it boil, then let it rest for a few minutes. ● Serve in the same pot.

* See footnote page 8.

174

Coca de verduras
Swiss chard and spinach tart

Coca de trempó
Pepper, onion and tomato tart

For 8 persons

Time: *preparation 50 min.* ● *cooking 30–40 min.*
Ingredients: *1 lb/500 g/Swiss chard* ● *1 lb/500 g spinach* ● *1 bunch young scallions (spring onions)* ● *salt* ● *1 tablespoon paprika* ● *olive oil* ● *1 tablespoon/½ oz/15 g lard* ● *1½ lb/750 g bread (or pizza) dough* ● *1 large tomato, peeled, seeded and chopped* ● *bunch of parsley, chopped*

For 8 persons

Time: *preparation 40 min.* ● *cooking 30–40 min.*
Ingredients: *1 lb/500 g tender young green peppers* ● *1 lb/500 g onions* ● *1 lb/500 g tomatoes* ● *bunch of parsley* ● *salt* ● *olive oil* ● *1 tablespoon/½ oz/15 g lard* ● *1½ lb/750 g bread (or pizza) dough.*

● Wash the Swiss chard, spinach and scallions (spring onions) thoroughly under running water. ● Slice finely, season and leave for several minutes, then squeeze hard to extract the water. ● Dress with the paprika and salt, and enough olive oil to coat the vegetables. ● Mix well. ● Combine 2 tablespoons olive oil and 1 tablespoon lard with the bread dough, working it well in. ● Roll the dough out thinly and line a large pie plate (flan tin), leaving a raised border all round. ● Fill with the vegetables, scatter with chopped tomato and parsley, and bake in a hot oven (425°F/mark 7/220°C) for 30–40 minutes.

● Cut up the vegetables, chop the parsley and mix well together, adding salt to taste. ● Mix 2 tablespoons oil and 1 tablespoon lard with the bread (or pizza) dough. ● Knead the dough well, then roll out thinly. ● Line a large pie plate (flan tin) with the dough, leaving a small raised border. ● Arrange the vegetables on top and bake in a hot oven (425°F/mark 7/220°C) for 30–40 minutes.

Sancocho canario
Fish and potatoes Canary Islands style

For 4 persons

Time: *preparation 10 min. + 15 min. for the sauce ● cooking 30 min.*
Ingredients: *1¼ lb/600 g sea bass or sea bream ● 1 lb/400 g potatoes ● salt ● 2 cloves garlic ● pinch of chili pepper ● ½ teaspoon cumin seeds ● 1 teaspoon paprika ● olive oil ● 2 tablespoons wine vinegar.*

● Clean the fish and cut into pieces. ● Peel and slice potatoes, and bring them to a boil in salted water. ● A few minutes after they begin to cook add the fish. ● Continue cooking till both are tender, about 30 minutes altogether. ● Meanwhile, pound the garlic, a pinch of salt, the chili pepper and the cumin to a fine paste in a mortar. ● Add the paprika and moisten all with a little olive oil. ● Pour in the vinegar and some of the fish stock. ● When ready to serve, drain the potatoes and fish, and serve accompanied by the chili sauce.

Rancho canario
Canary Islands stew

For 4–6 persons

Time: *preparation 20 min + 12 hours for soaking the beans ● cooking 2–3 hours.*
Ingredients: *1 cup/½ lb/200 g navy (haricot) beans ● 1 lb/500 g stewing beef ● 6 oz/150 g fat (streaky) bacon ● ¼ lb/100 g Chorizo sausage* ● salt ● 1 green pepper ● pinch of thyme ● pinch of saffron ● 1 clove garlic ● 1 tablespoon red wine ● 1 lb/500 g potatoes, peeled and chopped ● ½ lb/250 g spaghetti.*

● Soak the beans overnight. ● Trim the meat and cut into pieces. ● Place in a stewpan and cover with cold water. ● Bring to the boil, then add the bacon and the chopped Chorizo sausage. ● Let cook for a few minutes before adding the soaked beans with a little salt. ● Simmer for about 2 hours, or until meat is tender and beans are cooked. ● Strain the stock and put the beans and bacon to one side. ● Return the beef to the pan with the stock and chopped sausage. ● Bring to the boil. ● Add the chopped green pepper, thyme, saffron, garlic and wine. ● Throw in the potatoes and cook for 10–12 minutes, then add the spaghetti, broken into pieces. Continue cooking till all the ingredients are cooked. ● At the end, just before turning off the heat, add the beans and bacon and heat through.

*See footnote page 8.

"Greixera" de huevos
Soup with eggs

Pargo a la mallorquina
Pargo Majorcan style

For 6 persons

Time: *preparation 20 min. ● cooking 50 min.*
Ingredients: *1 lb/400 g stewing lamb ● 1 piece of fat bacon or fat salt pork ● olive oil ● 1 large onion, sliced ● 2 leeks, cleaned and sliced ● 1 carrot, chopped ● 3 ripe tomatoes, peeled and chopped ● 1 bay leaf ● 1 clove garlic, chopped ● pinch of oregano ● 4½ cups/1¾ pints/1 liter chicken stock ● a few lettuce leaves ● ½ lb/200 g potatoes, peeled and chopped ● 3 artichoke hearts ● salt. To garnish: hard-boiled eggs.*

For 4–5 persons

Time: *preparation 4 hours for marinating ● cooking 45 min.*
Ingredients: *3 lb/1.5 kg pargo* ● 1 glass dry white wine ● ½ cup/4 fl. oz/1 dl olive oil ● 1 teaspoon paprika ● 1 clove garlic, chopped ● salt ● pepper.* For the vegetable stew: *½ lb/450g spinach ● 1 lb/500 g Swiss chard ● 2 ripe tomatoes ● 2 bunches scallions (spring onions) ● 1 bunch parsley ● 2 cloves garlic ● 1 tablespoon paprika ● salt ● olive oil.* To garnish: *12 toasted almonds, chopped ● 1 clove garlic, crushed.*

● Trim the lamb and cut into cubes. ● Cut the fat bacon into pieces. ● In a large pan gently fry the lamb and bacon in a little oil. ● Add the sliced onion. ● Brown all the contents, then add the leeks, carrot, tomatoes, bay leaf, chopped garlic and oregano. ● As soon as all are nicely browned cover with the chicken stock and add the lettuce leaves cut in strips and the chopped potatoes. ● When nearly done add the artichoke hearts cut in segments. ● The end product should be a fairly thick soup. ● Before serving check the seasoning and garnish with segments of hard-boiled egg.

● Make a marinade of the white wine, olive oil, paprika, chopped garlic, salt and pepper. ● Cut the fish in half and marinate it for 4 hours. ● Meanwhile wash the spinach and Swiss chard very thoroughly and drain. ● Cut the other vegetables for the stew in small pieces. ● Take the fish out of the marinade, put it in a stewpan; add garlic, paprika, salt and olive oil and cover it with the mixed vegetables. ● Pour the marinade on top. ● Cook slowly for 45 minutes. ● Just before it is ready scatter chopped almonds and crushed garlic on top.

* Pargo is a kind of snapper. If unavailable, use red snapper or sea bream.

"Burrida de ratjada"
Skate with almonds

Filetes de gallo con dátiles de mar
Fillets of John Dory with mussels

For 6 persons

Time: *preparation 15 min. + 2 hours for marinating ● cooking 25 min.*
Ingredients: *1 skate weighing about 5½ lb/2.5 kg ● salt ● juice of 2 lemons ● 2 heads garlic, peeled ● 2 slices bread, fried ● 1 cup/¼ lb/100 g toasted almonds ● 2 tomatoes, peeled and chopped ● a sprig of parsley ● 2 eggs, beaten ● ½ cup/4 fl. oz/1 dl olive oil ● fish stock.*

For 2 persons

Time: *preparation 15 min. ● cooking 15 min.*
Ingredients: *1 John Dory* weighing about 2 lb/1 kg ● 1 pint/300 g mussels ● ¼ cup/2 oz/50 g butter, melted ● ¾ cup/6 fl. oz/1.5 dl light (single) cream ● salt ● 2 tablespoons fish stock.*

● Clean the skate and cut it into large slices. ● Leave to marinate in salt and lemon juice for 2 hours (to eliminate the typical ammoniac smell). ● Then scald in boiling water and arrange in a fireproof dish. ● Pound in a mortar the garlic, fried bread, the toasted almonds, the peeled and chopped tomatoes, the parsley, beaten eggs and oil. ● Combine this mixture with a little fish stock. ● Pour it on the skate slices and cook rapidly for 12 minutes.

● Fillet the fish. ● Scrub the mussels well, drop into a little boiling water, cover, and remove as soon as the shells open. Cool. ● Open the mussels, remove from the shell and put them on a plate with their own liquid and the melted butter. ● Lay the fillets in a casserole, skin side down. ● Season. ● Add the cream. ● Place the mussels on top of the fish. ● Moisten with the liquid remaining on the plate they were on. ● Put the casserole in an oven heated to 400°F/mark 6/205°C and bake for about 15 minutes. ● Remove from oven, check the seasoning of the sauce and dilute with a little fish stock.

*If unavailable, use turbot or sole.

Sama frita con mojo verde y "papas" arrugadas
Sea bream with green sauce and baked potatoes

"Cap roig" al hinojo marino
Scorpion fish with samphire

For 6 persons

Time: *preparation 30 min.* ● *cooking 40 min.*
Ingredients: *A 2 lb/1 kg sea bream* ● salt ● flour ● olive oil ● 4lb/2 kg new potatoes ● $\frac{1}{2}$ teaspoon cumin ● 1 head garlic ● 1 green pepper ● 8–10 sprigs parsley, chopped ● wine vinegar.*

For 1 person

Time: *preparation 15 min.* ● *cooking 18 min.*
Ingredients: *1 scorpion fish* weighing $\frac{3}{4}$–1 lb/300–400 g ● $\frac{1}{4}$ lb/100 g very fresh marsh or rock samphire** (sea fennel) ● salt ● 2 cloves garlic ● 1 egg yolk ● parsley ● $\frac{3}{4}$ cup/6 fl. oz/2 dl olive oil.*

● Skin and bone the bream. ● Cut in slices, season and coat with flour. ● Fry in olive oil. ● Drain and set aside. ● Keep warm. ● Wash the potatoes very thoroughly but do not scrape or peel. ● Place in a saucepan, only just cover with water, add a few handfuls salt, stir and boil. ● When cooked, drain, then put them back in the dry saucepan over a hot flame for a few minutes. ● This will cause the skin to wrinkle and dry. ● Keep them warm on a serving dish. ● Place in a mortar the cumin, peeled cloves of garlic, salt, green pepper seeded and cut into strips and chopped parsley. ● Pound them all very thoroughly. ● Moisten the resulting mixture with olive oil and stir well. ● Lastly add a few drops of vinegar and a little water. ● Pour this green sauce over the fried fish and serve with baked potatoes.

*Scup (porgy) can be used.

● Clean the fish. ● Place in a steamer saucepan with part of the samphire. ● When the water starts to boil add the remaining samphire (cleaned and salted). ● Steam for 10 minutes. ● Meanwhile, prepare the garlic sauce. ● Peel and crush the garlic. ● Place in a blender with egg yolks, salt and chopped parsley. ● Turn blender on and slowly add the oil through the top. ● Serve the fish with its own cooking liquid and the samphire, and serve the garlic sauce separately.

*The gurnard, or scorpion fish, is caught in the Atlantic and Mediterranean. It has a rather ugly, prehistoric-like head and there are grey, red and yellow varieties. If unavailable, use mullet or whiting.
**Samphire is a type of seaweed. If unavailable, a dried seaweed could be substituted—a health food shop or oriental delicatessen would be the best place to start looking.

Mariscada a la mallorquina
Majorcan seafood

Ensaimada con sobrasada
Majorcan sausage cake

For 4 persons

Time: *preparation 25 min.* ● *cooking 40 min.*
Ingredients: *3 large onions* ● *olive oil* ● *1 bouquet garni* ● *3 ripe tomatoes, peeled and seeded* ● *1 lobster weighing about 1¾ lb/800 g* ● *4 saltwater crayfish (scampi)* ● *4 pieces monkfish** ● *1 small glass brandy* ● *salt* ● *pepper* ● *2 cloves garlic* ● *12 toasted almonds* ● *parsley* ● *white wine.*

For 8 persons

Time: *preparation 20 min + 7 hours for the dough to rise* ● *cooking 20–25 min.*
Ingredients: *1 cup/½ lb/200 g sugar* ● *3 eggs* ● *3 teaspoons baking powder* ● *5 cups/1¼ lb/600 g all-purpose (plain) flour* ● *1 cup/½ lb/200 g lard.* For decoration: *thin slices of* Sobrasada, *a special Majorcan sausage (or any other spicy smoked sausage)* ● *confectioners' (icing) sugar.*

● Slice the onions in thin rings and sweat in oil in a flameproof casserole. ● Add the herbs and tomatoes. ● Cook gently till all are tender. ● Clean, boil and dismember the lobster. ● Brown the lobster, saltwater crayfish (scampi) and monkfish in a little oil. ● Moisten with the brandy and set alight. ● Transfer all the seafood to the casserole with the onions and tomatoes, and simmer, covered, over a low heat for 15 minutes. ● Season with salt and pepper. ● Five minutes before the end add a mixture of chopped garlic, almonds and parsley moistened with a few tablespoons of white wine.

*Or use bluefish.

● Mix all the ingredients except the lard together with 1 cup/8 fl. oz/2.5 dl water and knead until you obtain a smooth, pliable pastry. ● Lay the lard on the top and roll and fold till it is all absorbed. ● Roll the pastry out thinly, then roll it up like a jelly roll (Swiss roll) and twist into the spiral snailshell shape typical of the *ensaimada*. ● Leave it to rise for about 7 hours (if you want to be quicker, mix the dough with warmish water). ● Arrange thin slices of *sobrasada* sausage on top— more or fewer of them according to taste. ● (These can be added before baking, or 5 minutes before the cake is finished baking.) ● Place on a greased baking sheet (oven tray) and bake in a cool oven (300°F/mark 2/150°C) for 20–25 minutes. ● Cool, then dust with confectioners' (icing) sugar.

Sofrito ibicenco
Ibiza casserole

Lomo con leche
Loin of pork with milk

For 6 persons

Time: *preparation 20 min. ● cooking 1 hour.*
Ingredients: *½ leg of lamb weighing about 2 lb/1 kg ● 6 chicken legs ● ¼ cup/2 oz/50 g lard ● 6 oz/150 g Sobrasada (or other spicy smoked) sausage ● 6 oz/150 g pork sausage ● 1 lb/500 g small potatoes, peeled ● livers of 3 chickens, about ½ lb/250 g ● salt ● ⅓ cup/1½ oz/35 g almonds ● pinch of cumin ● pinch of saffron ● 3 cloves garlic ● chicken stock ● chopped parsley.*

For 4 persons

Time: *preparation 15 min. ● cooking 35–40 min.*
Ingredients: *1¼ lb/600 g loin of pork ● 1 cooked chicken breast ● 2 hard-boiled egg yolks ● 1 black truffle ● lard ● 1 cup/8 fl. oz/2.5 dl milk ● salt ● 1 cup/8 fl. oz/2.5 dl light (single) cream ● ½ cup/2 oz/50 g flaked almonds.*

● Clean and pat dry the leg of lamb and the chicken legs. ● Fry them lightly in lard with the *sobrasada*, pork sausage, potatoes and chicken livers. ● Check the seasoning. ● When well browned transfer all but the livers to a flameproof casserole. ● Separately, pound the almonds, cumin, saffron, garlic and cooked livers in a mortar. ● Add this mixture to the casserole with a little stock. ● Stir well. ● Bring to a boil and simmer till done, about an hour. ● Serve sprinkled with chopped parsley.

● Make long narrow openings going all the way through the pork loin and, with the help of a skewer, insert thin slices of cooked chicken breast, hard-boiled yolks and truffle. ● Brown it thoroughly in sizzling lard, then add the milk. ● Season, bring to a boil and continue to cook for 35–40 minutes. ● When the meat is tender remove from casserole. ● Add the cream and flaked almonds to the cooking juices. ● Carve the pork into slices and arrange on a serving dish. ● Keep hot. ● Stir well the sauce remaining in the casserole and pour it over the slices of pork. ● Serve.

Frito de menudillos
Giblet casserole

Conejo al salmorejo
Salmi of rabbit

For 4 persons

Time: *preparation 20 min. ● cooking 20 min.*
Ingredients: *the giblets of 4 chickens ● olive oil ● 3 cloves garlic, crushed ● 2 bay leaves ● bunch of scallions (spring onions) ● 1 lb/450 g potatoes, peeled and chopped ● 4 artichoke hearts ● salt ● pepper ● chopped fennel.*

For 4–6 persons

Time: *preparation 15 min. + 2 hours for marinating the rabbit ● cooking 30 min.*
Ingredients: *1 rabbit ● 1 cup/8 fl. oz/2.5 dl olive oil ● 1 head of garlic ● salt ● 1 bay leaf ● 1 sprig thyme ● 1 green pepper ● $\frac{1}{2}$ teaspoon cumin ● 1 teaspoon paprika ● few pieces of rabbit or other liver ● 1 tablespoon wine vinegar. As an accompaniment:* boiled potatoes.

● Place the gizzards in a pan of water, bring to a boil and simmer gently for 20 minutes. ● Drain and reserve stock. ● Brown the rest of the giblets (livers, hearts and kidneys) in olive oil in a flameproof casserole. ● Add the crushed garlic and the bay leaves. ● Trim the scallions (spring onions), slice them into 1 in./2 cm lengths and add them to the rest. ● Cover the casserole and cook gently. ● In a frying pan with a little oil lightly brown the potatoes and artichoke hearts. ● Add these to the casserole and stir thoroughly. ● Add some of the stock the gizzards were cooked in. ● Season with salt, pepper and chopped fennel, and continue to cook until everything is tender, about 20 minutes.

● Clean and joint the rabbit. ● Marinate for two hours in a mixture of $\frac{1}{2}$ cup/4 fl. oz/1 dl oil, half the chopped garlic, salt, bay leaf and thyme. ● Remove from marinade and pat dry. ● Heat the remaining oil and fry the rabbit until cooked. ● Drain and place on a serving dish. ● Keep warm. ● Prepare a sauce by pounding in a mortar the seeded green pepper, the rest of the garlic cloves, salt, cumin, paprika and previously cooked, chopped liver. ● Thin the mixture with a little oil, vinegar and a few drops of water. ● Pour this sauce over the rabbit, heat up if necessary and serve with potatoes boiled in their skins.

"Escaldums" de pavo con pasta de ensaimada
Turkey medallion pies

Truchas canarias
Canary Islands doughnuts

For 8 persons

Time: *preparation 45 mins. ● cooking 2 hours. For the pastry: preparation 15 min. + 30 min. rest ● cooking 10 min.*
Ingredients: *1 boned turkey or turkey roll weighing about 6½ lb/3 kg, or two smaller rolls ● 1 tablespoon flour ● ½ cup/4 fl. oz/1 dl olive oil ● ½ lb/200 g onions ● 2 carrots ● 2 ripe tomatoes, peeled ● 2 bay leaves ● 2 cups/1 pint/5 dl dry white wine ● 8¾ cups/3½ pints/2 liters stock from the turkey bones or chicken stock ● 2 cloves garlic ● few sprigs of parsley ● ¾ cup/3 oz/75 g almonds ● 2 hard-boiled egg yolks ● salt. For the pastry: ⅔ cup/5 oz/125 g sugar ● 1 egg ● 2 teaspoons baking powder ● 3 cups/¾ lb/300 g all-purpose (plain) flour.*

For 6–8 persons

Time: *preparation 40 min. + 24 hours for the filling ● cooking 1 hour.*
Ingredients: *1 lb/500 g sweet potatoes or yams ● 1 cup/½ lb/250 g sugar ● 1½ cups/6 oz/150 g chopped almonds ● pinch of cinnamon ● grated rind (peel) of 1 lemon ● 1 small glass aniseed liqueur (e.g., Pernod). For the dough: 8 cups/2 lb/1 kg all-purpose (plain) flour ● 3 teaspoons baking powder ● 1 cup/½ lb/200 g lard ● 1 cup/½ lb/200 g sugar ● grated rind (peel) of 1 lemon ● sunflower oil ● powdered (castor) sugar.*

● Cut "medallions" (round slices) from the boned turkey meat and season them. ● Coat the "medallions" in flour and brown in a little oil. ● Remove from pan and drain. ● Set aside. ● Chop the onions, carrots and tomatoes and fry them gently with the bay leaves in the oil used to fry the turkey slices. ● Add the wine, bring to a boil and cook rapidly to reduce the volume by half. ● Put the turkey slices back in the pan. ● Add enough stock to cover. ● Cook for 20 minutes. ● Remove turkey but leave the stock to cook for another 10 minutes. ● Then strain it and pour over the turkey meat, reserving vegetables. ● Make a chopped mixture of the peeled garlic cloves, parsley, almonds and hard-boiled egg yolks. ● Add to the turkey, bring to a boil and simmer very gently. ● Now it is time to make the pastry. ● Mix sugar, egg, baking powder and flour and gradually stir in ½ cup/4 fl. oz/1 dl water. ● Mix well and leave to rest for 30 minutes. ● Roll the pastry to a thickness of ¼ in./0.5 cm. ● Put the turkey slices with their sauce and the vegetables in an ovenproof casserole or 8 individual bowls, cover with pastry and bake in a fairly hot oven (400°F/mark 6/205°C) for 10 minutes or until the surface is golden brown.

● Peel and boil the sweet potatoes or yams. ● Drain and push through a wire sieve. ● Prepare a syrup by melting the sugar in a little water. ● Combine this with the sweet potato purée, chopped almonds, cinnamon, grated lemon rind (peel) and aniseed liqueur. ● Stir, cover with a cloth and leave for 24 hours. ● The next day, make the dough. ● Thoroughly mix the flour with the baking powder and lard. ● Add the sugar and lemon rind (peel), mix well again and leave to rest for 30 minutes. ● Dust the pastry board with flour and roll out the dough to a very thin sheet. ● Cut out circles with a pastry cutter, top them with the filling prepared the day before and close them by folding in half and pressing the borders with a fork, first having moistened them so that they will stick together. ● Deep-fry these doughnuts in deep, sizzling oil. ● Drain and sprinkle with powdered (castor) sugar.

"Greixonera de brossat"
Majorcan dessert

"Flaó"
Cheese flan

For 6 persons

Time: *preparation 15 min. ● cooking 1 hour.*
Ingredients: *2 cups/1 lb/450 g sugar ● butter ● 4½ cups/1¾ pints/1 liter milk ● 1 stick cinnamon ● rind (peel) of 1 lemon ● 6 eggs ● 6 small ensaimadas (a sort of bun—see recipe on p. 180).*

For 6 persons

Time: *preparation 30 min. ● cooking 25–30 min.*
Ingredients: *For the filling: 1 lb/500 g fresh cottage or cream cheese or ricotta ● 1 cup/½ lb/250 g sugar ● 4 eggs ● a few mint leaves ● 1 small glass aniseed liqueur (e.g., Pernod). For the pastry: 2 cups/½ lb/200 g all-purpose (plain) flour) ● ¼ cup/2 oz/50 g lard ● 1 egg ● 3 teaspoons sugar ● ½ cup/4 fl. oz/1 dl milk ● 1 teaspoon dried yeast.*

● Caramelize ½ cup/¼ lb/100 g sugar in a lightly buttered cast iron frying pan. ● Pour it into a casserole and leave it to cool. ● In another pan boil the milk with the cinnamon stick and lemon peel. ● Beat the eggs in a bowl together with the remaining sugar. ● Add to the milk when it is tepid and blend well. ● In the casserole containing the caramel place the *ensaimadas* cut into slices. ● Put egg and milk mixture through a fine sieve and pour over the *ensaimadas*. ● Bake in a moderate oven (350°F/mark 4/175°C) for 45 minutes. ● Serve cold in the casserole.

● Soften the cheese, and gradually mix the sugar in. ● Continue to beat until creamy. ● Gradually add the eggs, one at a time, beating well after each addition. ● Add some of the mint leaves, chopped, and the aniseed liqueur (Pernod). ● Set aside and prepare the pastry. ● Pile the flour on to a marble slab or in a bread bowl. ● Make a hollow in the center and into it drop the lard, egg, sugar, milk, and yeast, mixing well after each addition. ● Knead by hand till you obtain a smooth, homogeneous dough. ● Roll out and press into a previously greased large pie dish (flan tin). ● Fill with the prepared cheese mixture. ● Stud with the whole mint leaves and bake in a moderate oven (350°F/mark 4/175°C) for 25–30 minutes.

Hojaldre de plátanos
Almond and banana pastry

"Orelletes"
"Little ears"

For 4 persons

Time: *preparation 25 min. ● cooking 45 min.*
Ingredients: *1 cup/6 oz/150 g ground almonds ● 2 bananas ● a little light (single) cream ● ¼ cup/2 oz/50 g sugar ● 1 lb/500 g flaky or puff pastry ● 1 tablespoon/½ oz/15 g butter ● 1 egg, beaten ● ½ cup/2 oz/50 g coarsely chopped almonds ● confectioners' (icing) sugar.*

For 4 persons

Time: *preparation 30 min ● cooking 20 min.*
Ingredients: *3 eggs ● 1¼ cups/10 oz/285 g lard ● 1 cup/½ lb/200 g sugar ● essence of aniseed or liquorice ● 4 cups/1 lb/500 g all-purpose (plain) flour ● 2 cups/16 fl. oz/5 dl sunflower oil ● powdered (castor) sugar.*

● Put the ground almonds, bananas, cream and sugar in the blender and mix to a creamy texture. ● Set aside. ● Roll out a circle of the pastry ½ in./1 cm in thickness and 5 in./12 cm across. ● Lay it on a buttered baking sheet (oven tray). ● Brush pastry with beaten egg. ● Decorate with the coarsely chopped almonds. ● Bake in a slow oven (300°F/mark 2/150°C) for 45 minutes. ● Remove from the oven and leave to cool. ● When cold cut it in half *horizontally* and fill it with the cream mixture previously prepared. ● Sprinkle with confectioners' (icing) sugar and serve.

● Beat the eggs and blend them with 3 tablespoons/1½ oz/35 g melted lard and the sugar. ● Flavour the mixture with aniseed essence and add the flour. ● Mix together well and knead. ● Divide the dough into portions of about ½ cup/2 oz/50 g each, roll out and give them the shape desired (hearts, "ears," etc.). ● Fry these pieces of dough in a mixture of the oil and 1 cup/½ lb/250 g lard over a high heat. ● When the *orelletes* are golden brown on both sides sprinkle them with powdered (castor) sugar.

SWEET AND SAVOURY SAUCES

Caramel sauce

Time: *preparation 15 min.*
Ingredients: *½ cup/¼ lb/100 g sugar ● water.*

Melt the sugar in a little water and boil until it becomes dark brown, although it must not be allowed to burn. ● Add half a cup of hot water and stir well to melt the syrup anew. ● Lower the heat and continue to cook till the mixture becomes thick and homogeneous.

Egg custard

Time: *preparation and cooking 15 min. + the time needed for cooling.*
Ingredients: *4 egg yolks ● ½ cup/¼ lb/100 g sugar ● 1 tablespoon flour ● 2 cups/¾ pint/5 dl milk ● ½ teaspoon vanilla essence ● grated rind (peel) of ½ lemon.*

Mix egg yolks and sugar in a saucepan, stirring with a wooden spoon. ● Add the flour. ● In another pan bring to a boil the milk with the vanilla essence and grated lemon rind (peel). ● Strain the hot milk into the first saucepan, re-heat and simmer for about 5 minutes, stirring all the time. ● Leave to cool, stirring now and again to prevent skin formation.

Allioli (garlic) sauce

Time: *preparation 15 min.*
Ingredients: *3 cloves garlic ● 2 egg yolks ● salt ● pepper ● 1¼ cups/½ pint/3 dl olive oil ● juice of 1 lemon.*

Peel and crush the garlic. ● Put it in a bowl with the egg yolks, salt and pepper, and stir. ● Pour on the oil in a thin stream, beating continuously as if it were a mayonnaise. ● Add the lemon juice and stir to blend.

Sauce Hollandaise

Time: *preparation and cooking 50 min.*
Ingredients: *2 egg yolks ● 1 tablespoon wine vinegar ● salt ● pepper ● 1 cup/½ lb/200 g butter ● 1 tablespoon lemon juice.*

Stir the egg yolks, vinegar, salt and pepper together in a bowl. ● Place the bowl in a bain-marie (or use a double boiler (double saucepan)) and add the butter, cut in small pieces, a little at a time, stirring continuously. ● Without ever letting the water boil, continue cooking, still stirring, till the sauce is as thick as mayonnaise. ● Remove from the heat and add the lemon juice. ● Stir to blend.

Spanish sauce

Time: *preparation and cooking 3 hours.*
Ingredients: *¼ lb/100 g fat (streaky) bacon ● 1 onion ● 3 carrots ● 2 sticks celery ● 3 tablespoons/1½ oz/40 g dripping or bacon fat ● 3 tablespoons flour ● 6½ cups/2½ pints/1½ liters hot beef stock ● bouquet garni ● 1 clove garlic ● salt ● pepper.*

Slice the fat bacon, onion, carrots and celery. ● Brown them all in the dripping. ● Add the flour and, continuing to stir, cook over a moderate heat till the flour begins to turn colour. ● Add about a third of the steaming hot stock, the herbs and the garlic, and go on cooking and stirring until the sauce thickens. ● Add half the remaining stock, cover the pan and cook for about 2 hours. ● Skim and put back on the heat for a few more minutes. ● Strain the sauce and return it to the heat to simmer, skimming it occasionally till its volume is reduced to about 4½ cups/1¾ pints/1 litre. ● Season with pepper and salt.

Note. Although this sauce requires time and skill, it will keep very well in a refrigerator and of course it will also freeze. ● Thus it is advisable to make a fairly large quantity at a time (the above recipe is for 4½ cups/1¾ pints/1 liter).

Tomato sauce

Time: *preparation and cooking 50 min.*
Ingredients: *1 small onion ● 1 small carrot ● 1 stick celery ● a few leaves of basil ● sprig of parsley ● 1 teaspoon olive oil ● 2 cups/1 lb/500 g tomato pulp or canned tomatoes, mashed ● salt ● pepper.*

Wash and chop the onion, carrot, celery, basil and parsley. ● Sweat all in oil in a pan until the onion begins to colour. ● Add the tomato pulp and simmer for about 30 minutes, stirring occasionally. ● Season with pepper and salt.

White sauce

Time: *preparation and cooking 15 min.*
Ingredients: *3 tablespoons/1½ oz/40 g butter ● ¼ cup/1½ oz/40 g flour ● 2 cups/16 fl. oz/5 dl milk ● salt ● pepper.*

Melt butter in a saucepan. ● As soon as it is melted add the flour, stirring continuously to obtain a smooth, homogeneous texture. ● Do not let it colour. ● Pour in the milk a little at a time, still stirring. ● Season and bring to the boil. ● Lower the heat and simmer for 5 minutes.

LIST OF RECIPES